016.384 **Blum, Eleanor**
B6585b   Basic books in the mass media; an annotated, selected booklist covering general communications, book publishing, broadcasting, film, magazines, newspapers, advertising, indexes, and scholarly and professional periodicals. Urbana, University of Illinois Press [1972]

    ix, 252 p. 24 cm. $8.00

    1. Mass media—Bibliography.   I. Title.

Z5630.B55   016.30116′1   71-151998
ISBN 0-252-00178-8   MARC
Library of Congress   72 [4]

Basic Books in the Mass Media

Basic Books in the Mass Media

AN ANNOTATED, SELECTED BOOKLIST
COVERING GENERAL COMMUNICATIONS, BOOK PUBLISHING,
BROADCASTING, FILM, MAGAZINES, NEWSPAPERS, ADVERTISING,
INDEXES, AND SCHOLARLY AND PROFESSIONAL PERIODICALS

Eleanor Blum

UNIVERSITY OF ILLINOIS PRESS
Urbana   Chicago   London

© 1972 by The Board of Trustees of the University of Illinois
Manufactured in the United States of America
Library of Congress Catalog Card No. 71-151998
ISBN 0-252-00178-8

To Ted Peterson, my colleague and,
even more important, my friend

Preface

This book, intended to revise and update
Reference Books in the Mass Media, has become a completely new volume. Some of the old entries have been
deleted, and of those which remain many of the annotations have been rewritten, especially in the cases of
new editions and annuals. In addition, over 400 new
titles have been added. Scope has been broadened to
include material on theory, popular culture, the black
press, communication satellites, the underground press
and film, violence in the mass media, and similar current topics. Because of these many alterations, the
title has been changed to Basic Books in the Mass Media.
However, the reference function has by no means les-
sened; if anything, it has increased.

The book has three purposes: to serve as a
reference tool; to suggest materials for research,
especially to the layman; and to provide a checking or
buying list. A number of titles are primarily refer-
ence-handbooks, directories, manuals, indexes, reports,
bibliographies, yearbooks, and similar materials.
Others are surveys, anthologies, studies, and histories.
All in some way give information about background,
structure, function, content, and effects of the mass
media. None deals with techniques nor falls into the
"how to" category. Most entries contain bibliographies
leading to further sources. When they do, the annotation says so.

A work of this nature cannot be all-inclusive;
selection is inevitably somewhat eclectic, reflecting
the compiler's taste and knowledge. But all of the
books I have selected have one common factor -- they
treat the subject in broad, general terms. For example,

I have included books about news agencies, but not about a specific agency; I have included histories of journalism but not of specific newspapers. For this same reason, there are no biographies, either personal or institutional, nor books dealing with the media as a segment of a larger subject. Nor have I attempted to enter all of the media yearbooks published by foreign countries in the English language. This would be desirable, but there are so many that the task becomes impossible. Rather, I have selected a very few as examples.

By no means all the titles are new. Some were published years ago, but in my opinion have not dated, or have historical significance, or are classic in their field. Books published after April 1971 are not included.

A number of subjects are not covered. Among these are censorship, methodology, copyright, typography, photography, computer science, the post office, telephone and telegraph (although these last two categories are sometimes discussed in connection with telecommunications).

The first section, "General Communications," deals with theory or with books that apply to three or more media. The other sections deal with book publishing, broadcasting, film, magazines, newspapers, advertising (which, though not a medium, cuts across journalism and broadcasting), periodical indexes and other types of indexes, and scholarly and trade periodicals. In conclusion are a subject index and an author-title index.

Many titles fall under several categories and are therefore cross-referenced, except for most of the material in the communications section which is as a rule too general for cross-listing. Readers wanting material of a general nature should scan Section I, as well as Section VIII, "Indexes." They should also look under appropriate headings in the subject index, such as Anthologies, and Surveys, and Popular Culture -- to cite three illustrations.

A number of the books mentioned here are out of print -- a fact no longer so important as formerly because of the frequency with which books are reprinted in paperback and in hardcover, and because of the possibility of obtaining xeroxed copies or borrowing through interlibrary loan. For these reasons I have not stated price. I have not given pagination either, for this, too, changes with editions, particularly in paperbacks. Also, in cases of annuals and other continuations the paging varies with each issue. I have, however, specified pamphlet material in the annotation

Nor have I given publishers' addresses unless they may prove difficult to find. Most of them, however, can be easily obtained through such sources as Literary Market Place, American Book Trade Directory, and their equivalents.

In any work of this kind, many titles could have been included, and, conversely, many could have been omitted. My criteria for inclusion varied. Sometimes, though not always, a criterion was that elusive attribute, quality. The determination of quality, however, is subjective as well as elusive, and some books which I feel to lack it in greater or lesser degree have their place because little else exists on the subject or because they cover aspects not covered elsewhere. Also, to limit a bibliography to works of indubitable merit (and opinions differ as to what constitutes merit) would narrow its scope and usefulness. Even hackneyed anthologies usually contain some essays of value, and mediocre surveys may contain useful factual information not readily available elsewhere

In most cases all annotations are descriptive rather than evaluative because evaluation is too subjective. In addition, it becomes an impossible task when applied to hundreds of titles.

In conclusion, I would like to thank Prof. George Gerbner of the Annenberg College of Communications, University of Pennsylvania, for his suggestion years ago that this bibliography was needed; Prof. Theodore Peterson of the University of Illinois for his frequent guidance; Prof. Henry L. Mueller of the University of Illinois for his help with the section on film; Prof. Edward F. Douglass of the University of Illinois for his help with the section on broadcasting; Prof. Herbert Schiller of the University of California at San Diego, who suggested titles on communications satellites; Prof. Thomas E. Ratcliffe and his staff of the Reference Department of the University of Illinois Library for their frequent assistance; and the members of the Technical Processing departments for their assistance also, and for obtaining materials very quickly when it was necessary. I want also to express my gratitude to my assistant, Mrs. Margo Trumpeter, who ran down books for me to examine, checked my numbering and cross-referencing for accuracy, and helped in many other large and small ways.

Contents

General Communications

1. Asian Press. Seoul, Korea: Readership Research
   Center, Institute of Mass Communication, Seoul
   National University, annual.
   > Brings together information on many aspects
   of broadcasting, newspapers, and film in Asia
   today. Countries covered are Burma, Cambodia,
   Ceylon, Republic of China, Hong Kong, India,
   Indonesia, Japan, Republic of Korea, Laos,
   Malaysia and Singapore, Pakistan, Philippines,
   Thailand, and the Republic of Vietnam.

2. Bagdikian, Ben H. The Information Machines:
   Their Impact on Men and the Media. New York:
   Harper & Row, 1970.
   > A critical estimate of the past, present,
   and future of the communication media, sponsored by the Rand Corporation and written by
   the assistant managing editor for national
   news for the Washington Post. He discusses
   communication satellites, computers, conglom-
   erates, the future of print, and the long-
   range impacts of high density communication
   intervention on American society. Its power,
   he believes, will be tremendous, and poses
   consequences for both good and evil, which
   will ultimately rest with the public.
   > The author has backed his analysis with
   statistics and summaries of important studies
   and has included broadcast as well as newspaper
   journalism. The list of references serves as
   a bibliography, and there is an index.

3. Berelson, Bernard, and Morris Janowitz, eds.
   Reader in Public Opinion and Communication. 2d
   ed. New York: Free Press, 1966.
       Collection of over 50 articles by well-known
   social scientists on various phases of communication, grouped under the following headings:
   (1) theory of public opinion; (2) formation of
   public opinion; (3) impact of public opinion
   on public policy; (4) theory of communication;
   (5) communication media: structure and control; (6) communication content; (7) communication audiences; (8) communication effects;
   (9) public opinion, communication, and democratic objectives; (10) toward comparative
   analysis; (11) research methods.

4. Blum, Eleanor, comp. Communications Research in
   U.S. Universities. A Directory: 1969. 3d ed.
   Champaign-Urbana 61801: University of Illinois,
   Institute of Communications Research, 119 Gregory
   Hall, 1969.
       Brief summaries of the state of communi-
   cation research in the various schools and
   colleges which offer a formal curriculum either
   in journalism or communications. Contains a
   geographic index. Revised at irregular intervals.

5. Bryson, Lyman, ed. The Communication of Ideas:
   A Series of Lectures. New York: Cooper Square
   Publishers, c1948, 1964. (Religion and Civilization Series)
       One of the first anthologies in communi-
   cations. The editor attempts, through the
   articles selected, to place communication in a
   social context, past and present as well as
   cross-cultural, and to show what can be done
   with words and ideas via the media in contrast
   to what is actually done. Contributors include
   Harold D. Lasswell, Paul Lazarsfeld, Charles
   Siepmann, Robert D. Leigh, Margaret Mead,
   Lyman Bryson, and others. Indexed.

6. Canada. The Task Force on Government Information.
   To Know and Be Known. Ottawa: Queen's Printer,
   1969.
       "... presents analyses of the concept and
   role of information, public and official opinion
   of government information, problem areas, a
   descriptive analysis of information systems and
   methods, and proposals for new structures and

systems. Vol. I summarizes findings and recommendations, and Vol. II includes research papers." - <u>International Communications Bulletin</u>.

7. Cantor, Norman F., and Michael S. Wertham, eds. <u>The History of Popular Culture</u>. 2 vols. New York: Macmillan, 1968.
     An entertaining and illuminating anthology, covering a broad scope from ancient Greece (drama, athletics, sex and marriage) to today's mass media (Beatles and hippies). Much is touched upon briefly but expertly. There is no index nor bibliography; in this kind of book either would have been difficult -- perhaps impossible.

8. Cantril, Hadley, ed. <u>Public Opinion 1935-1946</u>. Princeton, N.J.: Princeton University Press, 1951.
     A compilation of opinion poll results, grouped under various subject headings, from 23 polling organizations in 16 countries, and covering the period from 1935 to 1946. The names of participating organizations form a useful list of international polling organizations as of 1946.
     This is updated to a degree by <u>Gallup Poll Reports 1935-1968</u> (No. 27), which can be kept current by the <u>Gallup Opinion Index</u> (No. 634), formerly <u>Gallup Political Index</u>. The last two cover only the Gallup organization's reports.

9. Casty, Alan, ed. <u>Mass Media and Mass Man</u>. New York: Holt, Rinehart & Winston, 1968.
     Anthology intended as a survey for the layman in and out of school. Part I focuses on the media in relation to culture, Part II in relation to information. Each part is divided into three sections: "Backgrounds and Perspectives," "Individual Media," and "Critiques and Cases." Contributors are social scientists and critics. There is a section, "Topics and Questions," for study groups or the classroom and a bibliography of books and articles.

10. Christenson, Reo M., and Robert O. McWilliams, eds. <u>Voice of the People: Readings in Public Opinion and Propaganda</u>. 2d ed. New York: McGraw-Hill, 1967.
     Described by the editors as "a nontechnical book of readings on public opinion and

propaganda designed to contribute broadly to
students' liberal education" rather than to
report quantitative studies, this anthology
covers such topics as the nature of public
opinion -- its cultural, social, and psychological background -- the role of the mass
media; the nature of censorship and propaganda;
the U.S. and world opinion; public relations
and advertising; polling; and the general
competence of public opinion. Contains bibliographical footnotes.

11. Clark, David D., and Earl R. Hutchison, eds.
    Mass Media and the Law: Freedom and Restraint.
    New York: Wiley-Interscience, 1970.
        A textbook for laymen which examines the
    law's regulation of the mass media from two
    aspects: what it does to enhance free expres-
    sion and what it does to restrain freedom.
    Highlights the strengths and reveals the
    weaknesses. There is a bibliography at the
    end of each chapter.

12. Clotfelter, James, comp. Communication Theory in
    the Study of Politics: A Review of the Litera-
    ture. Chapel Hill: University of North Carolina,
    School of Journalism, 1968. (Study No. 7)
        Essay-bibliography in which the author dis-
    cusses in the main text the literature over a
    period of time in this field of communication
    and gives elaborate footnotes containing
    entries and bibliographical information.
    Although only 18 pages, it is packed with facts
    and specific references. The last page is a
    selective bibliography of about 24 books.

13. Colle, Royal D., ed. Perspectives on Mass Media
    Systems: India, Japan, Nigeria, USSR, Worldvi-
    sion. Ithaca: Cornell University, New York
    State College of Agriculture, Department of Com-
    munication Arts, 1968. (Bulletin No. 4)
        A 69-page pamphlet which surveys the high-
    lights of some of the major media in the
    countries included. Media discussed in India
    and Japan are broadcasting, newspapers, and
    film; in Nigeria, broadcasting and newspapers;
    and, with the exception of a few sentences on
    the press, broadcasting only in the USSR.

14. Commission on Freedom of the Press. A Free and
    Responsible Press: A General Report on Mass
    Communication: Newspapers, Radio, Motion

4

Pictures, Magazines, and Books. Chicago: University of Chicago Press, 1947.
   A critique of the press as it existed in the 1940s, with "press" interpreted broadly. Emphasizes the responsibilities of owners and managers to use their media for the common good.

15. Couperie, Pierre, and others. A History of the Comic Strip. Trans. from the French by Eileen B. Hennessy. New York: Crown, 1968.
   The authors have done an excellent job of placing the comic strip genre in a historical, sociological, and aesthetic setting. Within the scope of their work it was impossible to cover everything, so they have concentrated upon artists who, in their opinion, are the principal creative talents. The American comic strip occupies a preeminent position because the U.S. has dominated the field. There are many illustrations and a detailed index. The book was created in conjunction with the exhibition of comic strip art at Musée des Arts Décoratifs, Palais du Louvre.

16. Danielson, Wayne A., and G.C. Wilhoit, Jr., comps. A Computerized Bibliography of Mass Communication Research, 1944-1964. New York 10022: Magazine Publishers Association, Inc., Magazine Center, 575 Lexington Ave., 1967.
   A monumental undertaking subsidized by the MPA, this computerized print-off bibliography leads the user to thousands of articles relating to the mass media from 1944 through 1964 which appeared in 48 social science periodicals.
   With thoughtful foresight the authors list the location in New York City libraries of the periodicals covered, on the assumption that users can have materials reproduced which are not available in their libraries.

17. Developing Information Media in Africa: Press, Radio, Film, Television. New York: UNESCO Publications Center, 1962. (Reports and Papers on Mass Communication No. 37)
   Report of a meeting of 200 experts (and part of a continuing survey by UNESCO encompassing underdeveloped areas on a worldwide scale) in which participants discuss methods by which mass communications may be strengthened and, where necessary, developed in Africa. Includes news

agencies and newspapers, film, radio and television broadcasting, and training and research
in mass communications.

18. Developing Mass Media in Asia: Papers of UNESCO
    Meeting at Bangkok, January 1960. UNESCO Publi-
    cations Center, 1960. (Reports and Papers on
    Mass Communication No. 30)
        Report of a meeting held by UNESCO to draw
    up a program for the development of information
    media in ,South East Asia. Information is
    grouped according to the four main subjects
    covered: (1) newspapers and periodicals; (2)
    news agencies and telecommunications; (3) radio
    broadcasting; (4) training in journalism and
    mass communication research. Special attention
    is given to the problems peculiar to each
    country participating.

19. Dexter, Lewis Anthony, and David Manning White,
    eds. People, Society and Mass Communications.
    New York: Free Press, 1964.
        Anthology of about 30 articles designed for
    professionals and scholars as well as students.
    Areas covered are: "Sociological Perspectives
    on Mass Communications," "The Communicator and
    His Audience," "Looking at the Media," "Social
    Institutions Studied in Terms of Communication
    Theory." In a lengthy introduction Dexter gives
    his interpretation of what constitutes mass
    communication.
        The bibliographical material is unorthodox.
    Apart from conventional footnotes, each article
    contains a list of selected publications by its
    author which treat the subject further. Con-
    cludes with "A Critique of Bibliographic
    Matter in Mass Communications." Indexed.

20. Directory of Communication Centers, Professional
    Societies, Programs Publications, and Scholars
    in the Field of Communication. Kansas City:
    University of Missouri at Kansas City, Center
    for the Advanced Study of Communication, 1968.
        Information on centers and societies which
    includes address, director, goals, and subject
    coverage. There are also sections giving names
    and addresses of related centers not dealing
    directly with communication; special projects
    and programs; professional associations and
    societies; serial and special publications,
    series, and so on; and major scholars and
    researchers. Indexed.

21. Dorfles, Gillo. _Kitsch: The World of Bad Taste_.
    New York: Universe, 1969.
         Kitsch -- "trash" or "cheap finery" in its
    original German sense -- has become very much a
    part of our mass culture due somewhat to propa-
    gation by the media. This book explains and
    illustrates with examples. It consists mainly
    of essays written by the author describing some
    of the many forms of kitsch. He has also added
    a few essays by other writers which he considers
    classic.
         Although Dorfles notes that as yet the
    bibliography on the subject is relatively
    small, he has included some of the leading
    works. There is an index of illustrations and
    of persons.

22. _Education for Journalism in Latin America_. New
    York 10017: Council on Higher Education in the
    American Republics, Institute of International
    Education, 809 United Nations Plaza, 1970.
         A 40-page survey of the situation in Latin
    America -- the growth of journalism schools; the
    influence of CIESPAL, one of the four regional
    centers sponsored by UNESCO; other forces at
    work; the dark and the bright sides of the
    picture. There are also conclusions and recom-
    mendations, a bibliography not limited to works
    about Latin America, and an appendix listing
    schools of journalism as of January 1970 which
    gives address, date of establishment, type,
    whether of university level, and number of
    years required to obtain a diploma or degree.

23. Emery, Edwin, Philip H. Ault, and Warren K. Agee.
    Introduction to Mass Communications. 3d ed. New
    York: Dodd, Mead, 1970.
         In this survey of the mass media as it re-
    lates to the development of a modern democratic
    society the authors state that their aim "is to
    answer in a positive, yet realistic, way the
    question: Is journalism a desirable profession,
    important to society?" They discuss its role,
    its history, its current problems and criti-
    cisms, and the mass communications industries
    and professions -- newspapers, broadcasting,
    photography, film, magazines, book publishing,
    advertising, public relations, press associa-
    tions, research, and education. There is a
    30-page bibliography in essay form and an
    index.

24. Ernst, Morris L. The First Freedom. New York:
    Macmillan, 1946.
        One of the earliest examinations of monopoly
    in the communications industry, which was then
    chiefly press, radio, and motion pictures. Up-
    dated in 1968 by Rucker's book by the same
    name, which concentrates on newspapers and
    broadcasting (No. 512).

25. Fischer, Heinz-Dietrich, and John C. Merrill,
    eds. International Communication: Media --
    Channel -- Functions. New York: Hastings House,
    1970.
        The editors state that their aim is to
    present articles and portions of books and
    theses relating to a dozen important aspects
    in the area of international communication,
    beginning with the broad and general and work-
    ing toward more specific concerns and areas.
    Emphasis is on overall concerns rather than
    those of any one country. Among the topics
    are communication systems and concepts, the
    flow of news, freedom and restriction, national
    development and mass media, propaganda and
    political communication, supranational com-
    munication efforts, the world's press, broad-
    casting, advertising and public relations,
    cultural communication, the future, and re-
    search. Contributors are from both the aca-
    demic and professional worlds. Contains a
    bibliography of bibliographies and an index.

26. Foremost Women in Communications; A Biographical
    Reference Work on Accomplished Women in Broad-
    casting, Publishing, Advertising, Public Rela-
    tions, and Allied Professions. Ed. by Barbara
    J. Love. New York: Foremost Americans Publish-
    ing Corporation, 1970.
        Gives biographical profiles of more than
    7,000 women prominent in communications fields.
    Contains geographical and subject cross-
    indexes.

27. Gallup Poll Reports 1935-1968. Princeton, N.J.:
    American Institute of Public Opinion (The Gallup
    Poll), 1969.
        Part I is a subject index of all 6,030
    Gallup Poll reports published between October
    20, 1935, and December 31, 1968, with cross-
    references. Part II is a listing of the re-
    ports in chronological order, with a brief sum-
    mary of each report. (1968 is listed separately,

both by subject and chronology, following Parts
I and II.) A note on the contents page tells
how and where copies of the original reports
may be obtained.

This is kept up to date by the Gallup
Opinion Index (No. 634), formerly the Gallup
Political Index. Cantril's Public Opinion
1935-1946 covers the same ground more widely
with a variety of indexes for a much shorter
period (No. 8).

28. Gillmor, Donald M., and Jerome A. Barron. Mass
Communication Law. St. Paul, Minn.: West Publishing Co., 1969. (American Casebook Series)
A professor of journalism and a professor of
law collaborate on a text for law of the press
courses which treat what the authors call "the
usual staples," with the significant new developments brought about by electronic media and
the equally significant new concepts which
have come into being recently. Contents
include: "The First Amendment Impact on Mass
Communication: The Theory, the Practice, the
Problem"; "Libel and the Newsman"; "The Puzzle
of Pornography"; "Free Press and Fair Trial";
"Selected Problems of Law and Journalism";
"The Regulation of Radio and Television Broadcasting: Some Problems of Law, Technology, and
Policy."

Appendices contain a report of the Committee
on the Operation of the Jury System of the
'Free Press -- Fair Trial' issue, the case of
Red Lion Broadcasting Co. vs. F.C.C., and
selected provisions of the FCC Act of 1934.
Indexed. For another book in this area see
Nelson's Law of Mass Communications: Freedom
and Control of Print and Broadcast Media (No.
61).

29. Hachten, William A. Muffled Drums: The News
Media in Africa. Ames: Iowa State University
Press, 1971.
Examination of the news media -- newspapers,
radio, television, magazines -- as they exist
in contemporary Africa, focusing on them as
institutions, and describing their establishment, their effectiveness, and their relations
with the government. Emphasis is on news and
public information rather than the cultural
and educational roles. In addition to the overview of the continent there are case studies
of news media systems in Nigeria, Ghana, the

Ivory Coast, Senegal, Kenya, Zambia, and South
Africa. Contains a bibliography and an index.

30. Hall, Stuart, and Paddy Whannel. The Popular
    Arts. Chicago: Hutchinson Educational, 1964.
          This book is intended to educate the younger
    reader and interested layman about today's
    mass culture -- or rather, day-before-yester-
    day's culture, for the rate of change is rapid.
          Part I defines the media's relation to
    society, minority art, folk art, and popular
    art and relates popular art to mass culture.
    Part II suggests topics for study -- "Violence
    on the Stage," "Falling in Love," "Fantasy
    and Romance," "Popular Forms and Popular
    Artists," among others. Part III discusses
    social themes -- the institutions, the critics
    and defenders of mass society, society and
    the hero, the world of pop, and so on. Some
    of these are suggested as teaching projects.
    Appendices contain bibliographies of books
    and journals, records, films and television
    materials, and organizations. Indexed.

31. Halloran, James D., Philip Elliott, and Graham
    Murdock. Demonstrations and Communication: A
    Case Study. London: Penguin, 1970.
          The authors have analyzed the manner in
    which the British news media covered an English
    demonstration against the Vietnam war. They
    also analyze certain underlying principles
    involved both in understanding and reporting
    news. Has bibliographic references and an
    index.

32. Halmos, Paul, ed. The Sociology of Mass-Media
    Communicators. Keele, Staffordshire, England:
    University of Keele, 1969. (The Sociological
    Review: Monograph No. 13)
          Emphasis here is divided between the theo-
    retical and the practical. Some of the essays
    broadly examine the factors which underlie a
    number of aspects of the communications system
    as it functions today; others concentrate upon
    television. All articles probe beneath the
    surface. There are footnotes at the end of
    each article but no bibliography.

33. Hansen, Donald A., and J. Herschel Parsons, comps.
    Mass Communication: A Research Bibliography.
    Santa Barbara, Calif.: Glendessary Press, 1968.

Selection of about 3,000 articles, books,
dissertations, and directories, grouped under
nine headings: (1) Bibliographies and Reference Materials; (2) Research and Methods; (3)
Media Development and Characteristics; (4)
Social Contexts of the Media; (5) Content;
(6) Media Organizations; (7) Roles and Processes; (8) Audience and Diffusion; (9) Effects
and Function. Entries are not annotated.
There is an author index.

34. Hoggart, Richard. The Uses of Literacy: Aspects
of Working-Class Life with Special Reference to
Publications and Entertainment. New York:
Oxford University Press, c1957, 1970.
In the earlier (1957) publication, this
socio-literary study was subtitled Changing
Patterns in English Mass Culture. It concerns
changes in working-class culture during the
last 30 or 40 years preceding the 1960s, telling in particular how these changes were being
encouraged by mass publications. Emphasis is
on periodicals and popular music, although the
author believes he would have obtained similar
results if film and commercial broadcasting had
been used. Contains "Notes and References,"
"A Select Bibliography," and an index.

35. Inkeles, Alex. Public Opinion in Soviet Russia:
A Study in Mass Persuasion. 2d ed. Cambridge,
Mass.: Harvard University Press, 1958.
The last two-thirds of this book analyzes
the structure, function, and contents of the
Soviet press, broadcasting, and films. A more
recent study which does not invalidate its use-
fulness is Hopkins's Mass Media in the Soviet
Union (No. 474). Contains bibliographic notes,
a bibliography, and an index.

36. Innis, Harold A. Empire and Communication.
Oxford: Clarendon Press, 1950; The Bias of Communication. Toronto, Canada: University of
Toronto Press, 1951; Changing Concepts of Time.
Toronto, Canada: University of Toronto Press,
1952.
One of Marshall McLuhan's outstanding contributions has been to bring into prominence
the works of the late Canadian economist,
Harold Innis. Innis's writings are best
treated as a group. His thesis is that the
communications systems of empires have in-
fluenced their rise and fall. In Empire and

11

Communication he discusses the possibility,
with emphasis on economics, that communication
may occupy "a crucial position in the organization and administration of government and in
turn of empires and of Western civilization."
The Bias of Communication is a collection
of papers supporting this theory in more
detail. Changing Concepts of Time attempts
to show that the communication system of a
given culture can affect the way in which its
people regard space-time concepts.

37. Irving, John A., ed. Mass Media in Canada. 2d
rev. ed. Toronto: Ryerson Press, 1969.
Anthology assessing the status of the mass
media in Canada. Contents include: "The
Development of Communications in Canada," "The
Press," "Books," "Film," "Radio," "Television,"
"Advertising," "The Electronic Age," "Communication, Communications and Community,"
"The Problems of the Mass Media." The chapters
on books, films, radio, and the electronic age
have bibliographies.

38. Jacobs, Norman, ed. Culture for the Millions?
Mass Media in Modern Society. Princeton, N.J.:
Van Nostrand, 1961.
Can pure culture survive the mass media and
mass society? This question is considered by
a notable list of contributors: Paul Lazarsfeld,
Edward Shils, Leo Lowenthal, Hannah Arendt,
Ernest van den Haag, Oscar Handlin, Leo
Rosten, Randall Jarrell, James Baldwin, Stanley
Edgar Hyman, Arthur Schlesinger, among others.

39. Jacobson, Howard Boone, ed. A Mass Communications Dictionary. New York: Philosophical
Library, 1961.
Gives terminologies for press, print, broadcasting, film, and communications research.
Neither sufficiently comprehensive nor abreast
with the field to make it useful for any except
elementary needs. A more definitive dictionary
remains to be written.

40. The Journalism Bibliography of the Journalism
Education Association's Bookshelf Commission
1970. Princeton, N.J. 08540: The Newspaper
Fund, P.O. Box 300, 1970.
"... instructor-advisor members of the
Journalism Education Association have compiled...a bibliography -- more as a beginning

12

than as the last word" for the use of the high
school journalism student who wishes to go
beyond texts. Forty-six pages long, it contains a list of suitable resource books
arranged under a number of subject headings --
advertising, broadcasting, the press and
society, photo-journalism, and so on. Both
theory and practice are included. Some of the
entries are annotated, others not. There is
also a listing of career books and high school
texts, periodicals, and yearbooks.

41. Katz, Elihu, and Paul F. Lazarsfeld. Personal
Influence: The Part Played by People in the
Flow of Communications. New York: Free Press,
1955.
        A theoretical analysis, backed by an empir-
ical study, of the effect of face-to-face
personal communication as distinguished from
the effects of mass communication and their
important interrelationships. Although 15
years old, the findings have remained valid.
Contains bibliographic notes, a bibliography,
and an index.

42. Klapper, Joseph T. The Effects of Mass Communication. New York: Free Press, 1960.
        Described by the publishers as "an analysis
of research on the effectiveness and limitations of mass media in influencing the opinions,
values, and behavior of their audiences," this
book, though published in 1960, still represents the most thorough survey of social
science findings on the subject.
        The first part is a report of the way the
mass media is known to change or reinforce
opinions and the differences among the various
media in bringing this about; the second part
deals with probable effects of specific types
of material presented over the media -- for
example, crime and violence and escapist
material, and adult TV fare when viewed by
children. Contains a bibliography and an
index.

43. Lacy, Dan. Freedom and Communications. 2d ed.
Urbana: University of Illinois Press, 1965.
(Seventh annual Windsor lecture)
        A broad picture of the American communica-
tions system, pointing out the problems
created by the revolutionary increase in

knowledge and assessing deficiencies in and possibilities of the current system.

44. Larsen, Otto N., ed. Violence and the Mass Media. New York: Harper & Row, 1968.
    Brings together articles dealing with important aspects of violence and the mass media, including content of the media, possible effects, and regulation. Bibliography.

45. Lasswell, Harold D., Ralph D. Casey, and Bruce Lannes Smith, comps. Propaganda and Promotional Activities: An Annotated Bibliography. Chicago: University of Chicago Press, c1935, 1969.
    Reprint of an extensive bibliography first published in 1935, with a 1969 introduction by Lasswell. Includes monographs in English and in foreign languages along with periodical articles. The authors note whether or not each entry has a bibliography.
    Arrangement: "The Study and Practice of Propaganda" (a long essay by Lasswell); "Propaganda Classified by the Name of the Promoting Group"; "Propaganda Classified by the Response to Be Elicited"; "The Symbols and Practices of Which Propaganda Makes Use or to Which It Adapts Itself"; "The Channels of Propaganda"; "The Measurements of the Effects of Propaganda"; "Propaganda and Censorship in Modern Society." There is a list of previous bibliographies on propaganda and an author and a subject index. For two bibliographies which update this somewhat <u>see</u> Nos. 83 and 84.

46. Levy, Milton L., comp. Media Awards Handbook. Berkeley, Calif.: Media Awards Handbook, Box 425, 1968.
    "... this handbook," says the author, "is designed to give as complete and comprehensive information as possible about the many Contests and Awards offered in radio, television, magazines, newspapers, allied fields, and industries." Information includes name of contest or award, sponsor, address, deadline, media, entry categories, form of entry, rules, awards, award date, and purpose. Listing is alphabetical, with an index by deadline. Earlier editions (1957, 1960, and 1964) were known as Honors Awards Handbook.

47. Lieberman, Elizabeth, ed. The Check-Log of
    Private Press Names. West New York, N.J.:
    Herity Press, 1967.
        Lists, with founding date, about 2,000
    names, including some commercial presses
    selected by a jury of distinguished typog-
    raphers as having done outstanding work in
    printing.

48. Lineberry, William P., ed. Mass Communications.
    New York: Wilson, 1969.
        "This compilation is designed to explore
    the status of mass communications in America --
    their impact on society, their achievements
    and shortcomings, and their potential for the
    future," says the editor. Among magazines from
    which he draws articles are the Annals of the
    American Academy of Political and Social
    Science, Commentary, Catholic World, New
    Leader, New York Times Magazine, Public Inter-
    est, Harper's, Atlantic, New Republic. Bib-
    liography.

49. Lippmann, Walter. Public Opinion. New York:
    Macmillan, 1922.
        Years have not dated Lippmann's basic con-
    cepts. His discussions of stereotypes, of the
    role of newspapers, and of various other as-
    pects remain classic. Indexed.

50. Literacy, 1965/1967. Paris: UNESCO, 1968.
    Literacy, 1967/1969: Progress Achieved in
    Literacy Throughout the World. Paris: UNESCO,
    1970.
        Both of these titles stress general liter-
    acy conditions rather than facts and figures
    on specific countries, although some are given.
    About half of the earlier book consists of
    good-will messages from the various heads of
    states to UNESCO; the rest, like the later book,
    concerns conditions, needs, and actions taken.
    The 1967/69 edition contains an appendix with
    statistical tables. (See also No. 101.)

51. McLuhan, Marshall. The Gutenberg Galaxy: The
    Making of Typographic Man. Toronto, Canada:
    University of Toronto Press, 1962.
        A lively and unconventionally organized his-
    tory of print, beginning with Gutenberg's press
    and skipping about eclectically through time
    and literature. For example, there are such
    headings for brief chapters as "King Lear is a

working model of the process of denudation by
which men translated themselves from a world
of roles to a world of jobs"; "Schizophrenia
may be a necessary consequence of literacy";
"The Greek point of view in both art and chronology has little in common with ours but was
much like that of the Middle Ages."

52. McLuhan, Marshall. Understanding Media: The
Extensions of Man. New York: McGraw-Hill, 1964.
No communications bibliography would be
complete without a book giving McLuhan's
theory. This one does so in a convoluted nut-
shell. It is the best single source.

53. McQuail, Denis. Toward a Sociology of Modern
Communications. New York: Collier-Macmillan,
1969.
Intended to acquaint the layman with the
field and to suggest guidelines for more
detailed study. It is the author's intention
to cover in breadth rather than depth. He
points out major issues and assesses the current state of discussion and research. Chapter
headings are "Mass Media in Modern Society,"
"Mass Society, Mass Culture and Mass Media,"
"The Empirical Tradition in the Sociology of
Mass Communications," "New Directions in Studies
of Mass Communications," "Toward a Sociology of
Mass Communications." There is a 23-page annotated bibliography. Indexed.

54. Markham, James W. Voices of the Red Giants:
Communications in Russia and China. Ames: Iowa
State University Press, 1967.
Investigation of Communist mass communication systems as exemplified by the Russian
Soviet and Communist Chinese models. The
author covers magazines, newspapers, radio and
television, the news agencies, and advertising.
A drawback is the use of secondary rather than
primary sources. Contains bibliographic notes
and an index.

55. Markham, James W., ed. International Communication as a Field of Study. Iowa City: University
of Iowa Press, 1970.
A symposium devoted to the problem of "inter-
nationalizing" the professional education of
communicators. The problem is approached from
two angles: the education of professionals
for international communication careers in

16

foreign countries or in the international
area, and the education of professionals for
careers primarily in American mass communications. Indexed.

56. Mass Media in Society: The Need of Research.
New York: UNESCO Publications Center, 1970.
(Reports and Papers on Mass Communication No.
59)
    In 1969 UNESCO called a meeting of experts
to examine the actual and potential role of
communication in society and to advise the
Secretariat on recent developments and probable trends in communication research. This
publication is a two-part report on their findings. The first part, by James Halloran, is a
general view of the impact of the means of
mass communication on the modern world and of
the present state and organization of communication research and the need for research in
new fields. The second part is a Final Report
in which discussions are summarized and suggestions and recommendations for future action
are outlined.

57. Mass Media in the Developing Countries: A UNESCO
Report to the United Nations. New York: UNESCO
Publications Center, 1961. (Reports and Papers
on Mass Communication No. 33)
    Tells of efforts already made to develop
information media and the problems met in
developing them. Material is separated into
the following regions -- South East Asia, Latin
America, Middle East, Oceania, and, very briefly,
certain European countries without sufficient
facilities. The latter portion gives conclusions and recommendations for improvement of
news agencies, newspapers and periodicals,
radio broadcasting, film, and television.

58. Mathison, Stuart L., and Philip M. Walker.
Computers and Telecommunications: Issues in
Public Policy. Englewood Cliffs, N.J.: Prentice-
Hall, 1970.
    Computers are having a direct effect on
communications. This book focuses upon certain issues of direct concern to the FCC: What
is the regulatory status of computer/communica-
tions services? Are common carrier communications services and tariffs responsive to the
requirements of the data processing industry?
Can privacy be protected against the increasing

phenomenon of concentration and the exchange
of data information? The authors attempt to
identify and explain the policy problems and
implications of alternative solutions, providing technical and regulatory background
information where needed. There is a very
comprehensive bibliography and an index.

59. Meeting of Experts on Development of Information
Media in Latin America. Paris: UNESCO, 1961.
     Report of a meeting held in Santiago,
Chile, at which participants discussed the
status of news agencies, newspapers, periodicals, radio broadcasting, television, film,
training of journalists, and scientific
research.

60. The National Publishing Directory: The Encyclopedia of the Canadian Publishing Industry.
Toronto: Presstige Books of Canada, biannual.
     Contains a brief history of Canadian pub-
lishing; biographies of prominent personnel;
and listings of advertising agencies, business,
trade,and consumer magazines, daily and weekly
newspapers, photographers, graphic arts and
book publishers, press associations and services.

61. Nelson, Harold L., and Dwight L. Teeter, Jr.
Law of Mass Communications: Freedom and Control
of Print and Broadcast Media. 5th ed. of Legal
Control of the Press. Mineola, N.Y.: The
Foundation Press, Inc., 1969.
     Although heralded as the fifth edition of
the late Frank Thayer's Legal Control of the
Press (No. 87), this is actually a new and
different book. "The immense changes in the
field of electronics, computers, microfilm,
have dictated a virtually complete reorganiza-
tion and presentation of largely new material,"
say the authors. Partial contents include the
principles and development of freedom of expression; defamation, libel,and slander; law of
privacy and the media; copyright; free press
and fair trial; contempt of court; obscenity;
access to government information; broadcasting
news and opinion; regulation of advertising;
antitrust law and the mass media; taxation and
licensing.
     Appendices give abbreviations; selected
court and pleading terms; a bibliography; and
background information on CATV, the FCC and

18

cigarette advertising, and the Failing Newspaper Act. Contains a table of cases and an
index. A similar although not overlapping
book, also published in 1969, is Mass Communication Law by Gillmor and Barron (No. 28).

62. Nye, Russel. The Unembarrassed Muse: The Popular Arts in America. New York: Dial, 1970.
        The author terms this "a historical study
of certain American popular arts, the arts of
commercial entertainment." It relates many
aspects of mass culture today and yesterday:
popular fiction (the Tarzan series and Zane
Grey, among other books), the pulps, radio and
television, comic books and comic strips, the
Wild West show, vaudeville, film, musical
comedy, poetry, even the "dream palace" architecture of movie theaters in the 1930s. He
explores some of the myths about our culture
which have not been widely discussed elsewhere.
        One of the most comprehensive works on the
subject. In addition to its reference value
it makes interesting reading. Contains a
section, "Bibliography and Sources," and an
index.

63. Overseas Press Club of America and American Correspondents Overseas. 1966 Directory. New York
10018: Overseas Press Club of America, 54 W.
40th St., 1966.
        Communications has no official biographical
directory that includes both sexes (No. 26),
and this roster of members of the Overseas
Press Club of America, with its brief, "who's
who" type of information about each, does not
fill the gap. But membership is wide and
varied, and a number of newspaper reporters,
magazine and free-lance writers, and broadcasters can be found here, along with a smaller
number of educators, public relations practitioners, and men and women in the business
end of the communications industry. There are
about 3,000 entries in all. Updated at irregular intervals.

64. Owen, Bruce M., David L. Grey, and James N. Rosse,
comps. A Selected Bibliography in the Economics
of the Mass Media. Stanford, Calif. 94305: Research Center in Economic Growth, 408 Encina Hall
West, 1970. (Studies in the Economics of Mass
Communication, Memorandum No. 99)

"What we have tried to do here is to present an extensive list of works known to exist by late Spring, 1970, which meet the following criteria: academic articles and books (often ten years of age or older) which appear to have been significant or early fundamental contributions to the literature; recent works which deal with the economics of the contemporary mass media on either academic or public policy levels." - Introduction.

Obviously the authors cannot be all-inclusive. They have dealt with the electronic media (radio, TV, cable, satellites), newspapers, magazines, and advertising, but not film and book publishing, and have treated these media under the following subjects: theory and concepts; analysis, description, empirics; law, regulation, public policy; data sources; trade publications and professional journals; technology and development; general and miscellaneous. They have omitted the purely methodological, articles and stories from popular and trade journals, and works by foreign authors or about foreign media. Entries are not annotated.

65. Perry, George, and Alan Aldridge. The Penguin Book of Comics: A Slight History. London: Penguin, 1967.

A substantial but lighthearted mixture of history, theory, and examples showing the evolution of the comic strip from its beginnings to today. The authors discuss its influence on pop art. Emphasis is on the 20th-century comic in Britain and the U.S. Indexed.

66. Peterson, Wilbur, comp. Organizations, Publications and Directories in the Mass Media of Communications. 3d ed. Iowa City: University of Iowa, School of Journalism, 1965.

Part 1 gives concise but extensive data on 235 organizations; Part 2 lists principal periodicals and gives brief information about each; Part 3 lists and annotates directories; Part 4 does the same for indexes and abstracts; Part 5, for state associations. Gives address for each entry and (except for directories) for the top official.

The various parts are arranged by media, which are broadly interpreted to include not only the newspaper and magazine press and

20

broadcasting but also film and advertising.
Coverage is extensive. Includes broadcasting
and newspaper unions.

67. Press, Film, Radio. 5 vols. and supps. 1-2. New
York: UNESCO Publications Center, 1947-51.
(Reports on the Facilities of Mass Communications)
A UNESCO survey originally designed to
determine the extent of damage suffered by the
equipment of news agencies, newspaper printing
works, broadcasting stations, and cinemas during World War II in the war-devastated countries,
as well as the nature and extent of those
countries' technical needs in these fields of
communication. This original purpose was later
broadened to include all countries and territories, and information was extended to cover
existing technical resources of mass communication. At the completion of the study 157
countries and territories had been surveyed.
A few could not be surveyed -- Albania, Bulgaria,
Byelo-Russian SSR, USSR, and Yemen. In addition, certain British and Portuguese colonies
failed to respond in time for inclusion of
their data.
Information, especially for the larger
countries, is detailed and thorough, with
historical background, tables, figures, and
maps. For a follow-up, concerned with newspapers only, see The Daily Press: A Survey of
the World Situation in 1952 (No. 454).

68. Pride, Armistead S., comp. The Black Press: A
Bibliography. Minneapolis 55455: Association
for Education in Journalism, School of Journalism,
Ad Hoc Committee on Minority Education, University
of Minnesota, 1968.
Thirty-seven pages of references, largely
from books and magazine articles, grouped under
the following headings: advertising and marketing, analysis and criticism, biography and
history, competition (coverage of black community by non-black media), employment, magazines, radio and television. Entries are not
annotated.

69. Professional Associations in the Mass Media:
Handbook of Press, Film, Radio, Television Organizations. New York: UNESCO Publications Center,
1959.
Gives details concerning 1,049 national
organizations in 93 states and territories and

64 international organizations. The survey
is preceded by an account of the rise of
the organizations and of their present-day
activities.

70. Professional Training for Mass Communication.
New York: UNESCO Publications Center, 1965.
(Reports and Papers on Mass Communication No.
45)
    Supplements The Training of Journalists
(No. 89), giving information about facilities
for training in mass communication, particularly in the developing regions of the world.
Also supplies details of training programs,
such as those of the International Centers
established with UNESCO assistance at
Strasbourg, France, and Quito, Ecuador. Contains a list: "Basic Books; Professional
Periodicals." (See also No. 90.)

71. Public Opinion and Propaganda: A Book of Readings. Edited for the Society of Psychological
Study of Social Issues by Daniel Katz and others.
New York: Dryden Press, 1954.
    Although parts of this anthology deal with
the political process and with methodology,
many of the articles directly concern the mass
media, and some of them are classic. In spite
of the fact that it was written in the mid-
1950s, the contents have dated surprisingly
little.

72. Removing Taxes on Knowledge. New York: UNESCO
Publications Center, 1969. (Reports and Papers
on Mass Communication No. 58)
    Updates Trade Barriers to Knowledge (No. 88).
This is more than a compendium of tariff regulations; UNESCO also states its case for free
flow of educational materials across national
boundaries. The term is broadly interpreted
to include products of printing and writing,
visual and auditory materials and equipment,
and various other items unrelated to the mass
media. There are statistics with a bibliography
of their sources.

73. Rivers, William L., Theodore Peterson, and Jay W.
Jensen. The Mass Media and Modern Society. 2d
ed. Corte Madera, Calif.: Rinehart Press, 1970.
    Three things make this book unusual: its
emphasis upon theory behind practice, its
broad view, and its adept style. Using a

sociological, economic, and political approach, it tells the large story of the impact of technological and social change upon America's mass media -- from print, broadcasting, and motion pictures to hard advertising and soft persuasion.

Although intended primarily as a text for undergraduates, its analytical coverage and its readability make it one of the best single sources for laymen wishing a guide through the intricate field of mass communications. Contains a bibliography and an index of names and subjects.

74. Rosenberg, Bernard, and David Manning White, eds. Mass Culture: The Popular Arts in America. New York: Free Press, 1957.

Although old, this collection of 51 essays designed to show the interplay between the mass media and society still remains timely because some of its articles focus upon basic issues and are classic. Contributors include literary critics, social scientists, journalists, and art critics whose works in this area have been scattered in relatively inaccessible scholarly journals and "little magazines." Not all are contemporary; there are essays by de Tocqueville and Walt Whitman. Among present-day authors are Gilbert Seldes, Ortega y Gasset, Frank Luther Mott, Dwight Macdonald, Leo Lowenthal, Edmund Wilson, David Riesman, Bernard Berelson, and George Orwell; among topics are books, magazines, detective fiction, comics, radio and television, motion pictures, and advertising. Contains a list of further readings at the end of each section and bibliography notes following most of the articles. (See also No. 75.)

75. Rosenberg, Bernard, and David Manning White, eds. Mass Culture Revisited. New York: Van Nostrand-Reinhold, 1971.

This is not an updating of Mass Culture (No. 74) but an entirely new book with new articles, some appearing for the first time, most of them of the same excellence that marked the earlier book. This second volume takes into account the many changes since 1957, including the increasing impetus of television, comic strips in the underground press, new trends in the old, established media like film, magazines and newspapers (an article on the underground press, for example), and so

on. One section, "The Overview," is
general.
Among the 27 contributors: Hannah Arendt,
Nicholas Johnson, Mordecai Richler, Nathan
Blumberg, Diana Trilling, Fred Friendly, Joe
McGinnis, and Samm Sinclair Baker.

76. Schools of Journalism and Communications Research
Centres. Paris: UNESCO, Division of Development of Mass Media, 1970. (CM/WS/134). Limited
distribution.
A worldwide listing without comment. Name
and address only is given for each.

77. Schramm, Wilbur, ed. Mass Communications: A
Book of Readings. 2d ed. Urbana: University
of Illinois Press, 1960.
Articles by authorities give background
material on the development, structure and
function, control and support, process, content, audience, effects, and responsibility
of newspapers, broadcasting, magazines, and
film. Additional useful features: the codes
of ethics of the American Society of Newspaper
Editors, the Motion Picture Association of
America, and the National Association of Broadcasters; a comparison of the size of mass
communications systems in 21 key countries;
and an extensive bibliography. Indexed.

78. Schramm, Wilbur, and Donald F. Roberts, eds.
The Process and Effects of Mass Communication.
Urbana: University of Illinois Press, 1971.
First published in 1954, this revised
edition contains only four articles from the
original volume. It represents the enormous
amount of communication research and theory
produced during the last 15 years, as well
as the work done earlier in this century
by prominent social scientists. Subjects
discussed include media, messages, and
audiences of mass communication; the effects
of communication on attitudes, politics,
public opinion, and social change; and the
technological future of mass communication.
Contains bibliography of 100 titles for
further reading and an index.

79. Schramm, Wilbur, ed. The Science of Human Communication: New Directions and New Findings in
Communication Research. New York: Basic Books,
1963.

A compilation of some of the findings in
communication research drawn from a series of
talks for the Voice of America by outstanding
American scholars.
Articles are by Wilbur Schramm, Leon
Festinger, Charles E. Osgood, Nathan Maccoby,
Irving Janis, Joseph Klapper, Elihu Katz, Paul
Lazarsfeld, Herbert Menzel, Eleanor Maccoby,
Ithiel de Sola Pool, and Arthur A. Lumsdaine.
There is a bibliography at the end of each
chapter and an index.

80. Seldes, Gilbert. The Great Audience. New York:
Viking, 1951.
Examines critically the state of mass
entertainment up to the 1950s -- its character
and the character of the special type of
audience it has created -- and finds it wanting. Much emphasis is on radio and on television, which is just appearing. This is a
perceptive study which has held up over the
years. See also his earlier book written when
he was more enchanted with the prospects of
the popular arts, The Seven Lively Arts (No.
81).

81. Seldes, Gilbert. The Seven Lively Arts. New
York: Harper, 1924.
Gilbert Seldes was the first person in the
20th century to take popular art seriously.
In a period when film had just come into its
own it held great promise to him as an inno-
vative art form. He was also excited with the
quality of entertainment in general -- the
comic strip, popular music, the Broadway
comedians. Among the "lively arts" he even
includes Picasso.
In the years that followed he lost much of
his optimism. But The Seven Lively Arts stands
as one of the best descriptions of popular
mass culture during and preceding the 1920s.

82. Siebert, Fred S., Theodore Peterson, and Wilbur
Schramm. Four Theories of the Press. Urbana:
University of Illinois Press, 1956.
"The thesis of this volume is that the press
always takes the form and coloration of the
social and political structures within which
it operates. Especially, it reflects the
social and political structures whereby the
relations of individuals and institutions are
adjusted." - Introduction. In the light of

this theory Siebert discusses both the
authoritarian and libertarian theories,
Peterson the social responsibility theory,
and Schramm the Soviet Communist theory.
      Press is interpreted broadly to include all
media of mass communication, although emphasis
is primarily upon print rather than broadcasting and film because it is the oldest medium.

83. Smith, Bruce Lannes, Harold D. Lasswell, and
Ralph D. Casey, comps. Propaganda, Communication, and Public Opinion: A Comprehensive
Reference Guide. Princeton, N.J.: Princeton
University Press, 1946.
      Covers the period 1934-43 and brings up to
date the compilers' Propaganda and Promotional
Activities: An Annotated Bibliography (No.
45). Continued by International Communications
and Political Opinion: A Guide to Literature
(No. 84).
      Contains four introductory essays by the
authors on the nature, contents, and effects
of communications with special reference to
propaganda followed by an extensive bibliography
which brings together over 2,500 selected books,
periodicals, and articles by advertisers,
educators, journalists, lawyers, political
leaders, psychologists, public administrators,
counselors, and representatives from the various
social sciences. The compilers have starred
150 titles they consider most outstanding.
Author and subject index.

84. Smith, Bruce Lannes, and Chita M. Smith, comps.
International Communications and Political
Opinion: A Guide to Literature. Princeton,
N.J.: Princeton University Press, 1956.
      Designed as a continuation to Propaganda,
Communication, and Public Opinion (No. 83)
though not so broad in scope. For example,
it concentrates on materials dealing with
international propaganda rather than on propaganda in general and emphasizes political
propaganda. Works indexed generally include
books, journals, and public affairs magazines
the editors consider scholarly and responsible.
A few popular magazines have also been included,
as have some government publications, unpublished materials, and foreign-language materials,
especially in French and German. Each entry
is annotated, and many of the annotations

26

amount to abstracts. Contains subject and
author indexes.

85. Steinberg, Charles S. The Communicative Arts:
An Introduction to Mass Media. New York:
Hastings House, 1970.
    Covering the subject in breadth rather than
depth, the author has surveyed many aspects of
mass communications, including some of the
theory. Subjects covered include mass media
and society, symbols, who says what to whom,
the book, the newspaper, the magazine, the
cartoon narrative, film, broadcasting (with
its supplementary systems -- public television
and CATV), the information industry, foreign
news and global communication, public opinion
and propaganda, advertising and public relations,
impact, freedom and control, and predictions
for the future. Each chapter contains a
fairly lengthy bibliography. Appendices give
codes for journalism, motion pictures, comics,
and television. Indexed.

86. Steinberg, Charles S., ed. Mass Media and Communication. New York: Hastings House, 1966.
    The editor's intent in this anthology is to
give an overview of mass communication, "pred-
icated on the conviction that there are affirm-
ative social values implicit in an understanding and proper utilization." He dwells briefly
upon a number of aspects, with about three
articles under each heading. The topics
include structure and development, public
opinion, the newspaper, the magazine, the
motion picture, broadcasting, book publishing
(two articles), international communication
(one), the motivation of assent, and effects.
Appendices give the canons of journalism, the
production code, and the television code.
Indexed.

87. Thayer, Frank. Legal Control of the Press Concerning Libel, Privacy, Contempt, Copyright,
Regulation of Advertising and Postal Laws. 4th
ed. Mineola, N.Y.: The Foundation Press, 1962.
    The author of this time-honored text (first
published in 1944) says that its function "is
not to serve as a digest of cases but rather
as an interpretation of the principles necessary in the solution of communication problems
in libel, privacy, contempt, copyright, and
regulation of advertising." Appendices include

abbreviations, selected court and pleading
terms, a bibliography, and a table of cases.
There is also an index.
    Eugene O. Gehl and Harold L. Nelson co-
operated with Mr. Thayer in preparing the
research for this last edition. In 1969 Prof.
Nelson and Dwight L. Teeter, Jr., updated the
fourth edition in what is virtually a new
book, Law of Mass Communications: Freedom
and Control of Print and Broadcast Media
(No. 61).

88. Trade Barriers to Knowledge: A Manual of Regulations Affecting Educational, Scientific, and
Cultural Materials. New and rev. ed. New York:
UNESCO Publications Center, 1955.
    Gives tariff and trade regulations in 91
states and territories as of mid-1954 which
affect the movement of educational, scientific,
and cultural material from one country to
another. For later information see UNESCO's
Removing Taxes on Knowledge (No. 72).

89. Training of Journalists. Strasbourg, France:
University of Strasbourg, International Centre
for Higher Education in Journalism, 1962.
(Journalisme, Journalism 12, Winter 1961-62.)
    Special issue giving training for journalists
in India, China, Japan, Thailand, Malaya,
Indonesia, the Philippines, Korea, and Pakistan.
Text in both French and English.

90. The Training of Journalists: A World-Wide Survey
on the Training of Personnel for the Mass Media.
New York: UNESCO Publications Center, 1958.
(Press, Film, and Radio in the World Today)
    Gives training programs for journalists in
21 countries and contains discussions of
UNESCO's role in journalism education and a
series of eight articles by authorities on
various aspects of journalism training, including a comparative analysis of recent curricula
trends.

91. Tunstall, Jeremy, ed. Media Sociology. Urbana:
University of Illinois Press, 1970.
    Anthology of 25 essays intended for students
taking introductory courses dealing with the
media, which in this anthology include newspapers, magazines, radio, records, television,
and books operating on a fairly large scale.
Although intended primarily for British

students, articles by and about the American media are included as well. Contents are: "Part One: Cross Media Patterns and Media Research," "Part Two: Communications Organizations and Communicators," "Part Three: Communicators, Performers and Content," "Part Four: Content and Audience," "Part Five: The Media and Politics." Contains a section, "Notes and Sources," on which the articles are based, a bibliography, and name and subject indexes.

92. U.S. Bureau of the Census. Census of Manufactures. Industry Statistics 1967: Newspapers, Periodicals, Books and Miscellaneous Publishing. Washington, D.C.: Government Printing Office, 1969.
   Detailed tables covering many aspects of production and consumption of printed media. Compares figures of current with previous editions -- in this case 1963 with 1967. Updated at approximately four-year intervals.

93. Violence and the Media. Prepared by Robert K. Baker and Sandra J. Ball. Washington, D.C.: Superintendent of Documents, Government Printing Office, 1969. (Mass Media and Violence: A Report to the National Commission on the Causes and Prevention of Violence. Vol. IX)
   A 370-page compendium with various sections and chapters written by experts. First, it approaches the problem from a historical perspective. Then it analyzes factually and often critically certain accepted values and practices such as function and credibility, intergroup communication, the marketplace myth (access to the mass media), coverage of civil disorders, journalism education. And finally it deals with television entertainment vis-à-vis violence, with emphasis on our limited knowledge of effects. Programming is analyzed and contrasted with the reality of violence in daily life.
   Each section has discussions, conclusions, and recommendations, as well as factual appendices. Among these are: codes, guidelines, and policies for news coverage; a review of recent literature on psychological effects of media portrayals of violence; outline of research required on effects; the content and context of violence in the mass media, with opposing views as to possible effects; content analysis procedures and results; the views,

29

standards, and practices of the television
industry. Includes bibliographical references.

94. Watt, Ian. The Rise of the Novel: Studies in
Defoe, Richardson and Fielding. London: Chatto
& Windus, 1957.
       The bounds of this study far exceed the
literary. In tracing the development of the
novel the author tells about social developments which made a new form of communication
necessary. Extensive footnotes and an index.

95. Wertham, Fredric. Seduction of the Innocent.
New York: Rinehart, 1953.
       When this book about what he believed to be
the effect of all kinds of crime comics upon
children first appeared, it generated much
excitement, soul-searching, and rebuttal. The
author was senior psychiatrist for the Department of Hospitals in New York City. Although
today television has taken the center of the
stage from crime comics, the book remains a
classic on the subject -- its findings never
definitely proved nor disproved. In any case
it provides a provocative insight into possible effects of violence in the mass media.
Because Dr. Wertham has drawn his material
from his own case studies he has not included
a bibliography.

96. White, David Manning, ed. Pop Culture in America.
Chicago: Quadrangle, 1970.
       Articles previously published in The New
York Times about what's happening in radio,
television, film, the theater, music, art, and
books, with a beginning section that deals with
the media in general and an introduction on
popular culture by the editor. A partial list
of contributors includes Marya Mannes, Tyrone
Guthrie, Robert Schnickel, Benjamin DeMott,
Richard Hoggart, Charles Siepmann, David
Dempsey. Contains a brief bibliography of
selected readings and an index.

97. White, Llewellyn, and Robert D. Leigh. Peoples
Speaking to Peoples: A Report on International
Mass Communication from the Commission on Freedom
of the Press. Chicago: University of Chicago
Press, 1946.
       A detailed analysis of the means by which
information, especially news, is gathered,

controlled, and distributed internationally.
Gives notes on sources.

98. Williams, Raymond. Communications. Rev. ed.
    London: Chatto & Windus, 1966.
        An analytical survey of communications,
    defined by the author as "the institutions
    and forms in which ideas, information, and
    attitudes are transmitted and received." He
    tells how the development of powerful new
    means of communication has coincided, histor-
    ically, with the extension of democracy;
    describes the interplay of various forces --
    government, business, and so on -- to obtain
    control; and discusses the relationship
    between communications and reality. Finally,
    he makes proposals about how he feels the
    mass media may best be used for the common
    good. Much of his orientation is toward
    education. Contains a bibliography, "Further
    Reading," and two appendices -- "Methods in
    TV Education" and "A Policy for the Arts."
    The earlier edition (1962) was called Britain
    in the Sixties: Communications and was pub-
    lished in paperback by Penguin.

99. Williams, Raymond. The Long Revolution. New
    York: Columbia University Press, 1961.
        One of the best background sources to
    interpret today's popular culture -- with the
    word "popular" used in a broad sense. Williams
    takes a long, perceptive look at the factors
    which have shaped this culture, with emphasis
    on the industrial revolution, particularly in
    relation to print media.
        Part One is concerned with abstracts -- with
    the nature of the creative mind, and with
    culture and society in general. Part Two deals
    with education, the reading public, the popu-
    lar press, the novel, and writers. Part Three
    surveys the state of culture in Britain in the
    1960s. Williams's orientation is British
    throughout, but his analyses are universal.
    Contains a reading list and an index.

100. World Communications: Press, Radio, Television,
     Film. 4th ed. New York: UNESCO Publications
     Center, 1964.
         Part I, "The Pattern of Communication," is
     a brief, overall treatment of the patterns of
     communication continent by continent; Part II,
     "Pictographs," illustrates Part I with

pictography; Part III, "Communication
Facilities, Country by Country," is the major
portion, discussing in detail communication
facilities including type of control, production, and consumption. Literacy figures are
also given. Appendices include a list of news
agencies throughout the world and a bibliography of books and periodicals.

101. World Illiteracy at Mid-Century: A Statistical
Study. New York: UNESCO Publications Center,
1957. (Monographs on Fundamental Education XI)
    "To our knowledge, the present study is the
first attempt to present estimates on the
extent of illiteracy in every country and
territory in the world. Detailed analyses are
also given in the present work for some 65
countries, based on available census data
since 1945." - Introduction.
    Although data are relatively old, it never-
theless remains valuable because up-to-date
information about literacy is hard to find
through conventional reference books. (See
also No. 50.)

102. Wright, Charles R. Mass Communication: A
Sociological Perspective. New York: Random
House, 1959.
    Intended as an introduction to the soci-
ology of communications with each chapter
presenting a major subdivision. The first
chapter deals with the nature and function of
mass communications in terms of audience, com-
municator experience, nature of the communica-
tor, surveillance of the environment, interpretation and prescription, and the transmission
of culture. The second discusses alternative
systems of mass communications through selected
case studies, using the Soviet Communist system
(broadcasting, film, press); British and
Canadian broadcasting; the American broadcasting system; and communication in nonindustrial
countries. The third chapter analyzes the
sociology of the audience. The fourth comments
on the cultural content of American mass communications. The fifth tells what is known
about social effects. Contains notes and
selected readings.

103. The Writers' and Artists' Year Book: A Directory
for Writers, Artists, Playwrights, Writers for

<u>Film, Radio and Television, Photographers and</u>
<u>Composers</u>. London: A. & C. Black, yearly.
     A British publication, resembling a composite
of our <u>Literary Market Place</u> and <u>Writer's</u>
<u>Market</u>, although somewhat more extensive geo-
graphically, covering not only the British Isles
but also the overseas market, including Canada,
Australia, South Africa, New Zealand, India,
Pakistan, and the U.S. A special markets section gives brief information on such legal and
economic aspects of authorship as copyright,
income tax, libel, and publishing agreements.
A valuable feature is the brief descriptive
annotation following the name of each publisher and journal.

104. <u>Writer's Market</u>. Ed. by Kirk Polking and Natalie
Hagen. Cincinnati, Ohio: Writer's Digest,
annual.
     "... a comprehensive guide to the editorial
requirement of consumer magazines, trade journals, play producers, greeting card companies,
book publishers, newspapers and syndicates....
This is a directory for paying markets. The
few exceptions are the prestige professional
journals and publications offering a vehicle
to those writers with interests in poetry or
politics who find doors closed to them in the
commercial press." So say the editors in
their preface. Canadian markets are included
along with the American ones. Magazines are
arranged primarily by subject, but certain
book publishers, play producers, syndicates,
cartoonists wanting gags, authors' agents,
and picture sources are listed.

Books and Book Publishing

105. Allworth, Edward. <u>Central Asian Publishing and
     the Rise of Nationalism: An Essay and a List of
     Publications in the New York Public Library</u>.
     New York: The New York Public Library, Astor,
     Lenox, and Tilden Foundations, 1965.
          The first half of this pamphlet consists of
     a 43-page analytical essay about the status of
     book publishing in Central Asia, or Western
     Turkistan. Contains many facts and figures,
     including those on literacy. Periodical pub-
     lications are mentioned briefly. The second
     half lists and describes 824 books and periodi-
     cals on the subject held by the New York
     Public Library.

106. Altick, Richard D. <u>The English Common Reader: A
     Social History of the Mass Reading Public 1800-
     1900</u>. Chicago: University of Chicago Press,
     1957.
          "This volume is an attempt to study, from
     the historian's viewpoint, the place of reading
     in an industrial and increasingly democratic
     society," says the author in this attempt at
     a systematically analyzed and documented work.
     In his approach he has not fallen back upon
     anecdotes nor attempted to analyze the appeal
     of the period's most popular authors. Rather,
     he has discussed the social background of the
     century -- its religion, its prevailing phi-
     losophy, its education, its labor movements,
     and its book, periodical, and newspaper trade.
          Appendices include a chronology of the mass
     reading public, 1774-1900; a chronology of
     best sellers with sales figures and notes; and

another chronology of periodical and newspaper
circulation. Contains a bibliography and an
index.

107. American Book Trade Directory 1969-1970: Lists
of Publishers and Booksellers. Ed. by Eleanor
F. Steiner-Prag and Helaine Mackeigan. New York:
Bowker, biennial.
    Deals primarily with the various agencies
involved in book selling and to a lesser degree
in book publishing.
    The current volume lists almost 4,000 pub-
lishers in the U.S., with addresses and areas
of interest; publishers' imprints, affiliated
companies, subsidiaries, and special distribution arrangements; inactive, out of business,
or merged publishers; about 10,000 retail out-
lets, with addresses, areas of interest,
specialties, and sidelines; book trade information such as dealers in foreign books,
exporters and importers, rental library chains,
wholesalers, auctioneers of literary property,
greeting card publishers; private book clubs;
British, Irish, and Canadian publishers and
booksellers; American representatives of British
publishers and British representatives of
American publishers; booksellers in other parts
of the world. Personnel are not given except
in some cases the owner or manager. A detailed
list of personnel in publishing firms can be
found in the Literary Market Place (No. 151).

108. The American Reading Public: What It Reads; Why
It Reads. Ed. by Roger H. Smith. New York:
Bowker, 1963.
    Subtitled "From Inside Education and Pub-
lishing: Views of Present Status, Future
Trends," most of the articles in this substantial
anthology originally appeared as a Daedalus
symposium. Rebuttals and new material have
been added to the book.
    Subjects dealt with are: "Educating the
Reader: From Grade School to Graduate School";
"Commerical Publishing"; "The University as
Publisher"; "The Reader and the Book: Areas
of Contact"; "The Mass Media of Print"; "Liter-
ary Criticism, the Publisher and the Reader."
Each section has from two to five articles on
various aspects. The authors, among whom are
Benjamin De Mott, Dan Lacy, Jason Epstein,
Frederick A. Praeger, Roger Shugg, Edward Shils,
Leo Bogart, and others equally expert, have an

analytical approach and pull no punches. The
result is a provocative and perceptive, as
well as descriptive, study. Indexed.

109. Anderson, Charles, and others, eds. A Manual on
Bookselling. New York: Bowker, 1969.
" ... a body of technical knowledge freely
offered by seasoned 'pros' not only to the
neophyte bookseller but to other 'pros' as
well." - Foreword. Excellent for its comprehensive account of all aspects of bookselling,
with an appendix on the role, purposes, and
services of the American Booksellers Association and a bibliography, "Books about Books:
A Bookman's Library." Indexed.

110. Astbury, Raymond, ed. Libraries & the Book Trade.
London: Clive Bingley, 1968.
Survey of the British book trade, centering
around publishing, censorship, and bookselling.
A final chapter includes the book trade and
the role of the library.

111. Bailey, Eric. The Economics of Bookselling.
London: Hutchinson, 1965.
Intended primarily for bookstore assistants,
this 59-page book is an excellent source of
data on the economic structure of the British
trade. Numerous statistics.

112. Bailey, Herbert S., Jr. The Art and Science of
Book Publishing. New York: Harper & Row, 1970.
"The ideas presented here . . . are meant
to focus analytically on the problems of management: organization, communication, external
and internal relationships, types of decisions,
work flow, personnel, finances, planning, new
technologies, and so on." So says the author,
drawing upon his experience of 15 years as
director of the Princeton University Press.
The result is one of the best possible inside
views of the structure and economics of book
publishing. One appendix suggests useful
business forms for publishing houses; another
is a bibliography. Indexed.

113. Barker, R. E. Books for All: A Study of International Book Trade. New York: UNESCO Publications Center, 1956.
On a worldwide basis, the author covers facts
and figures on the structure and economics of
book publishing, import and export, tariffs,

copyright, translations, libraries, and book
exchanges. Contains a bibliography and an
index.
Although a sequel to Barker has been written
(No. 134), its orientation is sociological rather
than statistical. In 1952 and from 1954 through
1961 UNESCO published Basic Facts and Figures,
which gave data on production of print media,
film, and broadcasting. This has now been
incorporated in UNESCO Statistical Yearbook:
Annaire Statistique, the best source for current data.

114. Bartlett, Gerald, ed. Better Bookselling: The
Collected Edition. London: Hutchinson, 1965.
Collection of pamphlets published in con-
sultation with the Booksellers Association of
Great Britain and Ireland. Covers most aspects
of British bookselling -- supply, economics,
accounting, careers, staffing, equipment, and
design. Although emphasis is on techniques,
it gives a good overall picture of the way the
system operates.

115. Bennett, H. S. English Books and Readers [1475 to
1640]. 3 vols. 2d ed. Cambridge, England:
Cambridge University Press, 1965, 1969, 1970.
History of the book trade in England for the
period covered. Vol. I deals with the years
from Caxton to the incorporation of the
Stationers' Company; Vol. II, the reign of
Elizabeth I; Vol. III, the reigns of James I
and Charles I.
The author discusses the kinds of books
being published, why they were written, and
for whom they were intended; the growth of
printers and booksellers; and the relationships
of printers, authors, patrons, and readers.
Each volume contains a bibliography and an
index.

116. Book Development in Africa: Problems and Perspectives. New York: UNESCO Publications
Center, 1969. (Reports and Papers on Mass Communication No. 56)
Report of a meeting held by UNESCO at
Accra to help formulate a program of action.
Discusses problems, the place of books in
economic and social development, measures to
promote discussion, demand and supply, prospects and priorities.

117. Book Development in Asia: A Report on the Production and Distribution of Books in the Region. New York: UNESCO Publications Center, 1967. (Reports and Papers on Mass Communication No. 52)

    Part I assesses Asia's book needs and the problems involved in meeting them and then discusses production, promotion and distribution, the international flow of books, and the need for training, research, and cooperation of professional organizations. Part II gives facts and figures and a general summary.

    The report includes the UNESCO member states only: Afghanistan, Burma, Cambodia, Ceylon, Taiwan, India, Indonesia, Iran, Nepal, Pakistan, Philippines, Singapore, Thailand, and the Republic of Vietnam.

118. The Book Industry in Yugoslavia: Report of the Delegation of U.S. Book Publishers Visiting Yugoslavia October 18-November 1, 1963. New York: American Book Publishers Council and the American Textbook Publishers Institute, 1964.

    Gives background and structure documented by facts and figures. Many of the statistics are contained in the appendices.

119. Book Publishing and Distribution in Rumania: Report of the Delegation of U.S. Book Publishers Visiting Rumania October 1-10, 1965. New York: American Book Publishers Council and American Textbook Publishers Institute, 1966.

    Succinct (60 pages) appraisal of the various facets of Rumanian book publishing placed within their social framework. Appendices.

120. Book Publishing in the U.S.S.R.: Report of the Delegation of U.S. Book Publishers Visiting the U.S.S.R. August 20-September 17, 1962. New York: American Book Publishers Council and American Textbook Publishers Institute, 1963.

    Includes: organization of book publishing, operation of a publishing house, book distribution, statistics on production and prices, foreign trade, manufacturing, belle lettres, scientific and technical books, textbooks for elementary and secondary schools, children's books, textbooks for higher education, encyclopedia and dictionary publishing, translations, authors' royalties, copyright.

121. The Bookman's Glossary. Ed. by Mary C. Turner.
     4th ed., rev. and enl. New York: Bowker, 1961.
         In the preface the publishers say that
     their object is to "provide a practical guide
     for those interested in the terminology used
     in the production and distribution of books
     new and old -- not necessarily the technical
     language of the printshop or the paper trade,
     but the words in common usage in the bookstore
     or publisher's office, in a library, or among
     book collectors." The latest edition includes
     new terms in book manufacturing, the graphic
     arts, advertising, publicity, and merchandis-
     ing. Appendices give foreign terms, proof-
     readers' marks, and a bibliography.

122. Books for the Developing Countries. Asia. Africa.
     New York: UNESCO Publications Center, 1965.
     (Reports and Papers on Mass Communication No. 47)
         Consists of two articles: "The Production
     and Flow of Books in South East Asia" by Om
     Prakash and "The Production and Flow of Books
     in Africa" by Clifford M. Fyle. Both authors
     emphasize such social aspects as literacy
     level and language difficulties and such
     economic aspects as copyright, trade barriers,
     and raw materials.

123. Books in West Africa: Report and Recommendations.
     New York: Franklin Books Programs, 1963.
         Report compiled by William E. Spaulding,
     president of Houghton Mifflin; Simon Michael
     Bessie, president of Atheneum; and Datus C.
     Smith, Jr., president of Franklin Books Pro-
     grams, which assesses conditions in West
     Africa relative to the setting up of an indig-
     enous book publishing industry. All manner
     of problems from linguistic and geographic to
     economic and literary are discussed. (See also
     No. 129.)

124. Bowker Annual of Library and Book Trade Infor-
     mation. New York: Bowker, annual.
         Although devoted mainly to information about
     libraries, this book contains a lengthy section
     about the book trade, giving general and miscel-
     laneous facts and figures on American book title
     output, trends in sales, prices of U.S. and
     foreign material, textbooks, British book pro-
     duction, best sellers, prices of book stock,
     the National Book Committee, mergers, inter-
     national book programs, the Frankfurt Fair,

acronyms, calendar of promotional events, meetings, library associations, appointments, retirements, resignations and deaths, National Library Week, trade associations, and other miscellaneous information. One of its most valuable features is the data on the number of new titles published in the U.S., broken down by subject and genre and in various other ways.

125. Bowker Lectures on Book Publishing. New York: Bowker, 1957.
      A collection of the first 17 Bowker Memorial Lectures on book publishing covering 1935-56. Even though a few are personal reminiscences and most of them are somewhat out of date, a number give a broad overview or a historical perspective of their subject. Among the most useful are those on paperback books by Freeman Lewis, university presses by Joseph Brandt, the economics of authorship by Elmer Davis, book clubs by Dorothy Canfield Fisher, and subscription books by F. E. Compton. The lectures delivered since 1956 are available as monographs from the New York Public Library.

126. Cazden, Robert E. German Exile Literature in America 1935-1950: A History of the Free German Press and Book Trade. Chicago: American Library Association, 1970.
      Describes the growth of a large and dynamic anti-Nazi press and book trade on an international scale; tells how thousands of German-language books and journals published outside the Third Reich were imported to the U.S.; and discusses the fate of the German emigré author in America. There are three bibliographic appendices: "Retail Distributors of Free German Publications in the United States 1933-1950"; "Free German and Free Austrian Newspapers and Periodicals in the United States 1933-1950 -- A Checklist"; "Free German Books and Pamphlets Published in the United States 1933-1954 -- A Checklist." There is also an extensive bibliography, footnotes following each chapter, and an index.

127. Cheney, O. H. Economic Survey of the Book Industry 1930-31. New York: Bowker, c1931, 1960.
      Reprint of an authoritative study done four decades ago but still unsurpassed as an analysis

40

of book publishing and book reading. This 1960
reprint contains a new bibliography, new statistical tables, and an introduction by Robert
Frase comparing the book industry in 1930 with
the book industry in 1960.

128. Clair, Colin. A Chronology of Printing. New
York: Praeger, 1969.
The author gives an excellent summation of
his book in the preface: "... this work . . .
is designed as a compendium of information on
matters connected with printing, its first
introduction into Europe and its spread throughout the world; being an attempt to set in
chronological order those matters judged most
important in the history of the printed book,
its manufacture, design and dissemination. Such
information is set out in the form of short and
factual entries, in an endeavour to provide the
widest range of information rather than to study
any one factor in depth. Under each year the
entries are grouped on a national basis, the
national entries being placed in order of
precedence based on the date of first printing
in that particular country."
Information has been drawn from many sources,
both standard works and articles in specialist
journals. Sometimes conflicts of authorities
occur, in which cases the author uses the most
recent findings. Information may be pulled
together through the comprehensive index of its
10,000 or more entries.

129. Clark, Alden H. Books in East Africa. New York:
Franklin Books Programs, 1964.
A thoroughgoing analysis of books and book
publishing as they now exist in Kenya, Tanganyika,
and Uganda, in which the author discusses present socioeconomic-geographic conditions as they
relate to the possibility of an indigenous publishing industry. Also contains an eight-page
interim report on Nigeria. (See also No.
123.)

130. Classified Catalogue of a Collection of Works on
Publishing and Bookselling in the British Library
of Political and Economic Science. London:
British Library of Political and Economic Science,
London School of Economics and Political Science,
1961.
Almost 4,000 entries under two main headings:
works on publishing not relating to particular

places and works relating to specific places.
Under the former come paper and papermaking,
binding, illustrations, the book trade (authorship, publishers and publishing, booksellers
and bookselling), press (journals and journalism), copyright and press law, libraries,
book collecting, books and reading, and
employees. Under the latter heading come
entries under 41 countries.

131. Dahl, Svend. _History of the Book._ 2d English ed.
Metuchen, N.J.: Scarecrow Press, 1968.
   The author describes his aim in the preface:
"Most of the existing works on the history of
the book present its various phases: manuscripts, printing, binding, illustration, the
book trade and libraries separately. In this
work I have attempted to present them all in
a unified account so that their interrelation-
ship will become apparent and the history of
the book will appear in perspective as an
essential factor in the history of culture."
Contains a bibliography and an index.

132. Downs, Robert B. _Books That Changed America._
New York: Macmillan, 1970.
   "The aim here is not to produce a list of
'best' books, 'great' books, or literary
gems, . . . but instead to identify those
writings which have exerted the greatest impact
on our national history, direct or indirect."
Emphasis is on the social sciences rather than
science or the humanities; the three novels
included -- Bellamy's _Looking Backward,_
Sinclair's _The Jungle,_ and Stowe's _Uncle Tom's
Cabin_ -- are essentially sociological. Twenty-
five works are analyzed, beginning with _Common
Sense_ and ending with _Silent Spring._ Each
essay is brief, but together they give an idea
of the power of the written word. (See also
the following item by the same author, _Books
That Changed the World._)

133. Downs, Robert B. _Books That Changed the World._
Chicago: American Library Association, 1956.
   How great is the power of the printed word
to influence men's minds and change the course
of history? The author has sought to pinpoint
16 books in the western world which have exerted
profound influence upon history, economics,
culture, civilization, and scientific thought

from, roughly, the Renaissance to the mid-twentieth century. Although he has definite criteria for selection, he points out that one must of necessity be selective. The books chosen make interesting case studies and highlight how the times can help to create the book and, conversely, how the book can affect the times. Indexed.

134. Escarpit, Robert. _The Book Revolution_. London: Harrap; Paris: UNESCO, 1966.
     Although intended as a sequel to Barker's _Books for All_ (No. 113), _The Book Revolution_, by a well-known French sociologist, makes no effort to update statistics but rather focuses on broad trends in general and the fate of the literary book in the mass market in particular. The result is a series of provocative essays about the way in which belle lettres fare in various countries.
     There is no bibliography as such, although notes at the end of each chapter contain references to other works, many of them European; there is no index.

135. Feehan, John M. _An Irish Publisher and His World_. Cork: Mercier, 1969.
     Books about contemporary Irish publishing are rare. The author emphasizes the problems that differentiate book publishing there from other countries and concludes with a chapter about his own press, Mercier.

136. Glaister, Geoffrey Ashall. _Encyclopedia of the Book_. New York: World Publishing Co., 1960.
     "Terms used in paper-making, printing, bookbinding and publishing, with notes on illuminated manuscripts, bibliophiles, private presses, and printing societies." - Subtitle. In its coverage of book publishing it not only defines terms but also identifies trade journals, prizes and awards, private (but not commercial) presses, and organizations from the Stationers' Company to the American Book Publishers Council. Although the emphasis is British, coverage for the United States is thorough.

137. Gorokhoff, Boris I. _Publishing in the U.S.S.R._ Bloomington: Indiana University Research Center in Anthropology, Folklore and Linguistics, 1959. (Indiana University Publications: Slavic and East European Series, Vol. 19)

"This study seeks to present a survey of
book, periodical, and newspaper publishing in
the Soviet Union, including some related
topics such as censorship, copyright, and
the book trade." - Preface. Emphasis is on
science and technology. Contains a bibliography and index.

138. Grannis, Chandler B., ed. What Happens in Book
Publishing. 2d ed. New York: Columbia University Press, 1967.
"This edition, like the first, is an outline
of the procedures in book publishing, not a
how-to book. It has been brought extensively
up to date by the contributors. Most chapters
have been largely rewritten, except for those
which have been replaced by new ones -- for
example, in the areas of sales and promotion,
children's books, paperbacks (two chapters
instead of one), and mail order publishing. . . .
New chapters on order fulfillment and internal
services, and on the future prospects of the
industry, have been added. And, of course, all
the statistics are new." - Preface.
Other aspects of publishing which are
included are the securing and selection of
manuscripts; copy editing; design; production;
manufacturing; advertising; publicity; business
management and accounting; subsidiary rights
and permission; the publisher and the law; the
distribution of American books abroad; religious
book publishing; textbook publishing; technical,
scientific, and medical publishing; university
presses; reference book publishing; and vanity
publishing. Two of the new chapters deal with
the extensive changes within the last ten years.

139. Griest, Guinevere L. Mudie's Circulating Library
and the Victorian Novel. Bloomington: Indiana
University Press, 1970.
Explains the book distribution system that
dominated the British fiction market for half
a century and in some ways determined the
course of development of popular English novels.

140. Gross, Gerald, ed. Publishers on Publishing.
New York: Bowker, 1961.
Selections on book publishing taken from
memoirs, autobiographies, and articles by
American and British publishers. Includes
such aspects as agents, writers, editing,
advertising, and history of publishing. The

compiler has added commentaries and biographical notes about author-publishers.

141. Hackett, Alice Payne. Seventy Years of Best Sellers: 1895-1965. 3d ed. New York: Bowker, 1968.

"The purpose of this book as of its predecessors, Fifty Years of Best Sellers and Sixty Years of Best Sellers, is to present as completely as possible the facts and figures about American best sellers during the period in which their records have been preserved, to interpret and comment to some extent upon the statistics and the trends, but not to evaluate them from a literary point of view," says the author.

Miss Hackett organizes the titles in many ways -- overall best sellers in paperback and in hardcover listed together and then separately; best sellers by subject; best sellers by years. There is also a bibliography about best sellers and an author-title index.

142. Hall, Max, ed. Made in New York: Case Studies in Metropolitan Manufacturing. Cambridge, Mass.: Harvard University Press, 1959.

One of a series of books on the forces that shape metropolitan areas. This volume is divided into three sections, one of which is "Printing and Publishing" by W. Eric Gustafson, another is "Electronics" by James M. Hund. Both show something of the structure and economics of the two industries, illustrating them with numerous statistics. Contains bibliographical references.

143. Hart, James D. The Popular Book: A History of America's Literary Taste. New York: Oxford University Press, 1950.

An attempt to relate America's popular reading to the social background of the times, from the mid-sixteenth century (Institutes of Christian Religion by John Calvin) to the late 1940s (This I Remember by Eleanor Roosevelt). The author pegs his discussions around specific books. Contains a bibliographical checklist, a chronological index of books discussed (but no sales figures), and an index.

144. Hiebert, Ray Eldon, ed. Books in Human Development. Washington, D.C.: Agency for International

Development, American University, Department of
Journalism, 1964.

    Final report of the Conference on the Role
of Books in Human Development sponsored by the
American University and the Agency for International Development. There is a discussion
of the problems involved, followed by inter-
regional and regional reports on the status
quo, U.S. government agency book programs,
the bilateral and multilateral book programs
of other governments, and a description of
private agency programs in the U.S. Contains
a comprehensive bibliography, including other
bibliographies, books and pamphlets, articles,
manuscripts, and monographs.

145. International Literary Market Place. European
ed. New York: Bowker, annual.

    The subtitle, "a directory of European pub-
lishers/ personnel/ addresses/ subsidiaries/
foreign representatives/ number of titles pub-
lished/ number of titles in stock/ subjects
published/ distributors/ book clubs/ bookstores," covers the contents except for a list
of international organizations which publish
books. The book clubs and bookstores are those
which belong to the various publishers; independent ones are not listed. Contains an
alphabetical index of publishers.

146. Jennison, Peter S., and William H. Kurth. Books
in the Americas: A Study of the Principal Barriers to the Booktrade in the Americas.
Washington, D.C.: Pan American Union, General
Secretariat, Organization of American States,
1960.

    Discusses the efforts to increase the circu-
lation of books in the Americas; book production; characteristics of book publishing and
distribution; imports and exports; Latin American market for books of U.S. origin and the
distribution of Latin American books in the
U.S.; import and export regulations; copyright
protection; political and informational barriers; general statistics. An appendix contains a list of current national bibliographies
for the various countries. The report was prepared as background information for the 11th
Inter-American Conference of the American Book
Publishers Council.

147. Jennison, Peter S., and Robert N. Sheridan. The Future of General Adult Books and Reading in America. Chicago: American Library Association, 1970.

Trends in readership as seen by a group of editors, critics, librarians, publishers, authors, and media specialists at a reading conference held in 1969 by the American Library Association.

148. Kerr, Chester. A Report on American University Presses. [Washington, D.C.:] The Association of American University Presses, 1949. (Obtain through University of North Carolina Press, Chapel Hill)

A report giving the results of a survey conducted in 1948-49 by the Association of American University Presses. Gives the history of university presses in this country, their status at the time of the report, their selection of manuscripts, their economics, their production and distribution, and their nonbook activities. A 51-page supplement appeared in 1956. The October 1969 issue of Scholarly Publishing (No. 654) carries a 25-page article by Mr. Kerr, "The Kerr Report Revisited."

149. Kingsford, R. J. L. The Publishers' Association 1896-1946, with an Epilogue. London: Cambridge University Press, 1970.

This story of England's book trade association from its founding to the mid-1940s, with an epilogue of six pages bringing it up to 1962, is also the story of the major events of the British book trade during the period.

Appendices give the first rules of the Association, the founding members and first Council, and the officers and secretaries from 1896 to 1962. There is a bibliography and an index.

150. Lehmann-Haupt, Hellmut, in collaboration with Lawrence C. Wroth and Rollo G. Silver. The Book in America: A History of the Making and Selling of Books in the United States. 2d ed. rev. and enl. New York: Bowker, 1951.

A history in which the author chronicles book production and distribution from the colonial period, 1638, to about 1950. Excellent for its identification and discussion of printers, publishers, and publishing houses in the U.S. during the time covered. For the

crowded events of the intervening 15 years
see Madison (No. 154).

151. Literary Market Place: The Business Directory
of American Book Publishing. New York: Bowker,
annual.
    An appropriate subtitle for this compendium
might also have been The Bible of American
Book Publishing. Perhaps its most-used feature
is an alphabetical list of the most active book
publishers in the country (vanity publishers
excluded), with addresses and telephone numbers,
a breakdown of personnel, a concise summary of
the kinds of publications the firm produces,
the yearly title output, foreign representatives,
and associations to which the firm belongs.
Further lists classify the publishers geographically and by type. A partial list of
other information includes: mergers; associations; book clubs; exporters and importers;
literary prizes and awards; authors' agents;
free-lance book salesmen; courses in book publishing; translators; newspapers, magazines,
and broadcasting stations which feature book
coverage; organizations which feature adult
and juvenile booklists; manufacturers; editorial
services; public relations services; government
agencies directly concerned with the book trade;
foundations closely associated with it; and
numerous other central and peripheral aspects.
It also contains a bibliography of reference
books of the trade.

152. Macmillan, Fiona. New Zealand. London:
Routledge & Kegan Paul, 1969. (The Spread of
Printing. Eastern Hemisphere)
    A 46-page history, treating the spread of
printing geographically except for sections on
a Maori Press and on government printing.

153. McMurtrie, Douglas. The Book: The Story of
Printing & Bookmaking. 3d ed., rev. New York:
Oxford University Press, 1943.
    Because of the close relationship between
printing and publishing, this account of book
design from the time of primitive human records
to the present is one of the best available
sources for information about the historical
development of the book, early printers, publishers and presses, and so on. Contains
extensive bibliographies and an index.

154. Madison, Charles A. Book Publishing in America.
New York: McGraw-Hill, 1966.
A thorough factual account of book publishing from its colonial beginnings to 1965, with
major emphasis on the period after 1900.
Complements and updates Lehmann-Haupt (No.
150); the two together give an excellent chronological picture of American book publishing and
major firms, past and present. No attempt is
made to place publishing in a social framework.
Useful features in the appendix are "Chronology
of Publishing Events," "All-Time Best Sellers,"
and a bibliography. Indexed.

Mason's Publishers. (See No. 488.)

155. Meeting of Experts on Book Development Planning
in Asia, Singapore 17-23, 1968. Final Report.
Paris: UNESCO, 1968.
Skeletal (15-page) résumé which pinpoints
what has been done and needs to be done to
develop a book publishing industry in those
Asian countries where little now exists.

156. Miller, William. The Book Industry: A Report of
the Public Library Inquiry. New York: Columbia
University Press, 1949.
The usefulness of this work is marred by
poor organization. Nevertheless, it gives an
insight into the structure of the book trade
in the 1940s. Chapters include: "Trade Publishing: A General View," "The Changing
Editorial Environment," "Book Manufacture and
Publishing Costs," "The Book Markets," and
"Trade Publishing and the Public Library."
Appendices contain notes on method and sources
and some book industry statistics. Indexed.

157. Mott, Frank Luther. Golden Multitudes: The
Story of Best Sellers in the United States. New
York: Bowker, c1947, 1960.
The author establishes a simple arithmetical
formula for determining best sellers and dis-
cusses them chronologically in their social
and literary context, from Michael Wigglesworth's
Day of Doom in 1662 to Kathleen Winsor's Forever
Amber in 1945.

158. Mumby, Frank. Publishing and Bookselling: A
History from Earliest Times to the Present Day.
4th ed. London: Jonathan Cape, 1956.

A history of book publishing in England,
with much attention to individual firms. The
first few chapters center around the book trade
in ancient times and the early Middle Ages.
Bibliography and index.

159. Names & Numbers: The Book Industry Telephone
Directory. New York: Bowker, annual.
    Supplement to Literary Market Place (No. 151),
indexing alphabetically some 15,000 names of
firms and individuals mentioned in it, with
addresses and telephone numbers. Formerly
called Book Industry Register.

160. Nunn, Godfrey Raymond. Publishing in Mainland
China. Cambridge, Mass.: M.I.T. Press, 1966.
(M.I.T. Report No. 4)
    "This study attempts to analyze the organi-
zation of book and periodical publishing in
China from 1949 to the end of 1964, with particular reference to publications in the
natural, applied, and social sciences." - Introduction.
    Gives as much information as can be obtained
from sources at Hong Kong about the structure
of the industry, the size of publishing houses,
the relative amounts of literature published in
minority and foreign languages, and the relative
amounts published by subjects. It also deals
with distribution systems -- retail, direct,
and through libraries. Contains four appendices,
a bibliography, and an index.

161. Page, Roger. Australian Bookselling. London:
Deitsch, 1970.
    A survey, including a historical retrospect,
of the Australian book trade as it affects the
booksellers. Contains chapters on educational
and library business and the trade in English,
American, and locally published books. The
author is manager of the Royal Melbourne Institute of Technology bookshop and a former president of the Australian Booksellers Association.
Contains appendices, a bibliography, and an
index.

162. Plant, Marjorie. The English Book Trade: An
Economic History of the Making and Sale of Books.
2d ed. London: Allen & Unwin, 1965.
    The author's comprehensive historical
analysis is mainly economic and, as the title
states, British. The book is divided into two

parts, the age of hand-printing and the age of
the mechanical printer. It discusses demand,
labor, trade organization, structure, paper,
bookbinding, and costs. The scope of the
second edition is like that of the first (1939),
but various statistics and other details have
been updated. There are bibliographical references and an index.

163. Publishers' International Year Book: World
Directory of Book Publishers. 5th ed. London:
Alexander P. Wales, annual.
      Listing of book publishers, publishing,
bookselling associations, and international
booksellers, from Aden to Zambia. Although the
listing appears to be comprehensive, the information about each firm is brief -- for publishers: name, address, telephone number, and
type of publishing emphasized; for associations
and booksellers: names and addresses.

164. Publishers' World. New York: Bowker, annual.
      For five years, between 1965 and 1970, this
annual covered book publishing around the world.
The type of information varied somewhat with
each issue, and ranged in style from features
to statistical material and lists. It always
contained latest developments, activities of
various associations, facts and figures for book
production and for export and import, news of
libraries, and "Essential Addresses" -- listings
of book industry associations, UN agencies which
work with book production, and between 5,000 and
6,000 of the most active publishers and exporters-
importers.
      In 1971 it ceased to exist as an annual.
Feature stories of the type it carried were
included in a special new issue of Publishers'
Weekly (No. 652), the International Edition,
and some of its listings and figures in the
International Literary Market Place (No. 145).

165. Reining, Conrad C. A Publication Survey Trip to
Central and East Africa. Washington, D.C.:
Library of Congress, Reference Department,
General Reference and Bibliography Division,
African Section, 1963.
      Report of a visit by the author to survey
trends in publishing and research in Africa
south of the Sahara. Specific countries in-
cluded are Rhodesia and Nyasaland, Tanganyika,
Zanzibar, Kenya, Uganda, and the Somali Republic.

The author states that his report deals only
superficially with the complex library and
publishing situations and does not always
represent an exhaustive account of the information collected. He offers to supply more
information if needed.

166. Sankaranarayanan, N., comp. and ed. Book Distri-
bution and Promotion Problems in South Asia.
New York: UNESCO Publications Center, 1964.
Survey of distribution and promotion in
Ceylon, Burma, Iran, East and West Pakistan,
North and South India, as well as in three
highly developed countries by way of contrast --
Holland, the United Kingdom, and the United
States.

167. Schick, Frank L. The Paperbound Book in America:
The History of Paperbacks and Their European
Background. New York: Bowker, 1958.
This book covers considerable ground superficially. Part I summarizes the history of
paperbound books in Europe and the U.S.; Part
II touches briefly upon technical production,
censorship, and other aspects; Part III gives
a short description of the majority of paperback firms and lines in business until the mid-
1950s. Its facts are not placed in a social
framework. It is especially useful for tracing
the first decade and a half of the growth of
paperback books in this country, beginning
with the late 1930s. Contains bibliographic
information.

168. Smith, Datus C., Jr. A Guide to Book Publishing.
New York: Bowker, 1966.
Intended especially for the developing
countries of Asia, Africa, and Latin America
in order to help them establish programs.
Traces the various steps in the process from
beginning to end, including economics, types
of publishing, literacy and reading development, the role of libraries, rights and con-
tracts, and distribution systems, including
retail bookstores and training. Contains a
bibliography and an index.

169. Steinberg, Sigfrid. Five Hundred Years of Printing. 2d ed. Baltimore, Md.: Penguin, 1961.
This history of printing from 1450 to the
present is also a history of book publishing
in the days when printer and publisher were

often the same. It is divided into three
sections: The First Century of Printing, The
Era of Consolidation, and The Nineteenth
Century and After. Contains a bibliography,
notes, and an index.

170. Strauss, Victor. The Printing Industry: An
Introduction to Its Many Branches, Processes
and Products. New York: Bowker, 1967.
     Encyclopedic treatment of printing, involv-
ing not only printing itself but also publishing,
advertising, and manufacturing of printed materials. Contains notes and references, a selective bibliography, and a subject index.

171. Taubert, Sigfred. Bibliopola: Pictures and Texts
about the Book Trade. 2 vols. New York: Bowker,
1966.
     Vol. I includes 306 illustrations with texts
arranged by themes such as symbols of the book
trade, the antiquarian bookman, the author,
bookshop interiors, and even headings like
"Drink" (the bibulous bookseller, with woodcut;
"An early specimen, this woodcut suggests that
drinking is another tradition among booksellers,
though less violent than the 16th-century
artist would have us believe"). Vol. II contains 258 plates arranged chronologically,
along with an anthology of writings covering
the book trade over the past 2,000 years.
Text is in French and German as well as English;
illustrations are charming.

172. Trends in American Book Publishing. Urbana: University of Illinois, Graduate School of Library
Science, 1958. (Library Trends, 7:1, July 1958)
     A compilation of articles by authorities on
various phases of book publishing in the late
1950s, including its economic development, the
physical development of bookmaking and printing,
trade book publishing, university press publishing, textbook publishing, private presses
and collectors' editions, book clubs, hard cover
reprints and paperback books, vanity presses,
government and foundation publishing, association publishing, reference book and subscription
book publishing, law book publishing, scientific
and technical book publishing, medical book
publishing, and children's book publishing.
Though obviously dated, some of its facts still
hold true and it is now useful historically.

173. <u>Trends in American Publishing</u>. Ed. by Kathryn
     Luther Henderson. Urbana: University of
     Illinois, Graduate School of Library Science,
     1968. (Allerton Park Institute No. 14)
         Discusses trends in book publishing, its
     economics, the problem of copyright, the role
     of computers, educational publishing, univer-
     sity presses, bookstores, and the viewpoint of
     the librarian. Among participants are Dan
     Lacy, Charles Madison, Robert W. Frase, Abe
     Goldman, Daniel Melcher, Robert J. R. Follett,
     Edwin Castagna, Louis Epstein, and Emily
     Schossberger.

174. Weber, Olga S., ed. <u>Literary and Library Prizes</u>.
     6th ed., rev. and enl. New York: Bowker, 1967.
         Full information on the history, conditions,
     and rules of literary prizes, library awards,
     fellowships, and grants in the U.S., Canada,
     and Great Britain, including awards of inter-
     national significance, with winning authors and
     titles from the establishment of the award to
     the date of the latest edition. Covers books,
     poems, and essays. Contains a comprehensive
     index arranged by names of donors, awards, and
     authors of books. The title has been changed
     several times. The first was <u>Famous Literary
     Prizes and Their Winners</u>, the second, <u>Literary
     Prizes and Their Winners</u>.

Broadcasting

Ainslie, Rosalynde. The Press in Africa: Communications Past and Present. (See No. 442.)

Alisky, Marvin. Latin American Journalism Bibliography. (See No. 443.)

175. Awards, Citations and Scholarships in Radio and Television. 5th ed. Washington, D.C. 20036: National Association of Broadcasters, 1771 N St., NW, 1967.
    Provides a list of broadcasting awards available primarily to radio and television stations, their management, and personnel. Also includes a listing of scholarships in radio and television. Contains an alphabetical index of awards and sponsors.

176. Awasthy, G. C. Broadcasting in India. Bombay 1: Allied Publishers Ltd., 15 Graham Road, Ballard Estate, 1965.
    The author, a former employee of All India Radio, calls this book "a critical narrative of AIR, its programmes, its policies, its ambitions and its failures since 1946." A five-page appendix deals with television.

177. Barnouw, Erik. A Tower in Babel. Vol. I: To 1933. New York: Oxford University Press, 1966.
    _____. The Golden Web. Vol. II: 1933-53. New York: Oxford University Press, 1968.
    _____. The Image Empire. Vol. III: From 1953. New York: Oxford University Press, 1970.

A three-volume massive chronological overview of American broadcasting which touches
upon practically every major event, trend, and
personality in its history. The author's style
makes for delightful reading. Vol. III takes
the history to the present. Appendices in
each volume include a chronology in outline
form, text of the major laws relating to broadcasting, an extensive bibliography, and an
index by performer, program, and topic.

178. BBC Handbook. London W. 1: British Broadcasting
Corporation, 35 Marylebone High St., annual.
(Formerly BBC Yearbook and BBC Annual)
    Concise and reliable guide to the structure
and operation of the British Broadcasting Corporation. Contains the following information:
BBC constitution; finances; domestic and overseas services; program policy and practice;
engineering activities; relations with the
public, including publicity and audience research; administration; a select list of broadcasts; a review of the year; financial accounts;
international relations with the European Broadcasting Union and other international bodies,
and European television program exchanges;
organization, addresses, and publications; texts
of the Royal Charter, License, and Agreement;
advisory councils and committees; and 20 pages
of maps, charts, tables, and analyses covering
many aspects. The 1933 issue gives a history
of the first ten years of the BBC.

179. Bluem, A. William. Religious Television Programs:
A Study of Relevance. New York: Hastings House,
1969.
    Explains the structure of religious broad-
casting and describes over 200 programs broadcast during one year by 430 stations throughout
the U.S. There is also an overview of syndicated and network programming. Appendices
list participating stations and give a brief
bibliography and a short history. Indexed.

180. Bogart, Leo. The Age of Television: A Study of
Viewing Habits and the Impact of Television on
American Life. 2d ed. New York: Frederick
Ungar, 1958.
    Brings together answers to questions fre-
quently asked about television viewing habits,
program content, effects on children, effects
on political thinking, and relationship to

reading, motion pictures, radio, and advertising.

181. Borchardt, Kurt. Structure and Performance of the U.S. Communications Industry: Government Regulation and Company Planning. Boston: Harvard University, Graduate School of Business Administration, Division of Research, 1970.
    Descriptive study aimed at evaluating and managing the structural problems in the U.S. communications industry that result from the interaction of public regulation and rapidly changing technology. The author traces the evolution of the present communications system, stressing the forces which have led to the status quo, and projecting their possible consequences. He gives no attention to the structure and performance of the U.S. communications industry in the public's interest. Rather, the book examines the struggle between corporate interests and the regulatory agency. There are no value judgments.
    Telegraph, telephone, and various private and land mobile systems, including private and point-to-point radio, are treated, as well as radio and television, including cable and pay TV. Contains brief appendices with apportionment charts and statistics. There are also reference footnotes.

182. Briggs, Asa. The Birth of Broadcasting. Vol. I. London: Oxford University Press, 1961. (History of Broadcasting in the United Kingdom)
    _____. The Golden Age of Broadcasting. Vol. II. London: Oxford University Press, 1965. (History of Broadcasting in the United Kingdom)
    _____. The War of Words. Vol. III. London: Oxford University Press, 1970. (History of Broadcasting in the United Kingdom)
    A multi-volume history of broadcasting in Britain, beginning with the 1920s and intended to extend to the passage of the Independent Television Act in 1954. It is written with full BBC cooperation, including access to all surviving records. Because British broadcasting before 1954 is synonymous with the BBC, the set constitutes a history of that institution as well.
    The first volume goes through 1926; the second, from 1927 to World War II; the third, from 1939 to 1945. A fourth and final volume is scheduled to appear within the next few years.

Each volume contains a section on bibliographical
sources and brief appendices consisting largely
of organizational charts, various statistics,
and miscellaneous information. All are indexed.

183. British Broadcasting: A Bibliography. London
W. 1: British Broadcasting Corporation, 35
Marylebone High St., 1958.
"This bibliography replaces 'Books about
Broadcasting' which was first issued in
September 1948. It covers books published in
this country on sound and television broadcasting, excluding those on engineering subjects.
A select list of articles on BBC policy in
monthly and quarterly periodicals, the more
important debates concerning the BBC in both
houses of Parliament, and all Government and
official publications relating to the BBC are
included." - Note by Librarian.

184. The Broadcasting and Television Yearbook: Who,
What, Where in . . . Broadcasting, Television,
Advertising. Sydney, NSW, Australia: Greater
Publications Pty. Ltd., Box 2608, GPO, annual.
Yearbook of Australian broadcasting, geared
mainly to the advertiser but, like most directories of advertising, has much information of
general value on the subject. Contains a full
section of statistics and facts, including
program trends; listings of radio and television stations and advertising representatives;
advertising agencies; a who's who section; and
a final section on broadcasting in New Zealand.

185. Broadcasting from Space. New York: UNESCO Publications Center, 1970. (Reports and Papers on
Mass Communication No. 60)
Report of a UNESCO-sponsored conference
which touched upon a number of aspects of space
communications, among which are: free flow
of information; action toward satellite television transmission (legal protection against
uses not authorized by the originating body);
assessment of the requirements of education,
science, and culture in the future allocation
of frequencies for space communication; and
the respective roles of the UN and the International Communication Union. Concluding is
an address by Arthur C. Clarke, "Beyond Babel:
The Century of the Communication Satellite."

186. <u>Broadcasting Yearbook</u>. Washington, D.C. 20036: Broadcasting Publications, Broadcasting-Telecasting Bldg., 1735 DeSales St., NW, annual.
This yearly supplement to <u>Broadcasting</u> magazine is an indispensable source of data on radio and television. Its main feature consists of separate directories of television and radio stations in the U.S. and Canada, giving for each date of founding, address, ownership, personnel, and other information. Educational as well as commercial stations are included.
It also provides a wealth of other facts, among which are: experimental TV stations; transfers of TV ownership; joint ownership of television and newspapers; group ownership; pending applications; a summary of television structure and statistics in over 50 foreign countries; equipment and FCC rules; NAB codes and program services, including foreign-language and Negro programming; a detailed list of network executives; government agencies concerned with broadcasting; associations, societies, unions, and labor groups concerned with it; attorneys and consulting engineers; professional schools, colleges, and universities offering courses; and a bibliography of recent outstanding books. One of its most useful features is a summary covering the year's important events with pertinent statistics.

187. Brown, Ronald. <u>Telecommunications: The Booming Technology</u>. New York: Doubleday, 1970.
Intended for the layman, this is a simplified account -- as untechnical as is possible -- which extends from the growth of early telegraph systems to the communication satellite. Contains many illustrations, a bibliography, and an index.

188. Canada. Committee on Broadcasting. <u>Report</u>. Ottawa: Queen's Printer, 1965.
Popularly known as the Fowler Report after Robert M. Fowler, Chairman of the Committee, this is a full-scale investigation of practically all facets of Canadian broadcasting, including both the Canadian Broadcasting System and the private sector.

189. Canada. Royal Commission on Broadcasting. <u>Report</u> 2 vols. Ottawa: Queen's Printer, 1957.

59

Inquiry, resulting from extensive hearings, into various facets of Canadian broadcasting in relation to Canada's geographic and socio-economic situation. Numerous appendices give the data from which much of the text is taken. Vol. II, Basic Tables: Television and Radio Programme Analysis compiled by Dallas W. Smythe, gives in tabular form a TV program log analysis.

Canada. Senate. Report on the Mass Media. (See No. 451.)

190. CATV & Station Coverage Atlas with 35-Mile Zone Maps. Washington, D.C. 20006: Television Digest, 2025 Eye St., NW, annual.
   "Designed to provide a quick, portable guide to: (1) Communities and areas in relation to the predicted coverage of TV stations, as expressed by Grade A and B contours; (2) 35-mile zone maps, depicting areas within 35 miles of TV markets, as employed by the Federal Communications Commission in its proposed CATV rules and by NAB, NCTA, and other industry groups seeking agreement on CATV operations."
   In accomplishing this, the following information is shown: CATV industry statistics; American Research Bureau market rankings; CATV and Bell System coordinator; a directory of NCTA, regional, and state associations; call letters of U.S. stations; amendments to FCC CATV rules; FCC-proposed CATV rules; copyright information.

191. CATV Systems: Directory and Service. Englewood, Colo. 80110: Communications Publishing Co., 1900 W. Yale, annual.
   This is an annual issue of TV Communications Magazine and CATV Magazine. The main portion is devoted to a listing of U.S. and Canadian CATV systems by state and province, with detailed information including chief personnel and rates for each. Another important section is the multiple system operators, which is a directory of CATV system group owners; still another gives maps of each state, locating CATV stations. Other features: CATV Operators' Association listings, FCC-approved top-100 market list, a guide to federal agencies and committees of Congress, and CATV regulations -- a summary of the FCC's rules.

192. Chester, Giraud, Garnet R. Garrison, and Edgar E.
     Willis. <u>Television and Radio</u>. 4th ed. New
     York: Appleton-Century-Crofts, 1971.
         The first third of this book surveys the
     structure of broadcasting in the United States
     in terms of its rise, programming, regulations,
     advertising, public, standard of criticism,
     and other such aspects. The rest is concerned
     with techniques.

193. Codding, George A., Jr. <u>Broadcasting without
     Barriers</u>. New York: UNESCO Publications Center,
     1959.
         A study to determine the extent to which
     radio broadcasting is available throughout the
     world as a means of communicating information
     and to examine ways of overcoming political,
     economic, and technological obstacles that
     impede its availability.
         Describes broadcasting systems in the various
     countries, broadcasting between countries, use
     of the radio spectrum, the sharing of frequencies,
     the quest for better techniques, and the impact
     of television on radio broadcasting. Contains
     a bibliography and an index.

194. Cole, Barry, ed. <u>Television: A Selection of
     Readings from TV Guide Magazine</u>. New York: Free
     Press, 1970.
         A substantial reader, with articles on news,
     programming, censorship and control, the
     audience, effects, and speculations about the
     future. Material has been updated in foot-
     notes or the introduction where necessary, and
     deleted when dated. Notes are at the end of
     each chapter, and there is an index.

195. <u>Commercial Television, Cinema and Radio Directory</u>.
     London: Admark Directories Ltd., 180 Fleet St.,
     annual.
         Subtitled "A comprehensive guide and direc-
     tory for all engaged in television, cinema and
     radio selling," this reference work is designed
     mainly for advertisers, but its list of names
     and addresses of many types of businesses con-
     nected with commercial broadcasting and film is
     useful for other purposes. There is, in addi-
     tion, a briefer international directory and a
     foreword about film and about broadcasting.
     The latter gives figures on the size of radio
     and television audiences.

61

196. Commercial Television Year Book and Directory.
London S.E. 1: Business Publications, Ltd.,
Mercury House, 103-119 Waterloo Road, annual.
      A British publication containing informa-
tion about the Independent Television Authority
and the British Broadcasting Corporation; production companies; advertising agents and TV
clients; research facilities; public relations
services; professional and trade organizations;
directories of performers, producers, script
writers, representatives, and newspaper correspondents. Also lists commercial television
stations throughout Europe.

Comprehensive Media Guide. Korea. (See No. 554.)

197. Dimensions of Radio. Washington, D.C. 20036:
National Association of Broadcasters, 1771 N
St., NW, annual.
      Gathering facts and figures on radio becomes
increasingly elusive. Therefore, this pamphlet
with simple data in tabular form from a variety
of sources, all cited, is valuable. Most of
the material is retroactive, giving comparisons
over a period of years. Some of it is hard to
locate elsewhere. Partial contents include:
commercial radio stations by states and other
regions; growth of FM stations broadcasting in
stereo, with breakdowns by states; stations
reporting payments to proprietors, etc.; revenue
and expense for the typical radio station,
nationwide; time sales; employment, both AM
and FM; audience dimensions; growth of radio
sets in use; total set sales, AM and FM, broken
down by home and car; world radio sets by
countries; and so on. Data will often be sufficient for the layman, but those researching
in depth will doubtless need to refer to the
original source, which is always given.

198. Dimensions of Television. Washington, D.C.:
National Association of Broadcasters, 1771 N
St., NW, annual.
      Like the preceding Dimensions of Radio,
this pamphlet gathers statistics on a number
of aspects of television from a number of
sources. Examples of type of material include:
growth of commercial and noncommercial stations;
time sales; revenues-expenses-profits from a
typical station; UHF and color penetration;
home viewing; markets; total employment for
both networks and stations; annual advertising

62

volume; TV households by states and a world
set count by country; and similar information.
Data are frequently retroactive. Sources are
cited.
   The same comment applies to this as applied
to Dimensions of Radio: facts and figures in
the pamphlet will often be sufficient for the
layman, but the researcher in depth will doubtless need to refer to the original sources.

199. Directory and Yearbook of Educational Broadcasting. Washington, D.C. 20036: National Association of Educational Broadcasters, 1346 Connecticut
   Ave., annual.
      The NAEB rightly terms this the most compre-
   hensive listing of institutions, organizations,
   and individuals involved in educational radio
   and television in the United States.
      Along with its information about stations,
   networks, program services, and individual and
   associate NAEB members, it gives related professional associations and colleges and universities offering courses in broadcasting.

200. Dizard, Wilson P. Television: A World View.
   Syracuse, N.Y.: Syracuse University Press, 1966.
      Factual account, giving history, present
   status, and current trends of television communications around the world, including underdeveloped and industrialized countries. The
   author is with the Foreign Service of the USIA,
   and as might be expected, his treatment emphasizes the role of the U.S. in making television
   a more effective means to further our national
   interests. Contains a lengthy bibliography and
   an index.

201. Drury, C. M. White Paper on a Domestic Satellite
   Communications System of Canada. Ottawa, Canada:
   Queen's Printer, 1968.
      Reviews the main factors involved in planning
   and establishing domestic satellite communications to meet Canada's needs, both in the
   immediate future and over the longer term. Discusses in general the significance and technique
   of communication by satellite; Canada's achieve-
   ments in satellite and communications technology;
   its present needs; a possible structure for the
   system; and international considerations.
   Appendices include a survey of satellite developments on an international level (INTELSAT,
   the Franco-German "SYMPHONIE," the USSR's

63

satellite communication system, the European
Launcher Development Organization (ELDO), and
the European Space Conference). There is a
glossary of terms. Text is in both English
and French.

202. Durham, F. Gayle. Amateur Radio Operation in the
Soviet Union. Cambridge, Mass.: Massachusetts
Institute of Technology, Center for International
Studies, Research Program on Problems of Communication and International Security, 1965. (Distributed by Clearinghouse for Federal Scientific
and Technical Information, U.S. Dept. of Commerce)
　　　Tells the importance, structure, and extent
of amateur radio activity. Contains bibliographical footnotes and extensive appendices
giving regulations and amateur radio competi-
tions.

203. Durham, F. Gayle. News Broadcasting on Soviet
Radio and Television. Cambridge, Mass.: Massachusetts Institute of Technology, Center for
International Studies, Research Program on Problems of Communication and International Security,
1965. (Distributed by Clearinghouse for Federal
Scientific and Technical Information, U.S. Dept.
of Commerce)
　　　An introduction gives the Soviet conception
of the function of broadcasting media and news.
This is followed by an analysis of the structure
and content of radio news broadcasting and a
shorter chapter on television broadcasting.
Contains copious bibliographical notes.

204. Durham, F. Gayle. Radio and Television in the
Soviet Union. Cambridge, Mass.: Massachusetts
Institute of Technology, Center for International
Studies, Research Program on Problems of Communication and International Security, 1965. (Distributed by Clearinghouse for Federal Scientific
and Technical Information, U.S. Dept. of Commerce)
　　　Gives information on many aspects of Soviet
broadcasting: structure, equipment, production
and repair, subscription fees, programs and
hours, educational television, relations with
Intervision, and audience. Detailed notes refer
to the original sources; and numerous charts,
graphs, and tables illustrate the text.

205. EBU Review. Part B -- General and Legal -- No.
     118B. November 1969. Geneva, Switzerland.
          This particular issue is devoted entirely
     to satellite broadcasting, with articles by
     authorities covering a number of phases and
     parts of the world.

206. Educational Television: The Next Ten Years.
     Stanford, Calif. 94305: Stanford University,
     Institute for Communication Research, Redwood
     Hall, 1962.
          Report and summary of major studies on the
     problems and potential of educational tele-
     vision in the early 1960s, conducted under the
     auspices of the United States Office of Educa-
     tion.

207. Emery, Walter B. Broadcasting and Government:
     Responsibilities and Regulations. 2d ed. East
     Lansing: Michigan State University Press, 1971.
          Although some of the same regulations relate
     to broadcasting that relate to the print media,
     broadcasting has nonetheless brought up a host
     of new problems because of the nature of its
     transmission which necessitates a certain amount
     of government regulation. The author discusses
     the various governmental agencies concerned
     with broadcasting and sets forth briefly their
     basic rules, policies, and any services they
     may provide to the American people. There are
     bibliographic notes at the end of each chapter;
     appendices which give important documents,
     requirements, definitions, codes, and so on; a
     selective bibliography; and an index.

208. Emery, Walter B. National and International
     Systems of Broadcasting: Their History, Operation
     and Control. East Lansing: Michigan State Uni-
     versity Press, 1969.
          The foreword states that this book represents
     the first attempt "to analyze in some depth the
     important broadcasting systems in all parts of
     the world, and to explain their origin, develop-
     ment and present operation." It covers the
     managerial and regulatory aspects of radio and
     television, both national and international, as
     well as the quantitative dimensions of the media
     and their programming patterns.
          Factual but not evaluative (and for some
     countries outdated -- i.e., Yugoslavia), it none-
     theless contains material not easily accessible
     in any other one place -- as, for example,

"pirate" stations. Countries or regions in-
cluded are the U.S., Mexico, Canada, the United
Kingdom, Ireland, Belgium, the Netherlands,
Luxembourg, Denmark, Iceland, Norway, Sweden,
Finland, France, Italy, Greece, Germany,
Austria, Switzerland, Spain, the USSR, Hungary,
Yugoslavia, Turkey, Africa (an overview), India,
Communist China, Japan, Australia.
    An appendix gives various broadcasting laws
and acts, codes for several nations, membership
of the European Broadcasting Union, and infor-
mation on satellite communications. There is
a detailed bibliography and a subject index.

209. The Focal Encyclopedia of Film and Television
Techniques. Ed. by Raymond Spottiswoode. New
York: Hastings House, 1969.
    Although much of the information in this
massive one-volume encyclopedia is highly
technical, much is also concerned with definitions and history. A considerable amount of
the technical information is useful to laymen
in understanding the technology behind current
happenings in television and, to a lesser
extent, the film. Contains about 1,600 entries
and covers both British and American practices.
A detailed index brings scattered material on
the same subject together.

Fowler, Robert M. See Canada. Committee on
Broadcasting. Report. 1965 (No. 188).

210. Garnett, Bernard E. How Soulful Is "Soul" Radio?
Nashville, Tenn. 37212: Race Relations Information Center, P.O. Box 6156, 1109 19th Ave.,
South, 1970.
    History, structure, programming, and present
extent of "black" radio which covers practically
all aspects.

211. Garry, Ralph, F. B. Rainsberry, and Charles
Winick, eds. For the Young Viewer: Television
Programming for Children . . . at the Local
Level. New York: McGraw-Hill, 1962.
    An educator, a program executive, and a
psychologist examine 425 local programs from
223 stations in 146 cities and suggest ways to
apply known principles of child development to
the production of children's programs. Although
old, it is one of the few studies of local
programming and is also interesting because of
its emphasis upon children's programs. It was

written under the auspices of the Television
Information Office. (See also No. 229.) Contains a bibliography.

212. Glick, Ira O., and Sidney J. Levy. Living with
Television. Chicago: Aldine, 1962. (Social
Research Studies in Contemporary Life Series)
Study of television viewers, based on over
13,000 interviews, designed to show how they
use the medium and how they feel about it.
Contains an appendix on methodology and an
index.

213. Gordon, George N. Educational Television. New
York 10011: Center for Applied Research in Education, 70 Fifth Ave., 1965.
History and appraisal which takes into account
growth, financial structure, public service
function, open- and closed-circuit television,
television in schools, and effect studies. Contains a brief bibliography and an index.

214. Great Britain. Committee on Broadcasting (1960).
Report. 2 vols. Appendices. London: Her Majesty's Stationery Office, 1962.
The purpose of this report, commonly known
as the Pilkington Report after its chairman,
Sir Harry Pilkington, considers the future of
broadcasting in the United Kingdom, the dissemination by wire of broadcasting and other
programs, and the possibility of television
for future showing; makes recommendations on
future services to be provided by the BBC and
ITV; recommends whether additional services
should be provided by any other organization;
and proposes financial and other conditions
which should be applied. A short version of
the total report, The Future of Sound Radio and
Television (Great Britain. Committee on Broadcasting. 1960), is a 47-page version of the
report of the Pilkington Committee.

Hall, Max, ed. Made in New York: Case Studies
in Metropolitan Manufacturing. (See No. 142.)

215. Halloran, James D. The Effects of Mass Communication with Special Reference to Television.
Leicester, England: Leicester University Press,
1964. (Television Research Committee Working
Paper No. 1)
An 80-page booklet giving an overview of the
major social-scientific studies, experiments,

67

and surveys that deal with the effects of television, especially upon children. The author deliberately omits certain aspects: the use of television in education (closed-circuit and school broadcasts) and its uses in propaganda and psychological warfare. He also limits himself to works with an empirical approach, and he stresses the gaps in verifiable evidence. Contains a bibliography and a rather sketchy index. (See also Halloran's later work on the effects of television, No. 216.)

216. Halloran, James D., ed. The Effects of Television. London: Panther, 1970.

Five British social scientists look at different areas or levels of the effects of television from their own particular standpoints. Contents include: "Introduction: Studying the Effects of Television" and "The Social Effects of Television," both by Halloran; "The Political Effects of Television" by Jay G. Blumler; "Television and the Arts" by Roger Brown; "The Effects of Television on Other Media" by Peter Masson; and "Television and Education" by Denis McQuail.

Those who wish definitive answers will not necessarily find them here, nor, as the authors point out, anywhere else, for the subject is elusive. But they cover much existing evidence and make a number of speculations, some of which raise provocative questions. There is a bibliography after each study. Indexed.

217. Halloran, James D. Mass Media and Delinquent Behavior. New York: Humanities Press, 1970. (Television Research Committee   Working Paper No. III-SBN391-00034-9)

An exploratory study of the television viewing habits of adolescents placed on probation by the courts. The second portion of the book is a report on research undertaken at the Centre for Mass Communication Research at the University of Leicester, Leicester, England. Gives special attention to the media portrayal ·of violence and aggression.

218. Harmon, Jim. The Great Radio Heroes. New York: Doubleday, 1967.

A lighthearted book which gives an excellent though informal account of the popular radio serials of yesteryear. The title,

incidentally, is a misnomer; heroines are
included as well.

219. Harris, Dale B. Children and Television: An
Annotated Bibliography. Washington, D.C. 20036:
National Association of Educational Broadcasters,
1346 Connecticut Ave., 1959.
Concise abstracts of a number of articles
and other materials, both popular and scholarly,
listed under the following headings: "Surveys
and Studies: General Approaches," "Surveys
and Studies: Educational and Character Effects
of TV," "Educational Outcomes of TV for Children," "Discussions for Parents," "General Comments and Opinions of Children's TV Programs,
Reviews, etc.," and "Principles and Recommendations Concerning Programs for Children."

220. Head, Sydney W. Broadcasting in America. A Survey
of Television and Radio. 2d rev. ed. Boston:
Houghton Mifflin, 1971.
One of the best books available to give background facts on broadcasting in the United
States. Drawing upon primary sources, the
author discusses in detail the physical basis
of broadcasting, its history and growth, its
economic structure, its regulation both by
government and by industry itself, the various
inter-media relationships between broadcasting
and film and press as well as the relationship
between radio and television, the role of
advertising, and what is known about effects.
This latter section is particularly strong. An
appendix gives a lengthy comparison of the
television, radio, and motion picture codes.
There is also a bibliography leading to primary
sources.

221. Heinz, Catherine, comp. Television and Education:
A Bibliography. Rev. ed. New York 10022: Television Information Office, The Library, 754 Fifth
Ave., 1962. (TIO Bibliography Series No. 1)
Over 100 annotated references to monographic
works of various sorts, grouped in the following categories: general; operational reports;
research; programming; production and technical;
reference sources -- general, bibliographies,
periodicals, and indexes; course directories;
audiovisual aids; directories of ETV facilities.
Emphasis is on the use of television in the
classroom.

222. Heinz, Catherine, comp. <u>Television Careers: A</u>
<u>Bibliography</u>. New York 10022: Television Infor-
mation Office, The Library, 745 Fifth Ave., 1966.
(TIO Bibliography Series No. 4)
    Comprehensive annotated bibliography of
books and pamphlets grouped as follows: general,
study and training, scholarships, fellowships,
internships, assistantships, occupational
specialties, employment opportunities by organization and by location, placement listings,
dissertations and theses, audiovisual aids.

223. Heinz, Catherine, comp. <u>Television: Freedom,</u>
<u>Responsibility, Regulation: A Bibliography</u>. New
York 10022: Television Information Office, The
Library, 745 Fifth Ave., 1962. (TIO Bibliography
Series No. 2)
    Pamphlet containing about 40 annotated
references to books, addresses, government
publications, pamphlets, and magazine articles.

224. Heinz, Catherine, comp. <u>Television in Government</u>
<u>and Politics: A Bibliography</u>. New York 10022:
Television Information Office, 745 Fifth Ave.,
1964. (TIO Bibliography Series No. 3)
    A 55-page pamphlet containing references to
books, pamphlets, government publications,
bibliographies, periodical articles, and dissertations.

225. Hill, Harold E. <u>The National Association of Edu-</u>
<u>cational Broadcasters</u>. Washington, D.C. 20036:
National Association of Educational Broadcasters,
1346 Connecticut Ave., 1954.
    Because of the close relationship of the NAEB
to educational broadcasting in general, this
history of the organization from its inception
as the Association of College and University
Broadcasting Stations in 1925 to the early
1950s serves also to trace the development of
the movement in the U.S. Contains a bibliography.

226. Himmelweit, Hilde T., A. N. Oppenheim, and Pamela
Vince. <u>Television and the Child: An Empirical</u>
<u>Study of the Effect of Television on the Young</u>.
London: Oxford University Press, 1958.
    Study based on a large sample of children in
five cities who were questioned about their
attitudes, interests, and behavior and re-
examined a year later to test changes that
might have occurred. The authors looked for

70

reactions to conflict, crime, and violence,
and for effects on values, outlook, knowledge,
school performance, leisure, interests, and so
on. Appendices describe methods and there is
a bibliography, glossary, and index. For a
study made in the U.S. shortly afterward see
Television in the Lives of Our Children by
Schramm, Lyle, and Parker (No. 267).

227. The History of Broadcasting in Japan. Tokyo:
Nippon Hoso Kyokai (Japanese Broadcasting Corporation), Radio & TV Culture Research Institute,
2-2 Uchisaiwai-oho Chiyoda-Ku, 1967.
    Comprehensive history dealing primarily
with the structure, control, programming, and
listenership of radio and television. Appendices
give broadcasting services in occupied areas,
development of commercial broadcasting, a
chronology, texts of historical documents
such as broadcast law and standards of NHK's
domestic broadcast programs, and an assortment
of statistical material.

Hopkins, Mark W. Mass Media in the Soviet Union.
(See No. 474.)

Hudson's Washington News Media Contacts Directory.
(See No. 475.)

228. India. Committee on Broadcasting and Information
Media. Radio and Television: Report of the Committee on Broadcasting Media. New Delhi: Ministry
of Information and Broadcasting, Government of
India, [1966].
    Overall survey of structure and content.

229. Interaction: Television Affairs Programming at
the Community Level. New York 10022: Television
Information Office, 745 Fifth Ave., 1960.
    Subject listing of 1,038 programs, both com-
mercial and educational, produced by local
stations. Robert Lewis Shayon, radio-television
critic of the Saturday Review, has written the
introduction and a description of each program.
    Although this study is by no means inclusive
(264 of the 562 stations questioned sent in
replies), and although it has not been brought
up to date, it nevertheless remains a valuable
source of information about local programming --
an area in which very little material exists.
(See also No. 211.)

230. International Television Almanac. Ed. by Charles
S. Aaronson. New York 10020: Quigley Publications, 1270 Sixth Ave., annual.
    The term "international" in the title is
misleading. Except for a section on Great
Britain and Canada and a brief one on the world
market, emphasis is on the United States.
    Gives a variety of data about nontechnical
aspects of television. A partial list of contents includes: a variety of statistics on
revenues, expenses, income, production and
sales, advertising, viewing habits, and users;
poll and award winners; a "who's who in motion
pictures and television"; a section on motion
pictures, giving feature releases from 1944
to about 1968; foreign film distribution in
the U.S.; television stations, with addresses,
chief personnel, and other data; channel allo-
cations; a listing of producers for programs,
commercials, feature films, and shorts; services
for producers, including marketing research,
and talent and literary agencies; publicity
representatives in the Los Angeles area; government film bureaus; programs, giving basic information about each; companies, including networks,
set manufacturers, major producers, and distributors; advertising agencies; station representatives; codes; organizations, including guilds
and unions. Some of the sections -- "who's
who," feature pictures, government film bureaus,
publicity representatives, and others -- are
identical with those in the same publisher's
International Motion Picture Almanac (No. 343).

231. Japan NAB Handbook. Tokyo: National Association
of Commercial Broadcasters in Japan, Bungei
Shunja Bldg. No. 3 Kiol-Cho, Chiyoda-Ku, annual.
    Each year contents vary slightly, but a
typical issue lists the history of the origin
of both government and private broadcasting,
the beginnings of commercial broadcasting, its
status today, the organization of Japan's
National Association of Broadcasting, its research center, numerous industry statistics,
and a directory of member companies. For information about Japan's public broadcasting system
see No. 252.

232. Johnson, Nicholas. How to Talk Back to Your Television Set. Boston: Little, Brown, 1969.
    A maverick member of the FCC reminds the
public that they own the airwaves, tells them

the facts of life about broadcasting as it now
exists, and states what he feels can be done
to improve it. Among other topics are: "The
Media Barons and the Public Interest," "New
Attitudes, New Understanding, New Will: The
Media and the Unheard," "A Concept of Communications: A Systems Approach," "Communications and the Year 2000," "Reforming Television:
Institutional Realignments," and a very practical "What You Can Do to Improve TV." There
follow two pages of specific instructions
about ways to change TV programming which include also a list of free materials, sources
of facts for local information, organizations
to which to write, and dates for license re-
newals. A useful and iconoclastic book which
makes interesting reading.

233. Kaftanov, S. V., and others, eds. Radio and Television in the USSR. Washington, D.C.: U.S. Joint
Publications Research Service, 1961. (Purchase
photocopies from Photoduplication Service, Library
of Congress.)
    Gives concise information about: radio and
television programs in the USSR; some of the
more important broadcasts of the central and
local services; radio and television newspapers
and magazines; the extent of the service; the
growing international ties; the activities of
the All-Union Scientific Research Sound Recording Institute and the State House of Radio
Broadcasting and Sound Recording in Moscow;
the basic material-technical means for radio
broadcasting and television broadcasting.

234. Kahn, Frank J., Jr., ed. Documents of American
Broadcasting. New York: Appleton-Century-
Crofts, 1968.
    Collection of primary reference sources
often difficult to obtain separately -- laws,
decisions, reports, and other documents in
their original form. An exceedingly valuable
resource book. Areas covered include broadcast
regulation, regulation of programming, broadcast journalism, regulation of competition,
educational broadcasting. Two-page bibliography.

235. Koenig, Allen E., ed. Broadcasting and Bargain-
ing: Labor Relations in Radio and Television.
Madison: University of Wisconsin Press, 1970.
    A study on broadcasting unions covering
four major areas: a historical overview, legal

73

decisions rendered by the National Labor Relations Board and the courts, specific problem areas confronting the industry and unions, and a look at the future. Contains appendices: "Report and Order of the FCC on Nondiscrimination in Broadcast Employment Practices," and "Further Notice of Proposed Rulemaking on Nondiscrimination in Broadcast Employment Practices." Indexed and with footnotes at the end of sections.

236. Lackmann, Ron. Remember Radio. New York: Norton, 1970.
    Intended to provide entertainment and provoke nostalgia through photographs, scripts, and radio listings of programs in pretelevision days, this covers a range of popular radio programs. Among other things, it provides about 300 pictures of characters known by voice rather than face.

237. Land, Herman W. Associates, Inc. Television and the "Wired City": A Study of the Implications of a Change in the Mode of Transmission. Washington, D.C. 20036: National Association of Broadcasters, Public Relations Service, 1771 N St., NW, 1968.
    Prepared for the President's Task Force on Communications Policy by the National Association of Broadcasters, this study reexamines the utilization of the useful electronic spectrum in the light of present and future technological breakthroughs such as communications satellites and coaxial cable transmission.

238. Laskin, Paul. Communicating by Satellite: Report of the Twentieth Century Fund Task Force on International Satellite Communications. New York 10021: Twentieth Century Fund, 41 East 70th St., 1969.
    A report which focuses on the way the international community can best be served by the communications satellite rather than on who should own it.

239. Lazarsfeld, Paul F. Radio and the Printed Page. New York: Duell, Sloan & Pearce, 1940.
    Subtitled "An Introduction to the Study of Radio and Its Role in the Communication of Ideas," this early study discusses the interplay of radio and reading.

Leading National Advertisers, Inc. LNA Television
Service. (See No. 570.)

Leading National Advertisers, Inc. Rorabaugh
Spot TV. (See No. 572.)

240. Levin, Harvey J. Broadcast Regulation and Joint
Ownership of Media. New York: New York University Press, 1960.
Discusses the character of intermedia competition, the pattern and trend of joint media
ownership, the case for separate ownership,
economics of joint ownership, impact of old
media on the new, competition in price and
quality, broadcast regulatory policy. An appendix giving sources of statistical data forms
a bibliography, and there are indexes to cases
cited and to subjects.

241. Lichty, Lawrence W., and Joseph M. Ripley II,
eds. American Broadcasting: Introduction and
Analysis Readings. 3 vols. Madison, Wis.:
College Printing and Typing Co., 1969.
Contains articles and statistics of many
sorts from many sources, covering such aspects
as revenues and profits, multiple control, and
TV station ownership vis-à-vis other communications interests. Information is factual, statistical, and documentary. Vol. II is concerned
largely with audience research, some of it data
from the research organizations, and also with
regulations, responsibility, goals, and effects.
Much of the material is again statistical.
Vol. II has a minimal section of obvious books.
Vol. III is a workbook.

242. Liu, Alan P. L. Radio Broadcasting in Communist
China. Cambridge, Mass.: Massachusetts Institute of Technology, 1964. (Distributed by Clearinghouse of Federal Scientific and Technical
Information, U.S. Dept. of Commerce, National
Bureau of Standards, Institute for Applied Technology.)
Gives background, monitoring system, broadcasting for minorities, growth of broadcasting
stations and power, control of equipment and
personnel, content and hours of broadcasting,
and audience feedback and listening behavior.
Data come from Taiwan, western sources, and
Chinese sources when they are available. Also
contains a map survey of the radio network, an

extensive bibliography, and an appendix, "Regulations governing the control of broadcasting."

243. MacCallum, Mungo, ed. <u>Ten Years of Television</u>. Melbourne, 3000, Australia: Sun Books, 44 La Trobe St., 1968.
   "This book is not meant to be a history of Australian television. It is a collection of comments on different aspects . . . at the end of its first decade of life." - Introduction.
   The contributors have written about aspects of television in which they are especially interested: profit and loss, entertainment, public affairs, drama, teenagers, the arts, education.

244. MacKay, Ian K. <u>Broadcasting in Australia</u>. Melbourne: Melbourne University Press, 1957.
   Description of the Australian system -- its background and origins, its national service, its commercial and network broadcasting, its listener research and surveys, its participating organizations, and what appears to be its impact. Appendices give Australian broadcasting stations (medium wave); number of national and commercial stations in relation to licensed listeners; listener licenses in relation to population; increase in ransmitting hours and extent of Australian broadcasting commission stations operation. There is an index to stations and a general index.

245. MacKay, Ian K. <u>Broadcasting in New Zealand</u>. Wellington, Australia: Reed, 1953.
   Gives history, structure, and programming. Because it predates television it is concerned primarily with radio. Indexed.

246. MacKay, Ian K. <u>Broadcasting in Nigeria</u>. Ibadan, Nigeria: Ibadan University Press, 1964.
   The last expatriate Director-General of the Nigerian Broadcasting Corporation tells its history, examines its present status, and gives some analytical criticism. Contains a bibliography and appendices giving the corporation ordinance and amendments and some key dates and figures.

247. <u>Meeting of Experts on the Use of Space Communication by the Mass Media</u>. New York: UNESCO Publications Center, 1966.

Report of a UNESCO meeting at which a number
of related subjects were discussed: technical
capabilities, economics, social implications,
transmission of news, radio and television
broadcasting, education, cultural exchange.

248. Membership Directory of the Radio-Television News
Directors Association. Iowa City: State University of Iowa, Communications Center, annual.
A nationwide list of members, arranged geographically.

Merrill, John C., Carter E. Bryan, and Marvin
Alisky. The Foreign Press: A Survey of World
Journalism. (See No. 491.)

249. Meyersohn, Rolf. Television Research: An Annotated Bibliography. New York: Columbia University, Bureau of Applied Social Research, 1954?
"This bibliography comprises an annotated
list of the research projects conducted on
television within the past few years. Sources
drawn upon included universities, advertising
agencies, trade organizations, and all available published material. Because of the widely
scattered and sometimes confidential nature of
research in this field, however, this bibliography should be looked upon as tentative rather
than exhaustive. . . .References are organized
around the traditional areas of communications
research: content, audience, and effect. Because of the considerable number of studies
concentrating on children and television, they
are grouped in a separate section (IV). This
final section comprises a selection of books,
articles, and studies on various aspects of
the mass media in general, many of which have
direct implication for television." - Introduction. One of the best sources in its field up
to about 1954.

250. Mitchell, Curtis. Cavalcade of Broadcasting.
Chicago: Follett, 1970. (A Benjamin Company/
Rutledge Book)
A simple, chronological history of radio
and television, profusely illustrated, and
intended for the high school and junior high
level.

Movies on TV. (See No. 374.)

251. Musolf, Lloyd D., ed. Communications Satellites in Political Orbit. San Francisco: Chandler, 1968.
    Beginning with the organization of the Communication Satellite Corporation in 1962 and progressing through the next half decade, the editor has traced its history through the use of official documents -- testimony of interested parties, both public and private, before congressional committees; reports made by these committees; interchanges between protagonists on the floor of the House or Senate; presidential messages and statements; and policy pronouncements by administrative agencies. Through use of these excerpts he has been successful in revealing some of the decision-making processes that structured an important technological innovation. A valuable sourcebook.

National Advertising Investments: Magazines. Newspaper Supplements. Network TV. Spot TV. (See No. 575.)

Network Rates and Data. (See No. 576.)

252. NHK Handbook. Tokyo: Nippon Hoso Kyokai (Japan Broadcasting Corporation), 2-2 Uchisaiwai-oho Chiyoda-Ku, annual.
    Comprehensive information about the public broadcasting corporation comparable to the British Broadcasting Corporation. Information for each year varies slightly; typical data include a discussion of the character and objectives of NHK, domestic and overseas broadcasts, interchanges with overseas countries, programs and programming services, engineering, research and investigation, audience, and a section giving documents such as broadcast laws and written standards. (For information about commercial broadcasting in Japan, see No. 231.)

Ogilvy & Mather Pocket Guide to Media. (See No. 582.)

253. Paulu, Burton. British Broadcasting in Transition. Minneapolis: University of Minnesota Press, 1961.
    A sequel to British Broadcasting: Radio and Television in the United Kingdom (No. 254), updating it and discussing the effects of competition on British broadcasting services.

254. Paulu, Burton. British Broadcasting: Radio and
     Television in the United Kingdom. Minneapolis:
     University of Minnesota Press, 1956.
        An analysis of British broadcasting from the
     standpoint of organization, history, type of
     programming, and audience. Discusses in
     detail the British Broadcasting Corporation and
     Independent Television Authority.

255. Paulu, Burton. Radio and Television Broadcasting
     on the European Continent. Minneapolis: Univer-
     sity of Minnesota Press, 1967.
        Survey, based on a firsthand study, of
     facilities, structure and organization, fi-
     nances, programming (both informational and
     entertainment) in the Soviet Union and other
     Communist countries, France, West Germany,
     Belgium, the Netherlands, Italy, Sweden, and
     Switzerland. Material is organized on these
     broad issues rather than on a country-by-
     country basis, and findings are placed within
     the framework of various interrelated factors
     such as geography, history, politics, inter-
     national relations, religious traditions,
     language, cultural and social life, and so on.
     Contains an excellent bibliography, extensive
     notes, and a detailed index.

256. Peers, Frank W. The Politics of Canadian Broad-
     casting 1920-1951. Toronto: University of Torontc
     Press, 1969.
        Analysis of the beginning and development
     of Canada's mixed system of private and public
     ownership. Copious footnotes serve in lieu of
     a bibliography; there is a detailed index.

257. Pennybacker, John H., and Waldo W. Braden, eds.
     Broadcasting and the Public Image. New York:
     Random House, 1969. (Random House Study in
     Speech)
        Although intended primarily as a tool for
     speech students in making presentations, this
     anthology brings together a number of position
     papers on broadcasting. Part I contains an
     article on the role of the FCC; Part II, pro-
     gramming; Part III, the Fairness Doctrine;
     Part IV, implications of the communications
     revolution. Each section has its own bibliog-
     raphy. Taken as a whole, the articles present
     a critical picture, intended for the young, the
     layman, or both.

258. <u>The People Look at Radio</u>. Chapel Hill: University of North Carolina Press, 1946.
    Report of an early survey conducted by the
National Opinion Research Center, University
of Denver, under the direction of Harry Field,
and analyzed and interpreted by the Bureau of
Applied Social Research at Columbia University
under the direction of Paul Lazarsfeld. Gives
an overall appraisal of program content, including advertising, along with the attitudes
of listeners toward both programming and
advertising, and a discussion of the role of
criticism. Appendices contain tables from
which the conclusions have been drawn. There
is an index.

Pilkington, Sir Harry. <u>See</u> Great Britain. Committee on Broadcasting (1960). <u>Report</u> (No. 214).

<u>"The Profitable Difference": A Study of the
Magazine Market . . . Its Size, Quality and Buy-
ing</u>. (<u>See</u> No. 585.)

259. <u>Public Television: A Program for Action</u>. New
York: Harper & Row; New York: Bantam, 1967.
    The report and recommendations of the Carnegie
Commission on Educational Television. Defines
the term "public television," summarizes the
report, and discusses the opportunity, the
present system, the Commission's proposal, and
the specific type of programming that could
emerge. Lists educational television stations
operating as of December 1966, also supplementary papers by various experts. These latter are "Memorandum of Law," telling the various legal aspects of the corporation of public
television; "Cost of Nationwide Educational
Television"; "Technology and Television"; "Tele-
vistas: Looking Ahead through Side Windows";
"Commercial Television"; "The Federal Communications Commission and Educational Television
Stations"; "Financial and Operating Reports of
Educational Television Stations, July 1965-
June 1966"; "Estimates of Educational Television
Audiences, 1965, 1966."

260. Quaal, Ward L. <u>Broadcast Management: Radio.
Television</u>. New York: Hastings House, 1968.
    In spite of the title, this is somewhat more
than a "how-to" book. The chapters on audience,
radio programming, television programming,
broadcast engineering, management for profit,

the manager and regulation, and the future are
particularly informative. There is no bibliography as such, although there are bibliographic
notes on the various chapters. Indexed.

261. Radio Listening in America: The People Look at
Radio -- Again. New York: Prentice-Hall, 1948.
   A follow-up of the survey, The People Look
at Radio (No. 258), conducted like its prede-
cessor by the National Opinion Research Center
in cooperation with the Bureau of Applied Social
Research, Columbia University, where Paul
Lazarsfeld and Patricia Kendall interpreted
the data. They trace the communications
behavior of the American people -- their reactions toward programming and attitudes --
and once again discuss means through which
radio may best be served by criticism. Data
are given in appendices. Indexed.

262. Radio Programming Profile. Glen Head, N.Y. 11545:
BF/Communication Services, 7 Cathy Court, 1967,
with quarterly revisions.
   Radio has become today's most neglected
medium from a reference-book point of view and
therefore this service is doubly valuable.
Although intended primarily for the time buyer,
it is a rich source of data for researchers in
popular culture.
   For AM and FM radio stations in the country's
top 100 markets (by metropolitan area population) it lists programs for every hour of the
day, identifying each by type, pinpointing
possible audience, and giving brief evaluations.
It also contains a personality sketch of the
station itself, highlighting its policies,
specialties, and so on. FM material was included beginning with the Fall 1969 issue.

263. Ray, Verne M., ed. Interpreting FCC Broadcast
Rules and Information. 2 vols. Thurmont, Md.:
TAB Books, 1966, 1968.
   These volumes are based on the belief that a
problem exists in understanding FCC rules and
regulations. Information in these volumes was
taken from the publisher's BM/E magazine. Contents include such topics as "Editorializing
and the 'Fairness Doctrine,'" "The Drive for
Diversified Ownership," "Rules on Fraudulent
Billing Practices," "The FCC's Position on
Television-CATV Cross-Ownership," and so on. One
volume complements, not supplants, the other.

Ross Reports -- Television Index. See Television
Index (No. 282).

Rucker, Bryce W. The First Freedom. (See No.
512.)

264. Schiller, Herbert I. Mass Communications and
American Empire. New York: Augustus M. Kelley,
1969.
    Books about the structure of the mass media
in the U.S. -- and there are too few -- tend
to be descriptive rather than analytical, and
if they are analytical they seldom question the
status quo. This book, however, does. But-
tressed with hard facts and figures, it examines
critically the past, present, and possible
future of American broadcasting, broadly defined.
    Chapter headings give an idea of its approach
and extent: "Electronics and Economics Serving
an American Century"; "The Rise of Commercial
Broadcast Communications"; "The Domestic Communications Complex" (as related to the mili-
tary-industrial complex and government); "The
Global American Electronics Invasion"; "The
International Commercialization of Broadcasting"; "The Developing World under Electronic
Siege"; "Comsat and Intelsat: The Structure
of International Communications Control";
"Toward a Democratic Reconstruction of Mass Communications: The Social Use of Technology."
Contains numerous footnotes but no bibliography as such. Indexed.

265. Schramm, Wilbur, ed. The Effects of Television
on Children and Adolescents. New York: UNESCO
Publications Center, 1964. (Reports and Papers
on Mass Communication No. 43)
    "An annotated bibliography with an intro-
ductory overview of research reports." - Subtitle. Contains a lengthy introduction summarizing the present state of research and
findings. Entries are international in scope
and include books and magazine articles.
Indexed.

266. Schramm, Wilbur, ed. The Impact of Educational
Television. Urbana: University of Illinois
Press, 1960.
    Anthology which discusses and summarizes
existing research on the content and audience
of educational television, its use in the

classroom, and its impact -- educational and
otherwise -- on children. Includes a bibliography and bibliographical footnotes.

267. Schramm, Wilbur, Jack Lyle, and Edwin B. Parker.
Television in the Lives of Our Children. Stanford, Calif.: Stanford University Press, 1961.
An analysis of the effects of television on
children, based on a study of over 6,000 children and on information obtained from some
2,300 parents, teachers, and school officials.
An appendix gives statistics and tabulations
and data on related topics (including children's use of other mass media). There is an
annotated bibliography, an index of names,
and a general index.
For its British counterpart see Himmelweit's
Television and the Child: An Empirical Study
of the Effect of Television on the Young (No.
226).

268. Settel, Irving, and William Lass. A Pictorial
History of Television. New York: Grosset &
Dunlap, 1969.
Pictures and text cover the history of tele-
vision in the U.S. in breadth rather than
depth. Indexed.

269. Siepmann, Charles A. Radio, Television, and
Society. New York: Oxford University Press,
1950.
Though 20 years old, this remains a classic
in the field for the ground it covers. Part
I, "Systems of Broadcasting," gives the early
history of radio in the U.S.; discusses the
Communications Act of 1934 and the FCC in
action, the radio industry, listenership in
the U.S., and the rights and duties of the
listener; and analyzes the British and Canadian
systems. Part II, "Social Implications of
Radio and Television," covers propaganda and
public opinion; freedom of speech in theory
and in practice; radio and education; world
listening; and, lastly, television. The
author's approach is analytical. Appendices
contain various documents important to broadcasting and tables on listenership and systems
in 21 other countries. Indexed.

270. Skornia, Harry. Television and Society: An In-
quest and Agenda for Improvement. New York:
McGraw-Hill, 1965.

83

With documented statements, the author contends that a television system controlled wholly by business cannot be expected to put public interest before profit. Bolstering his thesis, he discusses the structure of commercial television -- its leadership, its hidden economics, its rating system, its possible effects, including its possible effects on international relations. The last chapter is "An Agenda for Change: Some Proposals and Resolutions."

271. Skornia, Harry, and Jack Kitson, eds. Problems and Controversies in Television and Radio: Basic Readings. Palo Alto, Calif.: Pacific Books, 1968.

This anthology brings together articles, documents, position papers, and speeches from a number of viewpoints which give an overview of contemporary broadcasting and in doing so makes available certain materials which have become out of print or inaccessible.

Areas treated include: Frame of Reference, Criticism, Freedom and Responsibility, Educational Television and Radio, Criteria for Evaluation, Effects, News and Public Affairs, Advertising and Entertainment, International Television and Public Relations, New Problems and Alternatives: The Future.

272. Smith, Delbert, ed. International Telecommunication Control: International Law and the Ordering of Satellite and Other Forms of International Broadcasting. Leyden: A. W. Sijthoff, 1969.

Although intended as an investigation of present and future legal controls of international broadcasting, this book is additionally useful for tne background it gives on practically all forms of international broadcasting. The author feels that new concepts must be developed and applied and provides a framework through "an examination of the relevant general principles of international law, the activities of the International Telecommunication Union and other organizations, unauthorized international telecommunication and the applicable control theories and legislation, regional broadcasting groupings and national policy alternatives, and the problems created by satellite telecommunication. . . ." He also suggests a possible control system.

Contains appendices, charts, a bibliography, and an index.

Smythe, Dallas W. See Canada. Royal Commission on Broadcasting. Report. Vols. 1-2. 1957 (No. 189).

273. Sparks, Kenneth, comp. A Bibliography of Doctoral Dissertations in Television and Radio. 3d ed. Syracuse, N.Y.: Syracuse University, Newhouse Communications Center, School of Journalism, 1971.
Contains over 900 dissertation titles completed at American universities, grouped into 12 categories. Each entry gives author, title, university, and year completed. The author plans further additions at irregular intervals. There is an author index.

Spot Radio Rates and Data. (See No. 591.)

Spot Television Rates and Data. (See No. 592.)

274. State Broadcasters Associations. Directory. Washington, D.C. 20036: National Association of Broadcasters, 1771 N St., NW, annual.
Lists name, address, and telephone number of president, vice-president, secretary, legal counsel, and any other officers the state may have; tells when they are elected and assume duties; and where and when the coming meeting will be held.

275. Statistics on Radio and Television 1950-1960. New York: UNESCO Publications Center, 1963. (Statistical Reports and Studies)
Tables and charts give different types of broadcast organization throughout most nations of the world, transmitters and receivers, contents of programs both in general and for specific nations, and suggestions for possible content categories.

276. Steiner, Gary A. The People Look at Television: A Study of Audience Attitudes. New York: Knopf, 1963.
Report of a study at Columbia University's Bureau of Applied Social Research in which the author conducted personal interviews with a sample of about 2,500 adults to determine the respondent's attitude toward programs and commercials as well as toward himself as a viewer.

277. Survey of Broadcast Journalism. Ed. by Marvin
     Barrett. New York: Grosset & Dunlap, annual.
         "A penetrating and impartial look at how
     television and radio report the news, how they
     serve the public, and how they live with
     politicians, advertisers, and the FCC." This
     is the thumbnail description on the cover of
     the paperback publication sponsored by Alfred
     I. du Pont and Columbia University.
         The first volume, 1968-69, lives up to
     its aim. Emphasis in this particular issue
     is given to the many ramifications of the
     presidential election. Indexed.

278. Telecommunication Statistics -- General Telegraph
     Statistics -- General Telephone Statistics --
     Radiocommunication Statistics. Geneva: Publié
     par l'Union Internationale des Télécommunica-
     tions, annual.
         Statistics on the volume of business, both
     internal and external, for approximately 125
     countries. China and the USSR are among those
     not included.

279. Television: A World Survey. New York: UNESCO
     Publications Center, 1953. Supplement, 1955.
     (Reports on Facilities of Mass Communications)
         A country-by-country survey of the 52 nations
     and non-self-governing territories which had
     or were hoping to have television in the mid-
     1950s. For each country the book discusses
     such pertinent aspects as history of television,
     structure, censorship, technical facilities,
     and program content whenever these factors are
     applicable.

     Television Circulation and Rate Trends (1962-
     1968). (See No. 597.)

280. Television Factbook: The Authoritative Reference
     for Advertising, Television and Electronic
     Industries. 2 vols. Washington, D.C. 20006:
     Television Digest, 2025 Eye St., NW, annual.
         One of the most detailed factual sources for
     information about geographic, economic, and
     legal aspects of television in the U.S. The
     first volume pertains to services: allocations,
     associations, applications, CATV, colleges and
     universities offering degrees, Comsat, congres-
     sional committees, consulting engineers, edu-
     cational stations, electronic industries associa-
     tion, European Broadcasting Union, FCC

directory, group station ownership, instructional
TV, labor unions and guilds, market and audience
research organizations, manufacturers, National
Association of Broadcasters, networks, publications, statistics, and similar information.
The second volume, Stations, is a comprehensive
rundown on all TV stations in the U.S. and
Canada, containing maps and data such as
technical and recording facilities, news wire
and news film and facsimile services, licensee,
ownership, personnel, a digest of the rate card,
net weekly circulation, total households, and
total TV homes.

281. Television for the Family: A Comprehensive Guide
to Family Viewing. Los Angeles 90004: National
Association for Better Radio and Television,
373 North Western Ave., 1965--.
    Evaluation of about 300 available network
and "syndicated" program series televised weekly
throughout the U.S. The nine-member evaluating
committee includes teachers, a psychiatrist,
a librarian, a research journalist, and an M.D.
In 1969 the publication became part of the
quarterly magazine, Better Radio and Television.
    The trouble about evaluations of this sort
is that they are primarily keyed toward pres-
ence or absence of violence rather than overall quality, although they make an effort to
tackle this. An example of the problem en-
countered is the comment on My Three Sons:
"Bright, funny, entertaining, and apparently
everlasting." But there are those who might
add the adjectives "insipid" and "unrealistic."

282. Television Index. New York 10011: Television
Index, Inc., 150 Fifth Ave., weekly.
    A thoroughly comprehensive guide to individ-
ual television programs which have been produced in the U.S. since 1949 when the service
started as Ross Reports -- Television Index.
In newsletter form, it gives full information
on programs, program and production personnel,
talent, sponsors, and commercial production.
Arrangement is chronological by week. Each
entry tells whether the show is original,
adapted (and if so, by whom), or staff-directed
and gives a capsule résumé of the show's
character (not plot nor calibre), its production
staff, and its history. Every issue contains
a "Program and Production Report" with a one-
page summary of the week's news.

87

283. Third E.B.U. International Conference on Educational Radio and Television, Paris -- March 8th-22nd 1967. Paris: Office de Radiodiffusion-Télévision Française, no date.
    Lengthy and comprehensive summary of what is taking place in educational broadcasting around the world based on papers presented at a European Broadcasting Union Conference. Useful for anyone wishing to learn the status quo or wanting information about an individual country or continent. A list of working papers upon which the summaries are based is included with each section. Unfortunately there is no index.

284. TV Source Books. New York 10017: Broadcast Information Bureau, Inc., 535 Fifth Ave., annual.
    Gives details of the various kinds of films available for use on television. In three volumes: TV "Free" Film Source Book; Series, Serials & Packages; Feature Film Source Book. Information about each film varies according to whether the film is free or for rent. On free films it includes year, story line, stars, whether black and white or color, charges (if any), market restrictions (if any), underwriter, and distributor. For series, serials, and packages it includes, among other things, stars and story line, running time, leasing fee range, markets open, sponsors (if any), producer or original distributor, TV distributor. For feature films: stars, type, year, story line, running time, black and white or color, theatrical producer or original distributor, and TV distributor. Arrangement is such that films can be located by title and source. Main information is found under subject.

285. U.S. Department of Health, Education and Welfare. Office of Education. Educational AM and FM Radio, and Educational Stations, by State and City. Compiled by Gertrude Broderick. Washington, D.C.: Government Printing Office, 1965.
    Twenty-six-page pamphlet put out by the Office of Education with names of stations arranged alphabetically by city and state, giving for each entry call letters, frequency and power, licensee, station manager and director, and other pertinent information.

286. U.S. Department of Health, Education and Wel-
     fare. Office of Education. Radio and Tele-
     vision, a Selected Bibliography. Prepared by
     Patricia Beall Hamill under the direction of
     Gertrude G. Broderick. Washington, D.C.:
     Government Printing Office, 1960.
          Annotated bibliography which includes mate-
     rials reporting findings on research and experi-
     mentation, teaching with television, and pro-
     duction skills. Also contains a limited
     number of technical titles.

287. U.S. Federal Communications Commission. Broadcast
     Primer. "Evolution of Broadcasting." Washington,
     D.C.: Government Printing Office, 1964. (INF
     Bulletin No. 2-B)
          Concise (six-page) history of broadcasting
     in the U.S., citing trends, dates, and sta-
     tistics, some of which are hard to find else-
     where. Among statistics are: TV financial
     data 1952-62; number of commercial TV stations
     in operation from 1945 to 1964; same for com-
     mercial aural broadcast stations; AM-FM
     financial data 1952-62; noncommercial TV
     stations in operation 1955-64; noncommercial
     FM stations in operation 1945-63.

288. U.S. Federal Communications Commission. 25th
     Annual Report for Fiscal Year 1959. Washington,
     D.C.: Government Printing Office, 1960.
          The FCC's commemorative Silver Anniversary
     Report, tracing the history of its regulation.
     Excellent source of material on its growth
     and development from the FCC's own point of
     view.

289. U.S. Foreign Broadcast Information Service.
     Broadcasting Stations of the World. Pts. I-IV.
     Washington, D.C.: Government Printing Office,
     annual.
          Lists all reported radio broadcasting and
     television frequency assignments with the
     exception of those in the U.S. which broadcast
     on domestic channels.
          Part I, Amplitude Modulation Broadcasting
     Stations According to Country and City; Part
     II, Amplitude Modulation Broadcasting Stations
     According to Frequency; Part III, Frequency
     Modulation Broadcasting Stations, in two
     sections -- one alphabetical by country and
     city and the other by frequency; Part IV,
     Television Stations, in two sections as in

Part III and with the same information as in
the preceding parts plus additional data to
distinguish audio, video, polarization, and
other technical factors which apply.

290. U.S. President's Task Force on Communications
Policy. Final Report. Washington, D.C.: Government Printing Office, 1968.
"The report is organized around certain
topics: the organization of our international
telecommunications industry; policies to support and strengthen INTELSAT; telecommunications needs of less developed countries; uses
of domestic satellites; structure and regulation of the domestic carrier industry; future
opportunities for television; spectrum use and
management; and Federal Government role in
telecommunications." - Introduction.
Appendices contain the President's message
on communications policy, statements of partial
dissent of the task force's findings, and
various other comments and discussions.

291. Weil, Gordon L. Communicating by Satellite: An
International Discussion. New York 10021:
Carnegie Endowment for International Peace,
Twentieth Century Fund, 41 East 70th St., 1969.
Report of an international conference, dis-
cussing regulation and coordination of satel-
lite communication, operation, and management
and satellite broadcasting.

292. Weir, Earnest Austin. The Struggle for National
Broadcasting in Canada. Toronto: McClelland &
Stewart, 1965.
Lengthy history of Canadian broadcasting
from 1919 to the present. The author, who
was with the Canadian Broadcasting Corporation
from its beginnings to his retirement, has
used all available materials (he laments that
many of them have not been preserved) and has
interviewed a number of people who played
prominent parts in the development of
Canadian broadcasting.

293. Weiss, Fredric A. Sources of Information on
World and International Radio and Television.
Bloomington, Ind.: Mass Communication Program,
Indiana University, 1970.
Intended as a guide for the student of
international communications, this directory-
bibliography is a listing of publications and

90

professional agencies concerned with the broadcast systems of the world, as well as a selected listing of books and specific essays and articles in anthologies.

White, David Manning, and Richard Averson, eds. Sight, Sound and Society: Motion Pictures and Television in America. (See No. 406.)

294. White, Llewellyn. The American Radio: A Report on the Broadcasting Industry in the United States from the Commission on Freedom of the Press. Chicago: University of Chicago Press, 1947.
    A study of radio from its inception until the late 1940s, made by the Commission on Freedom of the Press to determine possible need for regulation and control. The author discusses history and structure, the attempts to establish educational broadcasting, academic and industrial research, and the efforts toward regulation both by government and by the industry itself. Appendices give regional networks and excerpts from the codes of 1929 and 1939. There are notes on sources.

Who's Who in Journalism 1969. (See No. 436.)

Williams, Francis. The Right to Know: The Rise of the World Press. (See No. 530.)

Wolseley, Roland E., ed. Journalism in Modern India. (See No. 335.)

295. Wood, Richard E. Shortwave Voices of the World. Park Ridge, N.J.: Gilfer Associates, Box 239, 1969.
    Guide to a fast-changing medium, providing information and illustrations on the existence and operation of shortwave stations in various countries.

296. The Working Press of the Nation. Radio and TV Directory. Vol. 3. Chicago 60601: National Research Bureau, 221 North LaSalle St., annual.
    Designed to give public relations officials necessary data about direct sources of broadcasting publicity, this furnishes detailed information on radio and television stations, networks, radio and television programs, sports directors, film buyers, newscasters, and program personnel. Data include names and descriptions of local programs with power,

news services, and executive personnel. Descriptions of local radio and TV programs tell
specific type -- children's, civic, entertainment, farm, and so on -- with name of program,
master of ceremonies, broadcast days and times,
and whether or not guests are used.

297. World Radio and Television. New York: UNESCO
Publications Center, 1965.
    Describes existing broadcasting facilities
in nearly 200 countries. Again material has
been drawn from UNESCO's more comprehensive
World Communications. There is a short bibliography.

298. World Radio-TV Handbook. New York 10036: World
Radio-TV Handbook, 165 West 46th St., annual.
    The first section of this handbook contains
an eclectic variety of articles and facts relating to broadcasting -- international organizations, Eurovision, the role of the UN in
space communications, religious broadcasting
organizations, standard frequency and time
signal stations, and so on. This changes somewhat from year to year. The main section of
several hundred pages gives detailed information, by country, of the radio stations and
broadcasting organizations of every country
in the world, with names and addresses of broadcasting companies; names and titles of leading
officials; lists of broadcasting stations in
each country, including frequencies, wave
lengths, transmitter power, call signs (if
used), and station names. Program information
is also listed, giving times, frequencies,
and beam areas of the broadcasts in each
language. There is other factual and statistical information, such as listings of long,
medium, and shortwave stations throughout the
world; program distributors and TV production
companies; and technical facts.

Film

299. American Film Institute. The American Film Institute Catalog: Feature Films 1921-1930. 2 vols.
New York: Bowker, 1970.
        The beginning of a vast project to provide a
filmographic record of features, short films,
and newsreels from 1893 through 1970. The current volumes list and describe about 700 feature
films so that they may be found by title, by
name of actor, director, producer, scenarist,
production company, and so on, and by subject.
The main entry is under author, and it gives
production credits, cast, and a brief synopsis.
The entire work is expected to be completed
around 1976.

300. The American Film Institute's Guide to College
Film Courses. Ed. by Linda B. Greenfelder.
Chicago 60611: American Library Association, 50
East Huron St., annual.
        Lists schools where students can major in
film (in 1970 there were 68) and additional
(233) schools where film courses are being
taught. Besides information on faculty,
courses, and equipment, there are statements
on philosophy, aims, and priorities of individual programs.
        Supplementary material gives a breakdown
of schools offering degrees, schools with
film-study courses for teachers, the American
Film Institute's program in education, and the
Fifth National Student Film Festival Award
Winners. Indexed.

301. Annals of the American Academy of Political and
Social Science. "The Motion Picture in Its
Economic and Social Aspects." Vol. 128. Philadelphia: The American Academy of Political and
Social Science, Nov. 1926.
     Compilation of articles, almost entirely by
business and professional men unconnected with
the film industry or universities. Emphasis is
on financial, technical, and educational factors,
with a final section on censorship, both volun-
tary and involuntary. Articles are, of course,
quite dated, which gives them historical value.
Examples: "What the Movies Mean to the Farmer,"
"Motion Pictures as Trade Getters," "Possibilities of the Cinema in Education," "Our
Foreign Trade in Motion Pictures," "What Are
Motion Pictures Doing for Industry?"

302. Annals of the American Academy of Political and
Social Science. "The Motion Picture Industry."
Vol. 254. Philadelphia: The American Academy of
Political and Social Science, Nov. 1947.
     Compilation of articles -- some by people
within the industry and the majority by social
scientists -- on the development of the motion
picture, its business and financial aspects, the
sources and production of motion pictures, the
possible effects, motion pictures and the public,
censorship and self-regulation, and suggestions
for further research.

303. Babitsky, Paul, and John Rimberg. The Soviet Film
Industry. New York: Praeger, 1955. (Studies of
the Research Program on the USSR, No. 12)
     Shows the principal steps by which the Com-
munist Party consolidated its power over the
Soviet motion picture industry; gives the
economic base and central administration; discusses scenarios and writers, imports and
exports, and production under the five-year
plan; and makes a quantitative content analysis
of heroes and villains in Soviet films, 1923-
50.

304. Baechlin, Peter, and Maurice Muller-Strauss.
Newsreels across the World. New York: UNESCO
Publications Center, 1952.
     "This book seeks to present an objective,
worldwide survey of news films as they are
today, and the problems they raise -- from the
production of the actual newsreels to their
projection on the cinema. It deals both with

94

international organization for production and
exhibition of newsreels and with the machinery
for exchange of newsreels between countries.
It was also considered useful to include an
analysis of the impact of television and certain types of documentary films upon the newsreel industry." - Preface. Its thoroughness,
its international scope, and the scarcity of
other materials on the subject make it
extremely valuable for this aspect of communication. Contains a bibliography and an
index.

305. Balshofer, Fred J., and Arthur C. Miller. One
Reel a Week. Berkeley and Los Angeles: University of California Press, 1967.
    As source material on the early days of movie
making, this is an important book. The authors,
veteran film makers who each give their accounts
in alternate chapters, tell of the power structure and the struggle for power -- the commercial
piracy which was taken for granted, the attempt
of a small group of men to monopolize the making
of pictures, and the methods used by the independent companies to survive.

306. Bardeche, Maurice, and Robert Brasillach. The
History of Motion Pictures. Trans. and ed. by Iris
Barry. New York: Norton and Museum of Modern Art,
1938.
    This book "attempts to survey the entire
history of film making in Europe and in America
and to describe the exchange of influences to
which the film as a whole has been subject.
That it surveys the field from a European angle,
even from a distinctly French angle, rather than
from our own native viewpoint, makes it a useful
check on other accounts of this art-industry." -
John E. Abbott, director of the Museum of Modern
Art Film Library. Beginning in 1895, the book
encompasses prewar and World War I films; the
emergence of film as an art (1919-23); the silent
film (1923-29); the talking film (1929-35); the
film as a world industry; and, in conclusion, a
summary of 40 years of film, "The Music of
Images." There is also an editorial postscript
for the years 1935-38, an index to film titles,
and a general index.

307. Barnouw, Erik, and Subrahmanyam Krishnaswamy.
Indian Film. New York: Columbia University Press,
1963.

Development of the motion picture industry
in India -- its economic structure, its censorship problems, its content.

308. Baxter, John. The Gangster Film. New York:
Barnes, 1970. (Screen Series)
Lists actors, directors, and others engaged
in the production of "gangster" films (defined
by the author as "films that deal, even in a
general way, with organized as opposed to conventional crime"), giving "who's who" type of
information and filmographies where pertinent,
along with some subject information -- e.g.,
Private Detectives, Saint Valentine's Day
Massacre. Indexed.

309. Baxter, John. Hollywood in the Thirties. New
York: Barnes, 1968.
Organizing his material around studios and
personalities, the author details events of
one of the American cinema's decades of great
change. This is part of a paperback series
which includes Hollywood in the Twenties and
Hollywood in the Forties (Nos. 386 and 339).

Blumer, Herbert. Movies and Conduct. See Payne
Fund Studies (No. 380).

Blumer, Herbert, and Philip M. Hauser. Movies,
Delinquency, and Crime. See Payne Fund Studies
(No. 380).

310. The British National Film Catalogue. Ed. by
Michael Moulds. London: British Industrial and
Scientific Film Association, quarterly with
annual cumulations.
Includes all nonfiction and short films
generally available in Britain for hire, loan,
or sale; films available to specialized or
limited audiences only, when permission is
given to include them; fiction and nonfiction
television programs available in film for nontheatrical release for loan or hire; film
magazines and certain nonfiction shorts which,
though made for theatrical release, frequently
become available on 16 mm at a later date;
British films distributed abroad through
British Information Services and the British
Council. From 1963 (Vol. 1) to 1969 features
covered by the Monthly Film Bulletin and newsreels are excluded. (Of newsreels the editor

says, "These have become increasingly super-
ficial and little purpose is served by listing
their content.")
    The catalogue lists entries by subject,
with a subject-title and a production index.
For each title information is given on distribution, date, production company and sponsor,
technical data, language version, credits,
length, and a synopsis.

311. Brownlow, Kevin. The Parade's Gone By. New York:
Knopf, 1968.
    History of the silent film based upon inter-
views with those who worked with them in one
capacity or another, profusely illustrated with
stills. Indexed.

312. Bucher, Felix. Germany. New York: Barnes, 1970.
(Screen Series)
    Directory of actors, actresses, and others
important in German films, with preference given
to those made before 1945 because most of the
important films were before that time. Gives
brief biographical data and a filmography.
Some of the leading movements in film -- e.g.,
"avant-garde" -- are discussed. There is a
detailed index to names and films.

313. Cameron, Ian, and Elisabeth Cameron. Dames. New
York: Praeger, 1969.
    Ranging across the past 25 years, the Camerons
discuss memorable Hollywood actresses who have
portrayed dolls, molls, floozies, and other un-
ladylike parts. There are photographic illustrations and filmographies for each actress.
This is a companion volume to The Heavies by the
same authors. (See No. 314.)

314. Cameron, Ian, and Elisabeth Cameron. The Heavies.
New York: Praeger, 1969.
    Presents a Hollywood rogues' gallery of cor-
rupt sheriffs, crooked lawyers, hired gunmen,
cattle rustlers, racketeers, and other dastardly
types. The authors have limited themselves to
the past 25 years and have omitted big names
like Bogart, Cagney, Raft, and Robinson (about
whom much material exists), in favor of middle-
bracket players.
    Biographical information is as complete as
possible for each, and includes a list of films
with dates. There are also photographs. A companion volume to Dames. (See No. 313.)

Charters, W. W. _Motion Pictures and Youth:_ _A_
Summary. See Payne Fund Studies (No. 380).

Commercial Television, Cinema and Radio Directory.
London: Admark Directories, annual. (See No.
195.)

315. Conant, Michael. _Antitrust in the Motion Picture_
Industry: _Economic and Legal Analysis_. Berkeley
and Los Angeles: University of California Press,
1960. (Publications of the Bureau of Business and
Economic Research)
    Analyzes and evaluates the impact of antitrust
actions on the structure, behavior, and performance of the industry. Updates Huettig (No. 340)
and is updated by about five years by Jobes (No.
348). Contains a bibliography, an index of
cases, and an index.

Cressey, Paul G., and Frederick M. Thrasher. _Boys,_
Movies, and City Streets. See Payne Fund Studies
(No. 380).

Dale, Edgar. _Children's Attendance at Motion_
Pictures. See Payne Fund Studies (No. 380).

Dale, Edgar. _The Content of Motion Pictures_. See
Payne Fund Studies (No. 380).

Dale, Edgar. _How to Appreciate Motion Pictures_.
See Payne Fund Studies (No. 380).

316. Dickinson, Thorold, and Catherine De La Roche.
Soviet Cinema. London: Falcon Press, 1948.
(National Cinema Series)
    An analysis of the Soviet film, beginning
shortly before the revolution and ending in the
mid-1940s. Discusses techniques, specific
pictures and producers, and the interplay between government and film makers.

317. Dimmitt, Richard Bertrand. _An Actor Guide to the_
Talkies: _A Comprehensive Listing of 8,000 Feature-_
Length Films from January, 1949, until December,
_1964_. 2 vols. Metuchen, N.J.: Scarecrow Press,
1967.
    Lists more than 8,000 foreign and domestic
films and 30,000 actors. Vol. I contains names
of films with complete cast of characters, pro-
ducing studio, and date of production. Vol. II,
the index, lists 30,000 actors in alphabetical
order, with references to the films in which

they appeared. The set will be expanded to
cover the period 1928-48.

318. Dimmitt, Richard Bertrand. A Title Guide to the
     Talkies: A Comprehensive Listing of 16,000
     Feature-Length Films from October, 1927, until
     December, 1963. 2 vols. Metuchen, N.J.: Scare-
     crow Press, 1965.
        The purpose of this list is to give origins
     of the screenplay from which the talking film
     was derived -- whether it was taken from a
     novel, short story, poem, teleplay, biography,
     or history, or whether it was an original
     script. Cross-references indicate changes in
     title. It is also possible to determine how
     many times a particular work has been made
     into a movie.
        The following information is given for each
     entry: title, original source, author's name,
     place of publication, publisher, date, and
     pagination. Contains an author index.

     Dysinger, W. S., and Christian A. Ruckmick. The
     Emotional Responses of Children to the Motion
     Picture Situation. See Payne Fund Studies (No.
     380).

319. Filmfacts. Ed. by Ernest Parmentier. New York
     10014: Village Station, Box 213, 1958--.
        Gives complete screen credits, synopses, and
     excerpts from reviews for a majority of com-
     mercial feature-length films, domestic and
     foreign, released in the United States. It was
     issued biweekly with quarterly indices and
     annual cumulations. The indices give, among
     other things, original titles, subtitles,
     alternate titles, and re-release titles, which
     help to track down certain films that otherwise
     might be difficult to find. At the end of the
     year it has a comprehensive list of awards and
     the major magazines' and newspapers' "best ten"
     lists.
        Although no issues with contemporary films
     have appeared since 1969, several retroactive
     issues have been published. The future of the
     publication is uncertain.

320. Film and Cinema Statistics: A Preliminary Report
     on Methodology with Tables Giving Current Sta-
     tistics. New York: UNESCO Publications Center,
     1955. (Statistical Reports and Studies No. 1)

"The object of the present report is to abstract for special study a small number of fundamental elements in the field of international film and cinema statistics, and, for each of these elements, to present existing statistics, to examine their scope and reference, and to make suggestions toward the adoption of certain standards and criteria designed to improve international comparability in the reporting of statistics." - Introduction.

Aspects chosen for special study are production and importation of films, facilities for film exhibition, cinema attendance, and box office receipts. Coverage is detailed and extensive. Appendix B is a list of sources.

321. Film Centre (London). <u>The Film Industry in Six European Countries</u>. New York: UNESCO Publications Center, 1950. (Press, Film and Radio in the World Today; a Series of Studies)

"A detailed study of the film industry in Denmark as compared with that in Norway, Sweden, Italy, France and the United Kingdom." Contains a brief bibliography.

322. <u>Film Daily Year Book of Motion Pictures</u>. New York 10019: Film and Television Daily, 1600 Broadway, annual.

Gives a wide assortment of facts about the motion picture industry. Some of these are: industry statistics (including the number of theaters in various areas of the world); awards; credits for feature releases, producers, screenplay writers, cinematographers, editors, players, music, and so on; a listing of industry personnel, including manufacturers, associations, guilds, corporations, and others; brief surveys of the film industry in each of a number of countries, followed by a country-by-country listing of producers, importer-distributors, and associations; labor organizations; events of the year in the Motion Picture Association of America, including information about codes and regulations; a long bibliography of books about the film -- not limited to the year; a list of trade, fan, and technical publications; motion picture newspaper editors; a financial section on stock market sales, financial histories, capitalizations, grosses, earnings, and dividends; a brief listing of over 33,000 features released since 1915; drive-in theaters; and theater circuits in the U.S. and Canada.

Another yearbook is International Motion
Picture Almanac (No. 343), which overlaps this
in certain areas and supplements it in a very
few. Major differences are that the International Motion Picture Almanac devotes much
space to a "who's who" in the industry; its
list of feature releases begins with 1944
rather than 1915; and it lacks the financial
section and the bibliography.

323. The Film Index: A Bibliography. Vol. 1: The
Film as Art. Compiled by the workers of the
Writers' Project of the Work Projects Administration in the City of New York. New York: Wilson
and Museum of Modern Art Film Library, 1941.
About 8,600 entries representing books,
magazine articles, and film reviews, arranged
by subject and with emphasis on the creative
rather than production, technological, or
purely sociological aspects.
An excellent source, not only for leads to
information about history and trends to 1940
but also for biographical information about
actors, directors, and other people connected
with films, or for identification, reviews, and
criticism of specific films. Although other
volumes were planned, this is the only one
carried through. It has never been brought up
to date.

324. Film Vocabulary. London S.W. 1: Western European
Union, 9 Grosvenor Place, 1958.
Multilingual vocabulary of some 900 cinema
terms in common use among those who work in the
fields of cultural and educational film and
audiovisual education. In cases where a word
in one language has no equivalent in the other
languages, a short description in the other
language is given.

The Focal Encyclopedia of Film and Television
Techniques. (See No. 209.)

Forman, Henry James. Our Movie Made Children.
See Payne Fund Studies (No. 380).

325. Fulton, Albert R. Motion Pictures: The Develop-
ment of an Art from Silent Films to the Age of
Television. Norman: University of Oklahoma
Press, 1960.
A history and analysis tracing the develop-
ment and techniques of the film. Emphasis is

on its art (or art entertainment) aspects
rather than on its entertainment function alone.

326. Gifford, Denis. <u>British Cinema: An Illustrated</u>
<u>Guide.</u> New York: Barnes, 1968.
"This book is the first attempt to put between
handy covers at a handy price the complete story
of British films in factual form. It is a kind
of All Time Who's Who of stars and directors,
546 of them, selected for their contribution to
the overall seventy-year scene." So says the
author in his introduction. His description
is accurate except for the use of the word
"complete." As he later states, he has dealt
with stars and directors who have a substantial
body of work in film rather than with bit
players or minor directors. For each entry he
gives a filmography. Writers and producers
are generally omitted. Contains a title index.

327. Graham, Peter. <u>A Dictionary of the Cinema.</u> Rev.
ed. New York: Barnes, 1968.
Hundreds of short biographical listings of
international film actors and actresses,
directors, script writers, and others prominent in films, with a list of their films and
dates. Also discusses certain of the terms
which describe cinema trends -- neo-realism,
new cinema, nouvelle vague, expressionism, for
example -- in fact-packed prose reminiscent of
"who's who" entries. There is a two-page
"Guide to Technical Terms." Scope is international.

328. Great Britain. House of Commons. Monopolies
Commission. <u>Films: A Report on the Supply of</u>
<u>Films for Exhibition in Cinemas.</u> London: Her
Majesty's Stationery Office, 1966.
An investigation into monopoly in Britain's
film industry, with recommendations to Parliament and an appendix filled with statistics
and documents on the industry.

329. Griffith, Mrs. D. W. <u>When the Movies Were Young.</u>
New York: Dutton, c1925, 1965.
". . . one of the earliest volumes containing eyewitness testimony to the conditions under
which early motion pictures were made." - Introduction to the Dover reprint edition, 1969.
First published in 1925. Indexed.

330. Griffith, Richard. <u>The Movie Stars</u>. New York:
Doubleday, 1970.
A mammoth, coffee-table-type book which
attempts to analyze the factors which constitute "star appeal," using past and present
illustrations and many photographs. Beginning
with "Early Fanfare" and going into "The
Heydey of the Stars," it concludes with "Death
and Transfiguration," the diminution of the
system. The author does more than tell a
story; he delves into the reasons for the rise
and fall of the institution of stardom. Indexed.

331. Griffith, Richard, and Arthur Mayer. <u>The Movies</u>.
Rev. ed. New York: Simon & Schuster, 1970.
The authors contend that the beginning of
motion pictures coincided with a high degree
of industrialization which the movies have
mirrored and in turn affected. Briefly and
chronologically they touch upon trends, with
profuse illustrations. Good for an overview
and for entertainment. Lack of space prevented
the authors from dealing with cartoons (including Walt Disney) and documentaries. Indexed.

332. Guback, Thomas H. <u>The International Film Industry:
Western Europe and America since 1945</u>. Bloomington:
Indiana University Press, 1969.
"The object of this study is to uncover and
analyze relationships between the American and
European film industries, keeping in mind the
financial stake American companies have in
Europe." - Introduction. To accomplish his aim,
the author penetrates economic, sociological,
and cultural factors which have a bearing.
Contains a bibliography of books, monographs,
pamphlets, documents, reports, and articles.
Also has a particularly useful index with a
minute subject breakdown.

333. Halliwell, Leslie. <u>The Filmgoer's Companion</u>. 3d
rev. and expanded ed. New York: Avon, 1971?
(Equinox)
An 850-page alphabetical index to old movies
of the 1930s and 1940s now being re-run on
television. Although the author much too
modestly claims that the book's main purpose is
to answer the late watcher's casual questions
about actors and actresses, he has produced an
impressive reference work which brings together
information about old films, players, directors,
producers, writers, photographers, title changes,
and so on. He has also eclectically included

entries about terminology, organizations, series,
and themes (e.g., horror, robberies, hotels,
sex, suicide, lesbianism, westerns).
 From time to time Mr. Halliwell lets his own
opinions slip in, as in his entry on The Robe.
"This solemn epic from Lloyd C. Douglas's novel
about the aftermath of the Crucifixion is
unremarkable except as the first film in Cinema-
scope (q.v.)."
 Emphasis is primarily Hollywood and British,
but some important films and film figures from
other parts of the world are included. Movie
buffs will find this a source of fun as well
as reference.

334. Handel, Leo A. Hollywood Looks at Its Audience:
A Report of Film Audience Research. Urbana:
University of Illinois Press, 1950.
 Summarizes many studies of motion picture
audiences of two decades ago and earlier --
their size, their preferences in stories and
players, the effect of motion pictures upon
them, and the advertising to which they were
exposed. Contains a bibliography, "Publications on Film Audience Research," and an index.

335. Hardy, Forsythe. Scandinavian Film. London:
Falcon Press, 1962. (National Cinema Series)
 As the author points out, Sweden and Denmark
have made a contribution to world cinema all
out of proportion to their size. He traces
the development of their film industry, stressing the influences that have made its products
different from those of other countries.

336. Hendricks, Gordon. Beginnings of the Biograph:
The Story of the Invention of the Mutoscope and
the Biograph and Their Supplying Camera. New
York 10011: The Beginnings of the American Film,
General Post Office 2552, 1964.
 Second in a series of books designed to
investigate the origin of the American film
(Nos. 337 and 338). This one begins in late
1894 and tells of the invention of a motion
picture camera, a projector, and a peep-hole
exhibiting machine. Indexed.

337. Hendricks, Gordon. The Edison Motion Picture Myth.
Berkeley and Los Angeles: University of California
Press, 1961.
 A history of the early motion picture, cover-
ing the years from 1888 to 1892. It concentrates

on the work of W. K. L. Dickson, an employee of
Thomas Edison whom Hendricks feels has not been
given sufficient credit for the invention of the
motion picture. His thesis is derived from the
first systematic examination of laboratory
records and other original sources.

338. Hendricks, Gordon. The Kinetoscope: America's
First Commercially Successful Motion Picture
Exhibitor. New York 10011: The Beginnings of
the American Film, General Post Office 2552, 1966.
This is the third in Hendricks's series of
books which go into detailed investigation of
the early technological history of the American
film; it documents the reasons he believes its
beginnings have been misrepresented.

339. Higham, Charles, and Joel Greenberg. Hollywood
in the Forties. New York: Barnes, 1968.
Second of a paperback series (Nos. 309 and
386) which defines and describes types of
films of the decade and personalities involved
with them. Following an introductory chapter
on trends, there are chapters on black cinema;
melodrama; fantasy and horror; problem and
sociological films; war propaganda; prestige
pictures; biographies and literary adaptations;
action, outdoor, and pastoral films; women's
pictures; comedy; musicals. Contains an index
to people and films.

Holaday, P. W. Getting Ideas from the Movies. See
Payne Fund Studies (No. 380).

340. Huettig, Mae D. Economic Control of the Motion
Picture Industry: A Study in Industrial Organiza-
tion. Philadelphia: University of Pennsylvania
Press, 1944.
One of the few studies that approaches the
American film strictly from the economic angle.
Gives a thorough analysis of the financial struc-
ture, including exhibition and distribution, up
to about 1944. Contains a bibliography. Conant
(No. 315) is useful for information up to 1960.
Jobes (No. 348) takes the subject to 1966.

341. Hull, David Steward. Film in the Third Reich: A
Study of the German Cinema 1933-1945. Berkeley
and Los Angeles: University of California Press,
1969.
Carefully documented study based on years of
research during which the author tracked down

and screened virtually all important films of
the period. Arranged chronologically beginning
with 1933, it shows the takeover of the film
industry by Goebbels as he abolished critics
and absorbed the industry, and the trends in
German films, such as war, escapism, and
antisemitism. Several useful sections are
the prologue, which reviews the literature
on the subject, the notes, the bibliography,
and the index.

342. International Film Guide. Ed. by Peter Cowie.
New York: Barnes, annual.
Briefly covers a variety of aspects and types
of film. Typical of the contents (which vary
from year to year): essays on five directors
of the year, short survey of each of 25 leading
composers of film music, world film production
country by country, festivals, short films,
films on 16 mm, film services, film schools,
archives, film magazines, art cinemas.

343. International Motion Picture Almanac. Fd. by
Charles S. Aaronson. New York: Quigley Publications, annual.
The term "international" is a misnomer.
Except for a section, "The Industry in Great
Britain and Ireland" (44 pages), and another,
"The World Market" (22 pages), this 800-page
yearbook is devoted primarily to the U.S.
Among an assortment of useful facts covered
are: various statistics; award winners; top-
grossing films; a lengthy "who's who" in motion
pictures and television; feature releases, 1944
to within about two years of the present;
foreign film distributors in the U.S.; motion
picture corporations; theater circuits and
drive-in theaters in the U.S. and Canada; services for producers, including market research,
talent and literary agencies, and publicity
representatives in the Los Angeles area; government; organizations, including guilds and unions;
codes and censorship; trade publications; fan
magazines; film writers and general representatives; and producers, distributors, and libraries of nontheatrical motion pictures.
Some of the sections -- "who's who," feature
pictures, government film bureaus, publicity
representatives, and others -- are identical
with those in the same publisher's International
Television Almanac (No. 230). For another book

of this nature see Film Daily Year Book of
Motion Pictures (No. 322).

344. Jacobs, Lewis, ed. The Emergence of Film Art:
The Evolution and Development of the Motion
Picture as an Art, from 1900 to the Present.
New York: Hopkinson & Blake, 1969.
  "The purpose of this book is two-fold,"
says Mr. Jacobs. "First, to provide insight
into creative film expression, and second, to
present an historical overview of the medium's
artistic development." It is divided into
three sections -- the silent film, the sound
and color film, the creative process -- with
each part consisting of essays by eminent film
makers, critics, and historians, and an introduction by Mr. Jacobs. The scope is international. Contains an index to names and titles.

345. Jacobs, Lewis. The Rise of the American Film: A
Critical History with an Essay, "Experimental
Cinema in America 1921-1947." New York: Teachers
College Press, c1939, 1948, 1967. (Studies in
Culture and Communication)
  Story of the motion picture in the United
States from its beginning at the turn of the
century to 1947. Although the author's main
stress is on the film as entertainment and as
art, with discussions of individual directors
and pictures that have helped shape its history,
he has also placed considerable emphasis on
its economic development. Contains an extensive bibliography and picture, name, and general
indices. The original edition and the 1948
printing are published by Harcourt, Brace.
"Experimental Cinema in America 1921-1947" has
been added to the 1967 edition.

346. Jarratt, Vernon. The Italian Cinema. New York:
Macmillan, 1951. (National Cinema Series)
  A history of the motion picture in Italy,
with special emphasis on the period after
World War II, when the new school of Italian
realism was becoming well known abroad.
Appendices list films directed from 1930 to
1946 by leading directors; cast and credit
lines of the more important postwar films are
given. Contains indices of film titles and
names.

347. Jarvie, I. C. Movies and Society. New York:
Basic Books, 1970.

"An essay, no more, toward the sociology of
the cinema." Thus the author views his non-
empirical study. In fitting it into this
framework, he has divided the problem into
four main areas -- the making, viewing, expe-
riencing, and evaluating of film. Its contents: Part I. Sociology of an industry: Who
makes films and why? Part II. Sociology of
an audience: Who sees films and why? Part III.
Sociology of an experience: Who experiences
movies and why? Part IV. Sociology of evaluation: How we learn about and appraise film.
   Mr. Jarvie says that he has drawn on published information, "good or bad, or as usual
fragmentary," and upon his own experience and
has included trash as well as art, for his aim
is not aesthetic. Although his data have been
used mainly to draw contrasts between Great
Britain and America, which is his central concern, he has included facts about the film
industry in a number of other countries --
France, Germany, India, Italy, Japan, Russia,
Poland, Hong Kong, Singapore, Taiwan, and
Thailand. Contains an appendix, "Film and
Communication of Values," a bibliography, and
an index of subjects, names, and films.

348. Jobes, Gertrude. <u>Motion Picture Empire</u>. Hamden,
     Conn.: Archon Books, Shoe String Press, 1966.
        Economics-based history, coupling careful
     research with firsthand knowledge. Contains
     an index of names and a bibliography. For
     other useful studies of the economics of film
     see Huettig (No. 340) and Conant (No. 315).

349. Kelly, Terence. <u>A Competitive Cinema</u>. London:
     Institute of Economic Affairs, 1966.
        Study of the economics, structure, and
     institutions of the British cinema industry,
     ranging from the financing of production to
     the exhibition of the film in theaters through-
     out the country. Contains a bibliography.

350. Knight, Arthur. <u>The Liveliest Art: A Panoramic
     History of the Movies</u>. New York: Macmillan,
     1957.
        Comprehensive history of the film, inter-
     national in scope, taking it from its beginning
     to the mid-1950s. Includes a 12-page section
     on documentaries, a bibliography of the 100
     books the author considers best on the subject,

and sources for 16-mm films. There is a general
index and an index to film titles.

351. Knight, Derrick, and Vincent Porter. A Long Long
Look at Short Films: An A.C.T.T. Report on the
Short Entertainment and Factual Film. New York:
Pergamon Press and the Association of Cinematograph, Television and Allied Technicians, 1967.
Factual report, written for a British trade
union, the Association of Cinematograph, Television and Allied Technicians, which documents
both the social and aesthetic need for short
films and their present plight. Contains many
facts and figures, both in the main body and
in the appendices. Bibliography and index.

352. Kracauer, Siegfried. From Caligari to Hitler: A
Psychological History of the German Film. Princeton, N.J.: Princeton University Press, c1947, 1966.
Although the author says that he is not concerned with German films merely for their own
sake but rather as a means to increase knowledge
of pre-Hitler Germany in a specific way, this
book nevertheless gives a great deal of information about structure and content of the
motion picture in Germany as well as about individual films.
Includes as a supplement "Propaganda and the
Nazi War Film," which with a few changes is a
reprint of the author's pamphlet of the same
title issued in 1942 by the Museum of Modern
Art Film Library. There is also a structural
analysis giving specific examples of the ways
in which propaganda is used, an excellent bibliography, and a name-subject index.

353. Kracauer, Siegfried. Theory of Film: The Redemption of Physical Reality. New York: Oxford University Press, 1960.
An aesthetic theory of film in which the
author's approach is through medium (photography) and content. He discusses types,
characteristics, highlights, and history. Has
notes, a bibliography, and an author-title-
subject index.

354. Lahue, Kalton C. Continued Next Week: A History
of the Moving Picture Serial. Norman: University
of Oklahoma Press, 1964.
Very little material exists about this genre,
which was once an important part of the film
industry. Mainly for this reason Mr. Lahue's

chronological story of the old-time serial is
useful. Following the text, a 123-page appendix
traces chronologically various serials from
1912 to 1930, giving for each the director,
cast, release date, company, and chapter titles.
There is an index.

In 1968 the author brought out a similar
book, Bound and Gagged: The Story of the
Silent Serials (Barnes). Profusely illustrated,
it is designed primarily to entertain all ages
and to promote nostalgia in those old enough
to remember the heydey of the serial.

355. Lahue, Kalton C. Worlds of Laughter: The Motion
Picture Comedy Short, 1910-1930. Norman: University of Oklahoma Press, 1966.

Account of the major films, firms, actors,
and directors of short comedy up to the advent
of sound. An appendix lists by date the films
of selected major comedians in this genre. There
is a very brief bibliography and a name-title
index. For a more definitive history which
covers long and short film comedy internationally
from its beginning to the present, see Robinson's The Great Funnies (No. 385).

356. Lahue, Kalton C., and Sam Gill. Clown Princes and
Court Jesters: Some Great Comics of the Silent
Screen. New York: Barnes, 1970.

Brief sketches with illustrations of 50 men
and women who played in short comedies during
the period just before World War I to the close
of the silent era. The chief value is that
information about early comedy shorts and their
major actors and actresses is not readily available elsewhere. Lacks either a bibliography
or an index.

357. Lejeune, Caroline A. Cinema. London: Alexander
Maclehose, 1931.

Even the contemporary portions of these
perceptive essays have now become history, and
as history they are excellent. Most of the
essays are about film personalities -- actors,
actresses, directors, producers -- and about
types of film, such as war, travel, the soil,
experimental, and so on, grouped into three
sections -- American, European, and miscellany --
in which latter category she has placed the
various genres. Contains a bibliography and
an index.

358. Leyda, Jay. Kino: A History of the Russian and
     Soviet Film. New York: Macmillan, 1960.
          Gives an intensive treatment of the back-
     ground, personalities, political interests,
     industrial growth, and artistic development.
     Concludes with the death of Eisenstein in
     1948. Has five appendices, one of the most
     useful of which is "Fifty Years of Russian and
     Soviet Films 1908-1958, a Select List." The
     list of sources for each chapter forms a bib-
     liography, and there is an index.

359. Lindsay, Vachel. The Art of the Motion Picture.
     New York: Macmillan, 1915.
          A delightful, informally written book about
     the early days of movies by the famous poet who
     wrote of them contemporarily. "This . . .
     might be entitled: 'How to Classify and Judge
     the Current Films,'" says Mr. Lindsay. "But I
     desire as well that the work shall have its
     influence upon producers, scenario-writers,
     actors, and those about to prepare and endow
     pictures for special crusades," he continues.
     His aim is to supply viewers with a social and
     aesthetic way of regarding film.
          The headings of the two parts into which the
     book is divided give an idea of Lindsay's
     approach and style: I, "This Outline Is Pro-
     posed as a Basis for Photoplay Criticism in
     America"; II, "More Personal Speculations and
     Afterthoughts Not Brought Forward So Dogmat-
     ically." (Under this latter heading come
     "The Orchestra, Conversation, and Censorship";
     "The Substitute for the Saloon"; and "California
     and America," in which he shows how California,
     "as the natural moving picture playground, has
     the possibility of developing a unique cultural
     leverage upon America.")

360. Liu, Alan P. L. The Film Industry in Communist
     China. Cambridge, Mass.: Massachusetts Institute
     of Technology, 1965. (Distributed by the Clearing-
     house for Federal Scientific and Technical Infor-
     mation, U.S. Dept. of Commerce, National Bureau
     of Standards, Institute for Applied Technology)
          Report, based almost exclusively on Chinese
     publications, which seeks to update the data on
     the subject and analyze the dynamics of the
     film industry. Deals briefly with Chinese films
     in the pre-Communist era and discusses at length
     the development, production, and audience under
     the present government, as well as the role of

foreign film in the country. An appendix charts
the distribution of the Film Copy System, and a
bibliography lists Communist Chinese books,
Chinese books from Hong Kong and Taiwan, articles
in western journals, and western books on China.

361. Low, Rachael. The History of the British Film.
4 vols. London: Allen & Unwin, 1948 --.
A multi-volume project, with four volumes
completed, covering thus far the period from
1896 through 1929. Roger Manvell collaborated
with Miss Low on Vol. I.
The series is published under the auspices
of the British Film Institute and includes
production, distribution, and exhibition information as well as discussions of specific films
and an excellent selection of stills. Each
volume is indexed, and Vol. IV contains a comprehensive film list of the 1920s, together with a
general index of 58 pages for that volume.
Further volumes are in preparation.

362. MacCann, Richard Dyer, ed. Film and Society. New
York: Scribner's, 1964.
Anthology designed as a controlled research
paper for undergraduates which gives an excellent overview of the historical, economic, and
social role of the American commercial motion
picture.
Topics include: Films past, present, and
future. What does the audience want? Does the
screen reflect society? Should the screen be
controlled? Should film distribution overseas
be restricted? Should films for television be
controlled?

363. MacCann, Richard Dyer, comp. Good Reading about
Motion Pictures: The 100 Best Books in English.
2d ed. Los Angeles: University of Southern
California, Department of Cinema, 1962.
Emphasizes film history, the documentary,
Hollywood, filmwriting, and film and society.
The author states that he has deliberately omitted novels, biographical material (except in a
few cases where it relates to history), audiovisual education, and periodicals. He has
included, whenever possible, only those books
which he considers to be written well and with
insight.

364. MacCann, Richard Dyer. Hollywood in Transition.
Boston: Houghton Mifflin, 1962.

An analysis of the motion picture industry,
taking into account television, foreign markets,
and so on.

365. Macgowan, Kenneth. Behind the Screen: The
History and Techniques of the Motion Picture. New
York: Delacorte, 1965.
Detailed history, with technical background,
of the invention and development of the motion
picture as a major industry. Emphasis is Amer-
ican, although brief sections are devoted to the
German, Scandinavian, and Russian film.

366. Malton, Leonard. Movie Comedy Teams. New York:
New American Library, 1970. (Signet original
paperback)
Intended both for nostalgic reading and historical research, this film history centers
around famous comedy teams -- the Marx Brothers,
Burns and Allen, Abbott and Costello, the Three
Stooges, and many others. The author gives a
picture of the old Hollywood through biographies
of the teams, peppered with anecdotes. There
are also synopses of major films by comedy
teams, along with painstaking filmographies
and over 200 still photographs.

367. Manvell, Roger. New Cinema in Europe. New York:
Dutton, 1966. (Vista paperback)
Deals with the film in Europe since the end
of World War II, with emphasis on the realistic
and naturalistic approach of major film makers.
Among nations included are Italy, Britain,
France, Russia, and Poland. Contains an index
of directors.

368. Manvell, Roger, and John Huntley. The Technique
of Film and Music. New York: Hastings House,
1957.
Traces the development of all kinds of film
music from early piano accompaniment of silent
films to contemporary orchestral scores especially composed. Appendices give an outline
history of film music from 1895 to 1955, a
selected list of film music recordings through
1955, two examples of film music criticism,
and a select bibliography of books and articles.
Indexed.

369. Michaels, Paul, editor-in-chief. The American
Movies Reference Book: The Sound Era. Englewood
Cliffs, N.J.: Prentice-Hall, 1969.

A combination coffee-table and reference book,
lavishly illustrated, covering the history,
players, films, directors, producers, and awards
of the film industry from the beginning of the
sound era to the present. For all its 629 pages,
it is not comprehensive, nor does the editor
claim it to be. In a "Note on Scope" he tells
his ground rules for selection. And for those
people and films represented, coverage is excellent. There is also a particularly useful
section on awards and the top-grossing films
of each year. On the other hand, the section
on history hits only the highlights. Has a
three-page bibliography and an index to players,
directors, and producers.

370. Montgomery, John. Comedy Films 1894-1954. 2d ed.
London: Allen & Unwin, 1968.
Factual history of comedy film in the United
States and England. The new edition has been
revised but covers the same period.

371. Morin, Edgar. The Stars. Trans. by Richard
Howard. New York: Grove Press, 1960.
Sociological study of stardom as an institution in which the author, using famous film
personalities as examples, discusses the sociology of stardom. There is a table of chronological landmarks. (See also Walker's Stardom,
No. 405.)

372. Motion Pictures 1894-1912, Identified from the
Records of the United States Copyright Office.
Ed. by Howard Lamarr Walls. Washington, D.C.:
Library of Congress, Copyright Office, 1953.
A catalog of copyrighted works identified as
motion pictures produced during the industry's
pioneer period. In two parts, with Part I an
alphabetical list under title, giving name of
claimant, date, and registration number, and
Part II an index of claimants, listing under
each the film copyrighted.
Useful not only to those seeking to establish copyright history and status of early
films but also to those studying the motion
picture as an art, a historical record, or a
form of communication.

373. Motion Pictures 1912-1939. Washington, D.C.:
Library of Congress, Copyright Office, 1951.
A list of films, both fiction and nonfiction,
registered in the Copyright Office between 24

August 1912 and 31 December 1929. In three
sections: the first, an alphabetical list
under title, giving date, length, credits,
producer, original source when from a book,
play, or other work, and in some cases a brief
summary of content; the second, an index listing
names of persons and organizations associated
with the productions and of the authors of
novels, dramas, or other works upon which they
may be based; and the third, the series contained in the main entries.
Motion Pictures 1940-49. Washington, D.C.:
Library of Congress, Copyright Office, 1953.
     A continuation of Motion Pictures 1894-1912
and Motion Pictures 1912-1939.
Motion Pictures 1950-59. Washington, D.C.:
Library of Congress, Copyright Office, 1960.
     A continuation of the three previous entries.
These four volumes form an unbroken record of
copyright registration of motion pictures and
an extensive though incomplete record of motion
picture production in the U.S.
Motion Pictures 1960-1969. Washington, D.C.:
Library of Congress, Copyright Office, 1971.
     Updates the series.

374. Movies on TV. Ed. by Steven H. Scheuer. Rev. ed.
New York: Bantam, annual.
     Brief, literate appraisals of more than 7,000
motion pictures, intended to guide the discriminat-
ing viewer. Lists each film alphabetically by
title and gives date, cast, a rating by *'s,
and succinct annotations which capture plot,
mood, and quality. For example, "Usual turf
story, pleasant in a familiar sort of way."
Or ". . . a medical expedition treks through
the African jungle to find a cure for sleeping
sickness. You may be stricken by the same
malady halfway through this film." Entries are
by name of film. Titles of the annual vary somewhat from year to year.

375. National Film Archive Catalogue. Part I: Silent
News Films 1895-1933, 2d ed.; Part II: Silent Non-
Fiction Films 1895-1934; Part III: Silent Fiction
Films 1895-1930. London, W. 1: British Film
Institute, 81 Dean St., 1960, 1965, 1966.
     Each film is arranged chronologically and
annotated. Part I contains a subject index so
that the films may be approached by historical
event; Part II an index to titles; and Part III --
fiction films -- an index to films, persons, and

companies. Thus far sound films have not been
cataloged. To quote the curator: "The complete
published catalogue of the Archive is . . .
gradually taking shape, but far too slowly owing
to our restricted resources. It will have taken
nearly twenty years to cover only our silent
films, and the accurate cataloguing of our
larger collection of sound films still stretches
before us."

376. New York Times Film Reviews (1913-1968). 5 vols.
and index vol. New York: The New York Times
Library Service and Information Division, 1970.
Fifty-six years of the Times film reviews,
arranged chronologically, with a separate cross-
referenced index by title of film, names of
persons connected with film (director, players,
screenwriter, and so on), and name of production
company. Date references tell users the particular volume and issue of the Times in which
the review originally appeared.

377. Niver, Kemp R. The First Twenty Years: A Segment
of Film History. Los Angeles 90046: Locare
Research Group, Box 46505, 1968.
"This book concerns over one hundred motion
pictures selected from the more than 3,000
films restored from the Library of Congress as
proof of copyright application prior to ratifica-
tion in 1912 of a motion picture copyright law.
Each film described was selected because, in
the author's opinion, it contributed something
of value to the progress of communication
through the new medium of moving photography."
Most of the films chosen for restoration were
16 mm. Contains a list of film titles in
alphabetical order.

378. Niver, Kemp R. Motion Pictures from the Library
of Congress Print Collection 1894-1912. Berkeley
and Los Angeles: University of California Press,
1967.
" . . . an index of films produced throughout
the world between 1894 and 1912, paper prints of
which were deposited with the Library of Congress
during those years for copyright purposes.
Altogether, some 3,000 titles are listed here,
representing more than two million linear feet
of film -- incunabula of the cinema."
Although intended as a guide to those who
want to view the original films (the celluloid
originals of which have been restored by Mr.

Niver through a unique process), the index itself is a valuable reference source, giving
cast, producer, and others concerned; date of
copyright; footage; and a variety of similar
useful information, including an abstract of
the content. There is also a subject-title
index.

379. Noble, Peter. The Negro in Films. London:
Skelton Robinson, 1948.
    Some years before the treatment of blacks in
the entertainment world became the burning
issue it is today, their status was undergoing
examination in Britain. This book examines
portrayals of and by Negroes on the stage beginning with the Federal period, and moves on to
the silent and then the sound film. It takes
up the Negro in song and dance roles, in independent and government films, and in European
films; discusses some of the leading Negro
players; and assays what the future may hold.
Appendices give a brief historical background
of the American Negro, a bibliography, a list
of films featuring Negroes or containing
important racial themes -- American, British,
and continental -- and a defense of The Birth
of a Nation made by D. W. Griffith. Indexed.

380. The Payne Fund Studies. Motion Pictures and Youth.
W. W. Charters, Chairman. New York: Macmillan,
1933, 1935.
    This is a series of empirical studies
decades old but still valuable both for what
has now become history and for their findings,
which hold up today and can even be applied to
television. A list of titles shows the depth,
scope, and content of the series. In some cases
two are combined within one book:
Blumer, Herbert. Movies and Conduct, 1933.
Blumer, Herbert, and Philip M. Hauser. Movies,
    Delinquency, and Crime, 1934.
Charters, W. W. Motion Pictures and Youth: A
    Summary, 1933, together with Holaday, P. W.,
    and George D. Stoddard. Getting Ideas from the
    Movies, 1933.
Cressey, Paul G., and Frederick M. Thrasher.
    Boys, Movies, and City Streets.
Dale, Edgar. Content of Motion Pictures, together
    with Dale, Edgar. Children's Attendance at
    Motion Pictures, 1935.
Dale, Edgar. How to Appreciate Motion Pictures,
    1934.

Dysinger, W. S., and Christian A. Ruckmick. The
    Emotional Responses of Children to the Motion
    Picture Situation, 1933, together with Peters,
    Charles C. Motion Pictures and Standards of
    Morality, 1933.
Forman, Henry James. Our Movie Made Children, 1933.
Peterson, Ruth C., and L. L. Thurstone. Motion
    Pictures and Social Attitudes of Children, 1933,
    together with Shuttleworth, Frank K., and Mark
    A. May. The Social Conduct and Attitude of
    Movie Fans, 1933.
Renshaw, Samuel, Vernon L. Miller, and Dorothy
    Marquis. Children's Sleep, 1933.
        This series, along with a number of other
    books of the same vintage about film, has been
    reissued by the Arno Press/New York Times in a
    package.

Peters, Charles C. Motion Pictures and Standards
of Morality. See Payne Fund Studies (No. 380).

Peterson, Ruth C., and L. L. Thurstone. Motion
Pictures and Social Attitudes of Children. See
Payne Fund Studies (No. 380).

381. Quigley, Martin, Jr. Magic Shadows: The Story
    of the Origin of Motion Pictures. New York:
    Biblo & Tannen, c1948, 1969.
        A pre-history of the motion picture, from
    ancient times through the kinetoscope. Con-
    tains a chronology from 6000 B.C. through 1896,
    a bibliography, and an index.

382. Quinn, James. The Film and Television as an
    Aspect of European Culture. Leyden: A. W.
    Sijthoff, 1968.
        Survey of the educational and cultural
    significance of film and television, commis-
    sioned by the Council for Cultural Co-operation
    of the Council of Europe. Gives different forms
    of governmental support, steps taken by educa-
    tional bodies in various countries to develop
    film and television studies, use of film and
    television in education, attitudes of the
    church and the public, and attitude of film
    industries of different countries toward the
    film as art.

383. Ramsaye, Terry. A Million and One Nights: A
    History of the Motion Picture. New York: Simon
    & Schuster, c1926, 1964.

First published in 1926, at a time when many
of the founders of the film were alive, this book
goes into detail about the history of the motion
picture in the United States from its inception
to 1926. The author, first connected with the
industry in 1913 as a journalist, used original
sources whenever possible and interviewed every
person then living whom he mentioned. Contains
an index but no bibliography or footnotes. Over
the years certain historical inaccuracies have
been found in Ramsaye, but it is still a useful
and interesting source.

384. Renan, Sheldon. An Introduction to the American
Underground Film. New York: Dutton Paperback,
1968.
    Comprehensive survey of an emerging form of
film on which most of the literature has existed
in scattered articles. Renan's work is substantial. Beginning with a lengthy definition
of the underground film in its many aspects, he
then gives its history in the U.S. and its
earlier European background and a gallery of its
chief film makers, its stars, and its "establishment"; and finally he discusses "expanded
cinema," which he defines as a spirit of inquiry
leading in many directions.
    An appendix lists the 400 to 500 films men-
tioned, telling their length, whether in color
or black and white, silent or sound, and availability for sales or rental, with source from
which they may be obtained. Contains a bibliography and an index.

Renshaw, Samuel. Children's Sleep. See Payne
Fund Studies (No. 380).

385. Robinson, David. The Great Funnies: A History
of Film Comedy. New York: Dutton, 1969.
    "This essay pretends to be no more than a
bird's-eye view, only lingering from time to
time over a figure of particular importance
or special attention," says the author with
too much modesty. For, building his history
around various well-known comedians, he packs
in a great deal of material in a succinct and
interesting fashion. The scope is international.
Indexed.

386. Robinson, David. Hollywood in the Twenties. New
York: Barnes, 1968.

". . . all that is really possible is a
bird's-eye view of things; and my concern has
been to show the films and film makers of this
period both in relationship to the industry and
to the general background of American life and
culture. . . . The sixty or seventy-five film
makers whose careers are treated in greater or
less detail are those whom I feel are most significant or at least most representative of the
period." - The author in his introduction.
Indexed by films and personalities mentioned.
This is the first of a series spanning the
1920s, 1930s, and 1940s. (See Nos. 309 and
339.)

387. Rosten, Leo C. Hollywood: The Movie Colony; the
Movie Makers. New York: Harcourt, Brace & World,
1941.
"This book is primarily concerned with put-
ting Hollywood under the microscopes of social
science. For Hollywood is an index to our
society and our culture. . . . 'A study of
Hollywood casts the profile of American society
into sharper relief.'" - Preface. The result
is a systematic analysis by the author and a
staff of social scientists, who combine statistical documentation with perception. Appendices contain data on such items as the following: the movies and Los Angeles; production
costs, analysis of movie companies, comparison
with other industries; annual earnings, weekly
salaries, and spending patterns; social data;
marriage and divorce data; comments and preference of movie makers; dogs, yachts, resorts;
fan mail. Useful both historically and for
certain eternal verities. Although three decades
old now, it remains a classic. Reference notes
form a bibliography, and there is an index of
subjects.

388. Rotha, Paul. Documentary Film. 3d ed. London:
Faber & Faber, 1952.
Subtitled "The use of the film medium to
interpret creatively and in social terms the
life of the people as it exists in reality,"
this is an intensive study of the documentary.
Limiting himself to no one country, the author
first gives a general introduction to the
cinema, then treats the following aspects of
documentary film: its evolution; certain basic
principles; techniques; developments, policies,
purposes; and a history from 1939 to the early

1950s. Three appendices include the use of
films by the U.S. Armed Forces, 100 important
documentary films, and a select bibliography.
Fully indexed. Sinclair Road and Richard
Griffith collaborated with Mr. Rotha.

389. Rotha, Paul. The Film Till Now: A Survey of
World Cinema. 3d ed. New York: Twayne, 1960.
   A history and analysis of the motion picture,
worldwide in scope, and treating both its
factual and theoretical backgrounds. Part I,
"The Actual," discusses its development, its
various forms, and its growth and characteristics in the U.S., USSR, Germany, France,
Britain, and other countries. Part II, "The
Theoretical," discusses its aims and influence
of form upon dramatic content. Part III, by
Richard Griffith, brings the first edition up
to 1948. An epilogue in the third edition goes
to 1958 and covers about 35 western and eastern
countries.

390. Sadoul, George. The Cinema in the Arab Countries.
Beirut, Lebanon: Interarab Centre of Cinema &
Television, P.O. Box 3434, 1966.
   Anthology, prepared for UNESCO, which pro-
vides the first general view of the cinema in the
Arab world. It is divided into six sections:
the cinema and Arab culture, history of the
Arab cinema, geography of the Arab cinema,
problems and future development, recommendations,
film lists and statistics.

391. Sarris, Andrew. The American Cinema: Directors
and Directions, 1929-1968. New York: Dutton,
1968.
   A brief but pointed examination of 200 American film directors. The author, a film critic,
rates his directors in categories ranging from
"pantheon" to "strained seriousness," "less
than meets the eye," and "oddities, one-shots,
and newcomers," and gives sound judgments as
well as facts. Taken as a whole, the book constitutes an excellent survey of the American
sound film. Special features are a directional
chronology of the most important films of each
year from 1929 through 1967 and an alphabetical
list of over 600 films with year of release and
director.

392. Schmidt, Georg, and others. The Film: Its
Economic, Social, and Artistic Problems. London:
Falcon Press, 1948.
A study of the contemporary film, limited
to what the authors term the fiction film
rather than the documentary, the newsreel, or
the advertising film, and showing its present
function, its technical and artistic means,
and the nature of its economic and social structure. Some history is also given as background.

393. Seldes, Gilbert. The Movies Come from America.
New York: Scribner's, 1937.
Intended as a guide to make the average
American movie-goer more sophisticated, this
critical history centers upon the United States
and upon personalities and films. The approach
is analytical. Indexed.

Shuttleworth, Frank K., and Mark A. May. The
Social Conduct and Attitude of Movie Fans. See
Payne Fund Studies (No. 380).

394. Slide, Anthony. Early American Cinema. New York:
Barnes, 1970.
From beginnings with Edison and Lubin to
Pearl White and serial queens, this 180-page
paperback describes and analyzes the Hollywood
of that period in terms of films of the period.
Contains a small bibliography and an index.

395. Spraos, John. The Decline of the Cinema: An
Economist's Report. London: Allen & Unwin, 1962.
One of the best economic studies of the film
industry in Britain, which the author contends
is declining -- a contention he bolsters with
facts and figures. He then proceeds to give
the reasons, some of which directly pertain to
the American film industry. Indexed.

396. Stedman, Raymond William. The Serials: Suspense
and Drama by Television. Norman: University of
Oklahoma Press, 1971.
"Here -- at times in broad brushstrokes -- is
the story of the dramatic serial in America, its
beginnings, its glorious cul-de-sacs, its continued good health in an electronic medium not
even in existence when the genre began." By
means of listening, viewing, studying published
research, and interviewing, the author traces
the births and, in most cases, ultimate demises
of the various types of serials -- film, magazine,

comic strip, radio, television. Although
emphasis is from 1912 to the present, he goes
further into history when necessary. Appendices
include a chronological list of daytime network
serials on radio and on television. There is a
bibliography and an index.

397. Svenska Filminstitutet; the Swedish Film Institute.
Stockholm: Ab Svensk Film Industri Kungsgatan,
36, 1964.
Twenty-page pamphlet packed with facts about
the Swedish film reform of 1963, giving present
economic and legal status of the industry and
the effect upon quality. In both French and
English languages.

398. Thorp, Margaret Farrand. America at the Movies.
New Haven, Conn.: Yale University Press, 1939.
A perceptive series of articles on the social
influence of the motion picture in America which
the author wrote during years before television,
when movies were at their peak. Chapter headings indicate scope and tone: "Eighty-five
Million a Week," "What Movie Tonight?," "Glamour,"
"Cinema Fashions," "The Industry," "Reforming
the Movies," "Taking the Movies Seriously," "The
Vampire Art," "The Lure of Propaganda." Indexed.

399. Tyler, Parker. Underground Film: A Critical
History. New York: Grove Press, 1969.
Intended as a definitive history of the experimental film movement whose center today is the
American underground. The author, a prominent
film critic, assesses the work of the leading
directors, discusses specific films, and shows
the variety of current aims and techniques, tracing the origins. Contains a filmography.

400. U.S. Department of Commerce. Business and Defense
Services Administration. Scientific, Motion
Picture, and Photographic Products Division. Motion
Pictures Abroad. Washington, D.C.: Government
Printing Office, 1959-61.
A series of pamphlets, each of which covers
a foreign country and discusses aspects of the
motion picture industry in that country. Includes
Argentina, Australia, Greece, Spain, and Belgium.
Among topics summarized are production, promo-
tion, exhibition, organization, distribution,
and so on.

401. U.S. Department of Commerce. Business and Defense
Services Administration. Scientific, Motion
Picture, and Photographic Products Division.
World Survey of Motion Picture Theater Facilities.
Washington, D.C.: Government Printing Office,
1960.
    A six-page pamphlet containing statistics on
    motion picture theater facilities throughout
    the world. Gives number of theaters, seating
    capacity, and U.S. percentage of screen time,
    by region and country, for 1955 and 1960.

402. Vallance, Tom. The American Musical. New York:
Barnes, 1970. (Screen Series)
    ". . . a guide to the artists who gave Holly-
    wood supremacy in the form of the musical. It
    lists their musical credits with a small amount
    of biographical material and comment. Though
    complete objectivity is probably impossible, I
    have generally tried to keep any controversial
    views in check and have given what are mainly
    widely held judgments and opinions on the
    artists involved." - The author in his intro-
    duction.
    Not all the entries are under performers.
    Some deal briefly with subject -- e.g.,
    "Animation in the Musical," "Band Leaders,"
    "Ghosting," "Composers on the Screen." Chor-
    eographers, directors, composers, and various
    others connected with the musical are listed
    along with the actors. Indexed.

403. Wagenknecht, Edward. The Movies in the Age of
Innocence. Norman: University of Oklahoma Press,
1962.
    "I wished to write this book most of all
    because I thought it high time that some Amer-
    ican should attempt to record what the first
    motion pictures looked like to the generation
    for which they were created. . . . I am not
    writing an all-inclusive study. I have chosen
    my materials upon a more or less personal basis;
    the films, the stars, the directors over which
    I linger longer are those that were important
    to me, and in many cases I have set down what I
    had to say about them in the manner of an essay-
    ist rather than a historian." He lingers over
    D. W. Griffith, Mary Pickford, and the Gish
    sisters and devotes two chapters to a number of
    stars, films, and directors of the 1920s and
    earlier. Informally written and profusely

illustrated. Contains an index to names and to
titles.

404. Waldron, Gloria. The Information Film. New
York: Columbia University Press, 1949. (A
Report of the Public Library Inquiry)
     "This survey is concerned primarily with
film as an instrument for adult education and
culture. It is necessarily concerned, too,
with the institutions -- particularly the public
library -- that are making films an educational
force," the author states in her first chapter.
She makes a comprehensive investigation of
production, distribution, and possibilities and
finds that possibilities far exceed production
and distribution, which had many problems to
overcome. A comprehensive and critical overview which has now become historical. Contains
appendices, a glossary, a bibliography, and an
index.

405. Walker, Alexander. Stardom: The Hollywood
Phenomenon. New York: Stein & Day, 1970.
     The author, film critic for the London Eve-
ning Standard, examines stardom and its implications, illustrating with case studies of past
and present Hollywood stars and how they are
made and broken, often at the expense of their
talent. Contains a bibliography and an index.
For another book dealing with the same subject
see Morin's The Stars (No. 371).

406. White, David Manning, and Richard Averson, eds.
Sight, Sound and Society: Motion Pictures and
Television in America. Boston: Beacon Press,
1968.
     Taken as a whole, this anthology gives an
overview of contemporary trends and theories;
taken by individual articles, it provides in-
sights into various aspects of television and
movies -- as, for instance, "Broadcasting and
the News" by Robert E. Kintner; "The FCC and
Program Regulation" by Lee Lovinger; "Violence
on the Cinema" by Philip French. Contains an
·appendix, "The Literature of Motion Pictures
and Television: A Critique and Recommendations,"
by the editors, and an index of names and subjects.

407. World Film Directory: Agencies Concerned with
Educational, Scientific and Cultural Film. New

York: UNESCO Publications Center, 1962. (Reports
and Papers on Mass Communication No. 35)
     Gives government offices, agencies, organiza-
tions, societies, and trade associations involved with film for 133 countries, along with
a short summary indicating the scope of the
activities of each agency. This edition contains and supplements information in a 1952-53
edition.

Magazines

408. An Advertiser's Guide to Scholarly Periodicals.
New York 10016: American University Press
Services, 1 Park Ave., annual.
     Probably the one single source bringing
together the majority of scholarly publications
in the United States. Intended as an aid to
members of the Association of American University Presses in placing advertising and book
reviews, it classifies over 350 scholarly publications, little magazines, and suitable
consumer magazines, giving for each, in addition to information about rates and deadlines
for ads, a brief description of content, circulation figures, analysis of subscribers, and
policy regarding book reviews.

Advertising and Press Annual of Africa. (See No.
542.)

Allworth, Edward. Central Asian Publishing and
the Rise of Nationalism: An Essay and a List of
Publications in the New York Public Library.
(See No. 105.)

Altick, Richard D. The English Common Reader: A
Social History of the Mass Reading Public 1800-
1900. (See No. 106.)

Arndt, Karl J. R., and May E. Olson. German-
American Newspapers and Periodicals, 1732-1955.
(See No. 445.)

409. The Associated Church Press. _Directory_. Chicago
     60610: The Associated Church Press, 875 North
     Dearborn, annual.
         Lists Protestant religious periodicals belong-
     ing to the Associated Church Press. For each
     periodical, gives address, personnel, frequency,
     circulation, and advertising policy and rates.

_Average Circulation and Rate Trends of Leading
Magazines, 1946-1966_. (_See_ No. 547.)

Ayer's. See _N. W. Ayer & Son_ (No. 495).

Bacon's Publicity Checker: Magazines, Newspapers.
(_See_ No. 548.)

410. _Bulletin of Bibliography and Magazine Notes_. Boston:
     Faxon, quarterly.
         Contains in each issue a section, "Births,
     Deaths, and Magazine Notes: A Record of New
     Titles, Changed Titles, and Deaths in the
     Periodical World," by Albert H. Davis, Jr. Cov-
     erage is comprehensive, including trade journals,
     scholarly journals, consumer magazines, and
     paperback and hardcover periodicals.

Business Publications Rates and Data. (_See_ No.
552.)

411. Canada. Royal Commission on Publications. _Report_.
     Ottawa: Queen's Printer for the Royal Commission
     on Publications, 1961.
         Investigation of Canadian periodical publish-
     ing, placed in the general context of Canadian
     communications. Emphasis is economic and cul-
     tural. Contains 11 appendices and an index.

412. Cannon, Carl L., comp. _Journalism: A Bibliog-
     raphy_. New York 10018: New York Public Library,
     Fifth Ave. & 42d St., 1924.
         Annotated list of books and magazine articles
     "intended to be useful to the American newspaper
     man actively engaged in his profession, or to
     the student of journalism." The author has
     emphasized the present rather than the historical
     in his selections, which means that his bibliog-
     raphy is now an excellent source for references
     to the state of journalism in the early 1920s.

413. _Catholic Press Directory_. New York 10016: Catho-
     lic Press Association, 432 Park Ave. South, annual.

Official media reference guide to Catholic
newspapers, magazines, and diocesan directories
in the U.S. and Canada. For most entries, provides address, key personnel, rates, and circulation.

Cazden, Robert. German Exile Literature in
America 1935-1950: A History of the Free German
Press and Book Trade. (See No. 126.)

Comprehensive Media Guide. Korea. (See No. 554.)

Consumer Magazine and Farm Publication Rates and
Data. (See No. 556.)

Consumer Magazine Report. (See No. 557.)

Demographics Report. (See No. 558.)

414. Directory of Little Magazines and Small Presses.
Ed. by Len Fulton. Paradise, Calif. 95969: Dustbooks, 5218 Scottswood Road, annual.
    One of the most elusive forms of printed
material is the little magazine, largely because
most of them are ephemeral and without financial
stability. The compilers of this directory have
done an admirable job of listing about 600 such
publications throughout the world, with emphasis
on the U.S., Latin America, and Great Britain.
Data for each entry vary from name and address
only to editor, price, frequency, circulation,
size, typography, date first published, nature
of content, payment (if any), and similar information.
    Some of the directories have special features.
The third edition (1967) carries a preface in
which the editor discusses the sources he used
to unearth the existence of little magazines and
gives advice to would-be editors and contributors. The fifth edition (1969) lists names
and addresses of underground newspapers in the
U.S. and Europe. For continuity on the subject
see Hoffman (No. 423) and Gerstenberger and
Hendrick (No. 421).

415. Directory of Members. International Council of
Industrial Editors. Akron, Ohio 44313: International Council of Industrial Editors, 2108
Braewick Circle, annual.
    Alphabetical list of editors with their pub-
lication and address, followed by lists of

organizations and of associations with membership.

Directory of the College Student Press of America.
(See No. 456.)

Directory of the Jewish Press in America. (See
No. 457.)

416. Drewry, John E. "Magazine Journalism: A Selected
Bibliography." Journalism Quarterly 25 (Sept.
1948):260-77.
    Includes references to both books and articles.
The former are briefly annotated; the latter
are classified under the specific magazines to
which they refer.

417. Elfenbein, Julien. Business Journalism. 2d rev.
ed. New York: Harper, 1960.
    A discussion of trade publications, both
magazine and newspaper. Defines the business
press, tells how it serves industry, and gives
its history and present status not only in the
U.S. but in other countries as well.

Emery, Edwin, and Henry Ladd Smith. The Press and
America: An Interpretative History of Journalism.
(See No. 461.)

The European Press Today. (See No. 462.)

418. First National Directory of "Rightist" Groups,
Publications and Some Individuals in the United
States (and Some Foreign Countries). 5th ed.
Los Angeles 90005: Noontide Press, P.O. Box
76062, 1965.
    Alphabetical listing of several thousand
educational, social, and religious organizations
and their publications where one exists -- all
of which represent a protest of some sort
against prevailing "leftist" political or
social trends. Information for each item includes name and address. Every publication has
a separate entry and is entered again under the
name of the organization. Compiled by the Alert
Americans Association.

419. Ford, James C. L. Magazines for Millions: The
Story of Specialized Publications. Carbondale:
Southern Illinois University Press, 1969.
    A practical survey of today's biggest trend
in the magazine field -- the specialized

publication, defined by the author as those
magazines and newspapers which deal with a particular subject matter of interest to a specialized audience which can be very small or very
large. The result is a compendium of facts,
with the various classes of magazines treated
within their subject fields. Among the types
are communications; industrial; technical;
business; the professional, occupational, and
association publications; and farm magazines.
Satisfactory for the history, scope, and content of specific publications, but disappoint-
ing as an analysis of the trends which are
fragmenting the magazine audience.
    Information contained in the appendices
includes instruction for authors issued by
certain of the magazines; lists of American
Business Press member publications, specialized publishing associations, Bureau of Independent Publishers and Distributors; and a
flow-chart of production schedules for Better
Homes and Gardens. Indexed.

Fulton, Len. See Directory of Little Magazines
and Small Presses (No. 414).

420. Gebbie House Magazine Directory: A Public Relations and Free-Lance Guide to the Nation's Leading House Magazines. 6th ed. Sioux City, Iowa
51102: Gebbie Directory, P.O. Box 1111, 1968.
    Lists house organs alphabetically under the
name of the issuing company or organization,
which is briefly described. Information about
each includes name, address, editor, printer,
type of print, frequency, length, and circulation figures, along with a description of
the type of material published and rates.
There is also a title list, a geographical
grouping, a grouping by type of industry, and
various miscellaneous information. An earlier
book in this area, long out of print, is The
Printers' Ink Directory of House Organs (New
York: Printers' Ink, 1954).

421. Gerstenberger, Donna, and George Hendrick. Third
Directory of Periodicals Publishing Articles in
English and American Literature and Language. 3d
ed. Chicago: Swallow Press, 1970.
    Although the purpose of this book is to pro-
vide information both for scholars wishing to
submit articles for publication and for graduate
students in English who may wish to use it as a

guide to the extensive publications in English
and American literature and language, it is
also useful in tracking down and tracing the
history of literary magazines.

There are over 500 entries in this latest
edition as well as a subject index. Earlier
editions contain information about periodicals
no long extant. Data given include title,
address, price, year of founding and sponsor,
major field of interest, manuscript information,
payment, and copyright policy. See Hoffman (No.
423) and Directory of Little Magazines and Small
Presses (No. 414) for continuity on this elusive
subject.

Glessing, Robert J. The Underground Press in
America. (See No. 465.)

422. Goldwater, Walter. Radical Periodicals in America
1890-1950: A Bibliography with Brief Notes. Rev.
ed. New Haven, Conn.: Yale University Library,
1966.

Consists of a listing of 321 periodicals with
a genealogical chart and a concise lexicon of
the parties and groups which issued each. Every
entry has a brief annotation giving contributors and character. Contains a bibliography,
"A Short List of Useful Books."

Gorokhoff, Boris I. Publishing in the U.S.S.R.
(See No. 137.)

Great Britain. Royal Commission on the Press.
Minutes of Oral Evidence Taken before the Royal
Commission on the Press. (See No. 468.)

Hall, Max, ed. Made in New York: Case Studies
in Metropolitan Manufacturing. (See No. 142.)

423. Hoffman, Frederick J., Charles Allen, and Carolyn
F. Ulrich. The Little Magazine: A History and
a Bibliography. Princeton, N.J.: Princeton
University Press, 1946.

The best single source for the history of
little magazines in the U.S. and for bibliographic data on specific titles up to 1946.
After this date information must be pieced
together from a variety of publications. One
of the best of these is the literary magazine
Trace (London: Villiers Publications Ltd.;
Hollywood, Calif.: P.O. Box 1068), each issue
of which contains a section, "The Chronicle:

An Evolving Directory of Magazines and Publishers of Literary Intent," which, in addition
to books, lists little magazines in the English
language stressing literature and poetry. In
1967 Trace Hardback cumulated this column.
For further information see Gerstenberger's
and Hendrick's Third Directory of Periodicals
Publishing Articles in English and American
Literature and Language (No. 421) and Len
Fulton's annual Directory of Little Magazines
and Small Presses (No. 414), popularly known
as Dustbooks. Because of the ephemeral nature
of little magazines, none of these sources can
be definitive.

Hoggart, Richard. The Uses of Literacy: Aspects
of Working-Class Life with Special Reference to
Publications and Entertainment. (See No. 34.)

Hopkins, Mark W. Mass Media in the Soviet Union.
(See No. 474.)

Hudson's Washington News Media Contacts Directory.
(See No. 475.)

424. ILPA Directory of Member Publications. Washington,
D.C. 20006: International Labor Press Association,
815 16th St., NW, biennial.
Lists some 400 bulletins, newspapers, and
magazines published by trade union bodies
associated under the banner of AFL-CIO. For
each entry, gives name, address, telephone
number, editor, size, circulation, and whether
or not it accepts advertising. Also gives
Canadian labor publications, associate members,
regional and industrial associations, radio
stations, and the Press Code of Ethics.

Leading Advertisers in Business Publications.
(See No. 569.)

Leading National Advertisers, Inc. P.I.B. Magazine Service. (See No. 571.)

Liu, Alan P. L. The Press and Journals in Communist China. (See No. 487.)

Magazine Circulation and Rate Trends 1940-1967.
(See No. 573.)

425. Magazine Editorial Reports. Analysis of the
Editorial Content of General, News, Women's, Home,

Fashion, and Farm Magazines. New York 10016:
Lloyd G. Hall Co., 216 Madison Ave., monthly,
with annual cumulations.

Monthly report classifying the editorial
content of over 50 large-circulation consumer
magazines according to 18 main subject groupings and nearly 200 subclassifications in
terms of lines, pages, and percentage of
total editorial content for each. Ratio of
total editorial to total content is also given.

426. Marty, Martin E., and others. The Religious
Press in America. New York: Holt, Rinehart &
Winston, 1963.

The aim of the authors is to familiarize
readers of denominational publications, both
newspapers and magazines, with the way in
which they interpret the world in terms of
religious commitments. In chapters both
descriptive and broadly analytical, Mr. Marty
discusses "The Protestant Press: Limitations
and Possibilities"; John G. Deedy, Jr., "The
Catholic Press: The Why and the Wherefore";
David Wolf Silverman, "The Jewish Press: A
Quadrilingual Phenomenon"; and Robert Lekach-
man, "The Secular Uses of the Religious Press."
The book is particularly good because it puts
the subject in a social perspective. There
are footnotes but no bibliography or index.

Mason's Publishers. (See No. 488.)

Merrill, John C., Carter E. Bryan, and Marvin
Alisky. The Foreign Press: A Survey of the
World's Journalism. (See No. 491.)

427. Mott, Frank Luther. A History of American Magazines. 5 vols. Cambridge, Mass.: Harvard University Press, 1930-68. (Vol. I, 1741-1850;
Vol. II, 1850-65; Vol. III, 1865-85; Vol. IV,
1885-1905; Vol. V, 1885-1905.)

A thorough and comprehensive history of the
American magazine from pre-Revolutionary times
to 1900. Arrangement is chronological. Vol.
V, published posthumously and edited by the
author's daughter, Mildred Mott Wedel, assisted
by Theodore Peterson and John T. Frederick, is
somewhat different, consisting of a series of
sketches of 25 of the most prominent magazines
of the period.

The appendices of the first four volumes contain a chronological list of magazines covered,

with dates of establishment and demise (except
in the rare cases where they are extant). Vol.
V indexes the entire series. For the period
from 1900 on see Peterson's Magazines in the
Twentieth Century (No. 428).

Murthy, Nadig Krishna. Indian Journalism: Origin,
Growth and Development of Indian Journalism from
Asoka to Nehru. (See No. 494.)

National Advertising Investments: Magazines.
Newspaper Supplements. Network TV. Spot TV.
(See No. 575.)

The Newspaper Press Directory and Advertisers'
Guide. (See No. 500.)

N. W. Ayer & Son. Directory of Newspapers and
Periodicals. (See No. 495.)

Ogilvy & Mather Pocket Guide to Media. (See No.
582.)

P&D Overseas Newspaper and Periodicals Guide
Book. (See No. 504.)

428. Peterson, Theodore. Magazines in the Twentieth
Century. 2d rev. ed. Urbana: University of
Illinois Press, 1964.
        The best single source for detailed informa-
tion on trends in consumer magazines over the
past 60 years and for the history of specific
ones. The author deals with special-interest
as well as big-name magazines, tracing their
development and placing them in historical
and economic context. Arrangement is broadly
by aspects of magazine publishing and types
of magazines -- for example, "Advertising: Its
Growth and Effects," "The Economic Structure
of the Industry," "The Old Leaders That Died,"
"The New Leaders That Survived," "New Leaders:
The Missionaries," "New Leaders: The Mer-
chants," "Success by Compression," "Magazines
for Cultural Minorities," and so on. The first
edition (1956) contained a lengthy bibliography
which has been omitted from the second. However, footnotes somewhat replace it. There is
an index.

Press and Advertisers Year Book. (See No. 506.)

Price, Warren C. The Literature of Journalism:
An Annotated Bibliography. (See No. 508.)

The Rome Report of Business Publication Advertising. (See No. 586.)

429. Schacht, John H. A Bibliography for the Study of
Magazines. 2d ed. Urbana: University of Illinois,
College of Communications, 119 Gregory Hall, 1968.
Selective, annotated 37-page bibliography
of periodical articles and monographs, arranged
by subject. Updated at irregular intervals.

430. Serial Publications in Large Libraries. Ed. by
Walter C. Allen. Urbana: University of Illinois,
Graduate School of Library Science, 1970. (Aller-
ton Park Institute No. 16)
Although the bulk of this symposium is concerned with technical treatment of periodicals
in libraries, it contains two articles which
are of general interest: "The Bright, Bleak
Future of American Magazines" by Theodore
Peterson, summarizing trends, and "Serials
Selection" by William A. Katz, dealing with
the failure of libraries to preserve magazines
unsanctified by periodical indexes -- as, for
example, pulps, comics, "stag mags," and so
on -- which are a part of our popular culture
and as such have scholarly value.

431. Sources of Consumer Magazine Information. 3d ed.
New York 10022: Magazine Advertising Bureau of
Magazine Publishers Association, Inc., 575
Lexington Ave., 1969.
Résumé of selected general sources of information about consumer magazines. Brief summaries of the references available are given
under the following headings: circulation,
advertising volume, advertising rates and
mechanical specifications, magazine audience
size and characteristics, marketing information,
advertising ratings and advertising effectiveness, miscellaneous.

432. Standard Periodical Directory. Ed. by Leon
Garry. 3d ed. New York: Oxbridge, 1969.
The subtitle for this book, "The Most Complete Guide to United States & Canadian
Periodicals . . . Information on More Than
50,000 Publications," is not boastful. The word
"periodical" has been defined broadly as any
publication with a regular frequency of at least

136

once every two years. Within this definition
are: magazines and journals, newsletters,
government publications, advisory services,
house organs, directories, serials, transactions
and proceedings of professional societies, bulletins, yearbooks, and publications of museums
and religious, ethnic, social, and literary
groups.

Information includes title; address and
telephone number; names of editor, publisher,
advertising director; a description of editorial
content and scope; year founded; frequency;
subscription and advertising rates; circulation;
auditing organization. Entries are arranged
by subject categories and in a few cases by
form -- e.g., house organs. There is an alphabetical index to titles.

Statistics of Newspapers and Other Periodicals.
(See No. 517.)

433. Tebbel, John. The American Magazine: A Compact
History. New York: Hawthorn Press, 1969.
The author has described his book perfectly:
"What I am offering here is a narrative history
that necessarily depends in large part on the
scholarship of others, but does what the others
were of course not intending to do, that is, to
tell the story of the magazine business in
America from 1749 to the present, within the
scope of a single volume, in terms the general
reader, and especially the preprofessional
reader, will find helpful in his study and
understanding." Contains a short list of
recommended readings and an index.

434. Ulrich's International Periodicals Directory. 2
vols. New York: Bowker, biennial with supplement between editions.
The current edition (each one grows) gives
full and concise information on 40,000 periodicals from practically all parts of the world.
Includes for each: full name; subtitle; change
of name (where relevant); sponsoring organization (if any); year first published; frequency;
subscription rate; editor; publisher, with
full address; whether it carries abstracts,
reviews, bibliographies, advertising; format;
whether indexed or abstracted. Arrangement
is by subject, with an alphabetical index which
includes former names of periodicals if they
have changed since the previous edition.

435. Union List of Serials in Libraries of the United
States and Canada. 3d ed. Ed. by Edna Brown
Titus. 5 vols. New York: Wilson, 1965.
    Listing of over 156,000 periodicals available
in libraries in the U.S. and Canada. In addition to telling where they may be found, it
gives dates and changes in titles.
    Among some of the types of publications omit-
ted are: government (except periodicals and
monograph series issued by governments); United
Nations publications; administrative reports of
various sorts; almanacs; law reports and di-
gests; house organs; national and international
conferences and congresses, etc.; and, in brief,
various other types of publications having
limited or ephemeral value.
    This third edition carries periodicals up to
1949. After that date new periodicals appear in a
cumulative publication, New Serials Titles.
This has cumulated into a 10-year volume covering 1950-60 and is continued by monthly issues
which cumulate yearly. A section at the back
of each cumulation lists "Changes in Serials"
and notes changes regardless of their beginning
date. These changes include titles, cessations,
suspensions, resumptions, and so on.

436. Who's Who in Journalism 1969. London W. 1:
Campaign, Gillow House, 5 Winsley St., 1969.
    This title is somewhat a misnomer, for the
book gives no biographical data. Rather, it
lists British journalists under the headings of
their specialties (among categories is "Wine
Writers"), and it gives magazines, newspapers,
and broadcasting stations with personnel and
(for magazines) areas of specialization where
they exist. It also contains an assortment of
other useful information -- news agencies; photo
agencies; newsreels; liaison groups; information
sources; British Information Service (overseas);
foreign information services (home); foreign
correspondents in Britain; reception, conference,
and exhibition centers; business services; model
agencies. This supersedes the annual Directory
of Newspaper and Magazine Personnel and Data.

Willing's European Press Guide. (See No. 532.)

Willing's Press Guide. (See No. 533.)

437. Wolseley, Roland E. Understanding Magazines. Ames:
Iowa State University Press, 1965.
"The purpose of Understanding Magazines is to
provide at least four kinds of readers with an
overview of magazines in the United States --
their history, functions, organization, types,
responsibilities, problems, vocational opportunities, and future." - Author's preface.
Complements Mott (No. 427) and Peterson (No.
428) covering different material and with a
different organization.

438. Wood, James Playsted. Magazines in the United
States. 2d ed. New York: Ronald Press, 1956.
A one-volume history of magazine publishing,
tracing origins in England and in this country
and discussing trends, types, and certain titles.
It covers a long period of time and a wide scope
briefly and eclectically. Contains a bibliography and an index.

439. Working Press of the Nation. Feature Writer and
Syndicate Directory. Vol. 4. Chicago 60601:
National Research Bureau, 221 North LaSalle St.,
annual.
Directory of free-lance writers and feature
syndicates intended as a guide to public relations men. This edition lists over 800 leading
feature writers who appear regularly in prominent national magazines, gives home addresses,
and classifies them by the kind of features
they write and the publications for which they
write. There are also listings of free-lance
photographers and leading feature syndicates.
A section also contains the editorial requirements of about 35 of the large-circulation consumer magazines.

440. The Working Press of the Nation. Magazine and
Editorial Directory. Vol. 2. Chicago 60601:
National Research Bureau, 221 North LaSalle St.,
annual.
The purpose of this volume is to list those
magazines of importance to public relations
officials and to give pertinent facts about
each. The main section is arranged first by
groups of interest and then alphabetically
within the groups. This is preceded by an
alphabetical index.
Each listing covers name, address, phone
number, personnel (in some detail), deadlines,
circulation, subscription rates, and both an

editorial and a circulation analysis, along with
an indication by the editor of the general types
of editorial and departmental features of interest to them. This particular edition contains
over 3,200 publications in the U.S. and Canada.

Newspapers

Advertising and Press Annual of Africa. (See No.
542.)

441. African Newspapers in Selected American Libraries:
A Union List. Comp. by Rozanne M. Barry. 3d ed.
Washington, D.C.: Library of Congress, Reference
Department, Serials Division, 1965.
Current and retrospective holdings of 708
African newspapers in 33 selected libraries.
For each paper, tells frequency of publication
and, where available, date of establishment.

442. Ainslie, Rosalynde. The Press in Africa: Communications Past and Present. New York: Walker,
1967.
Analytical study of the history and structure
of the African press, with press broadly defined
to include broadcasting and news agencies as
well as newspapers. Contains a bibliography of
published and unpublished material on the subject and a table showing African broadcasting
stations, news agencies, and daily newspapers.
Certain countries are omitted, among which are
Israel, Syria, and Lebanon. Indexed.

443. Alisky, Marvin. Latin American Journalism Bibliography. Ann Arbor, Mich. 48103: University Micro-
films, LASA Project No. 12, 1958.
An annotated bibliography, with emphasis on
newspapers, radio and television, printing, and
freedom of the press.

Altick, Richard D. The English Common Reader: A Social History of the Mass Reading Public 1800-1900. (See No. 106.)

American Newspaper Markets' Circulation. (See No. 546.)

444. American Newspapers 1821-1936: A Union List of Files Available in the United States and Canada. Ed. by Winifred Gregory. New York: Wilson, 1937.
   A list of newspapers, beginning where Brigham (No. 448) leaves off, giving their location in libraries of the U.S. and Canada, dates when they began and ceased publication (if no longer extant), and changes in names or mergers that have occurred. Information about their history is not, however, as full as in Brigham.

445. Arndt, Karl J. R., and May E. Olson. German-American Newspapers and Periodicals, 1732-1955. 2d rev. ed. New York: Johnson Reprint Corp., 1965.
   State-by-state listing of the German-American press, giving dates, circulation, library holdings, and considerable data for each item. The second revised edition differs from the first (1961) in that a 14-page appendix has been added on refugee and POW camp publications. The earlier edition was published in Germany by Quelle & Meyer of Heidelberg.

Ayer's Directory. See N. W. Ayer & Son (No. 495).

Bacon's Publicity Checker: Magazines, Newspapers. (See No. 548.)

446. Barns, Margarita. The Indian Press: A History of the Growth of Public Opinion in India. London: Allen & Unwin, 1940.
   Contending that a history of the Indian press must, to some extent, also be a history of the British occupation of India, the author traces the development of the newspaper in India and its relationship to public opinion. Chapters are devoted to censorship, the news agencies, and scientific and technical journalism. There is also a list of old newspapers to be found in Calcutta, Bombay, and London. Indexed.

447. Brandsberg, George. The Free Papers: A Comprehensive Study of America's Shopping Guide and

142

<u>Free Circulation Newspaper Industry</u>. Ames, Iowa
50010: Wordsmith Books, University Station, 1969.
     So little has been written on the free-distri-
bution newspaper that this analysis, worthwhile
in itself, becomes doubly valuable. Interspers-
ing statistics throughout, the author discusses
the following aspects: history, publishers,
advertisers, readers, good and bad points, and
ethical and research problems. He ends with a
review and conclusions. There is a bibliography.

448. Brigham, Clarence S. <u>History and Bibliography of</u>
<u>American Newspapers, 1690-1820</u>. Worcester, Mass.:
American Antiquarian Society, 1947.
     A geographical list of newspapers for the
period covered, locating the libraries where
they may be found and giving the history of
each paper in a concise descriptive annotation.
Brought up to date by <u>American Newspapers 1821-</u>
<u>1936</u>. A 50-page book of additions and correc-
tions appeared in 1961. (<u>See</u> No. 444.) Each
volume contains a list of libraries and of
private owners mentioned and an index of titles
and of printers; Vol. II has a general index.

449. Brooks, Maxwell R. <u>The Negro Press Re-Examined:</u>
<u>Political Content of Leading Negro Newspapers</u>.
Boston 02120: Christopher Publishing House, 401
Walnut St., 1959.
     An empirical content analysis. Contains a
bibliography.

450. Bryan, Carter R. <u>Journalism in America before</u>
<u>Emancipation</u>. Minneapolis: University of Minne-
sota, School of Journalism, AEJ Publications
Business Manager, 1969 (Journalism Monographs
No. 12)
     A 33-page monograph intended as a survey of
a neglected, scantily researched subject. As
the author puts it, ". . . it is the writer's
hope that as a result of this brief survey
other scholars will turn their attention to
the subject and that, consequently, lost newspapers and their forgotten editors . . . will
be found and restored to their rightful place
in history." Footnotes serve as an excellent
bibliography, and there is a checklist of Negro
newspapers published before emancipation.

451. Canada. Senate. <u>Report on the Mass Media</u>. Vols.
I-III. Ottawa: Information Canada, 171 Slater
St., 1970.

Vol. I, The Uncertain Mirror, summarizes and
evaluates the economics of the media in Canada
and makes proposals, one of which involves the
teaching of journalism. Vol. II, Good, Bad, or
Simply Inevitable, gives raw data on the economics of newspapers and advertising. Vol.
III, Words, Music and Dollars, is a question-
naire distributed in an effort to learn how
Canadian people feel about the mass media.
Results are broken down by province. Although
much of the contents concerns broadcasting, more
of the emphasis is on newspapers because broadcasting was covered in 1965 by the Report of
the Committee on Broadcasting (No. 188). The
three volumes constitute a comprehensive and
excellent picture of the structure and function
of the media and how the people feel about them.
Contains appendices and an index.

Catholic Press Directory. (See No. 413.)

452. Chen, Mong-Hock. The Early Chinese Newspapers of
Singapore 1881-1912. Singapore: University of
Malaya Press, 1967. (Distributed by Oxford University Press, London)
     Details of the development of the Chinese
press are related to the social and commercial
background of Singapore during a period of
rapid expansion. Contains an excellent bibliography of primary and secondary source
material in both English and Chinese. Indexed.

Comprehensive Media Guide. Korea. (See No. 554.)

453. The Daily Newspaper and Its Reading Public. New
York 10017: American Newspaper Association, Bureau
of Advertising Research, 485 Lexington Ave., 1961.
     Report of a study defining the newspaper
audience in terms of size, kind, location, and
reading interests and habits.

454. The Daily Press: A Survey of the World Situation
in 1952. New York: UNESCO Publications Center,
1953. (Reports and Papers on Mass Communication
No. 7)
     A follow-up, concerned only with newspapers,
to the five-volume series, Press, Film and
Radio (No. 67). Consists of 13 graphs and
tables, with detailed explanatory texts, and
covers the majority of countries and territories
throughout the world. Also lists countries where
no daily paper was published at that time.

455. Dann, Martin, ed. The Black Press (1827-1890):
A Quest for National Identity. New York: Putnam,
1971.
Although the editor's primary aim in this
anthology of articles of the nineteenth-century
black press is to provide an insight into black
history, it also tells a great deal about the
Negro press. A sizable portion -- 67 pages --
is taken up with its role; the five remaining
sections -- "The Black View of American History,"
"The Black Man and Politics," "The Black Man
and Labor," "The Black Exodus," and "Creating
a Black Community" -- present in chronological
order the articles, editorials, advertisements,
and political cartoons of the period. Selections
are almost exclusively from newspapers available
on microfilm in the Schomburg Collection of the
New York Public Library. Indexed.

Directory of Little Magazines and Small Presses.
(See No. 414.)

456. Directory of the College Student Press in America.
Ed. by Dario Politella. 2d ed. New York:
Oxbridge, 1970.
The main part of this directory consists of
a listing by institution of its newspapers,
magazines, and yearbooks, giving faculty adviser,
budget, press run, date of founding, size, and
design. Other information includes a summary
of basic statistical data; guidelines for
principles of conduct; and lists of collegiate
press groups, high school press associations,
scholastic press associations, journalistic
societies, and suppliers and venders. Also
contains a seven-page bibliography of the college press.

457. Directory of the Jewish Press in America. New
York 10017: Joseph Jacobs Organization, 342
Madison Ave., 1970.
Contains detailed advertising and publicity
information about major Jewish weekly newspapers
and monthly magazines in the U.S. and Canada.
Gives names of editors, editorial requirements,
special publicity and photo needs, and special-
feature issues. In addition, it has a history
of the Jewish press in America and an article on
ethnic marketing during the past 50 years.
Indexed.

Durham, F. Gayle. News Broadcasting on Soviet
Radio and Television. (See No. 203.)

458. Editor & Publisher International Yearbook. New
York 10022: Editor & Publisher Co., 850 Third
Ave., annual.
   Properly subtitled "The Encyclopedia of the
Newspaper Industry," this annual supplement to
Editor & Publisher magazine is devoted primarily
to a listing of daily newspapers in the United
States and Canada, with detailed information
about advertising and editorial personnel. In
addition, it tells addresses, circulation, date
of establishment, flat line advertising rates,
types of advertising not accepted, special
editions, mechanical facilities available,
broadcast affiliates, political leanings, news
agency service, and name of Sunday magazine if
it carries one.
   It also gives a variety of other data about
the newspaper world. Among these are a brief
summary of circulation trends for the year in
the U.S. and a review of the British newspaper
year; groups of daily papers under common ownership; offset newspapers; Negro newspapers in
the U.S.; weekly newspapers; newspapers published only on Sunday; special-service dailies,
including college dailies; foreign-language
papers; employee and carrier publications; newspaper-distributed magazine sections, group
units, and newspaper networks; comic section
groups and networks; national newspaper representatives; a section on mechanical equipment,
supplies, and services; mat services; a selected
listing of advertising agencies that buy newspaper space; the names, addresses, and principal
personnel of daily newspapers throughout the
world; foreign press and radio-TV correspondents
in the U.S.; the members of the United Nations
Correspondents Association; a feature, news,
and syndicate directory; a listing of journalism
schools and departments; standards of education
for journalism; the Code of Practice of the
Newspaper Advertising Executives Association;
trade unions; advertising clubs and associations
in the U.S. and Canada; contests and awards,
with current winners; and newsprint statistics.

459. Editor & Publisher Syndicate Directory. New York
10022: Editor & Publisher Co., 850 Third Ave.,
annual.

Each July an issue of Editor & Publisher carries a directory of more than 200 syndicates broken down as follows: an alphabetical list of syndicates with addresses, names of editor or director, and features handled; a classified list of features arranged by a number of subject headings ranging from astrology to women's pages; an alphabetical list of features, with name of author and syndicate for each; and, conversely, an alphabetical list of authors, giving their features and syndicates.

460. Editorial Research Reports. Washington, D.C. 20006: Congressional Quarterly, Inc., 1735 K St., NW, weekly with semiannual cumulations.
    Intended primarily as background material for newspaper articles and features, this staff-written weekly service gives concise information on current news and trends. For example, among numerous other topics discussed recently were federal budget making, street crime in America, movies as art, Arab guerrillas, chemical-biological weaponry, economic nationalism in Latin America, the future of psychiatry, the regional theater, waste disposal, and so on. Each subject is well documented with bibliographical footnotes. Twice a year the pamphlets cumulate into bound volumes.

Elfenbein, Julien. Business Journalism. (See No. 417.)

461. Emery, Edwin, and Henry Ladd Smith. The Press and America: An Interpretative History of Journalism. 2d ed. Englewood Cliffs, N.J.: Prentice-Hall, 1962.
    Copious history of journalism in the United States, beginning with its European heritage and extending to the present. In their foreword the authors state, "The first portion, covering the long time-span ending with the Civil War, is concerned less with details than with an exposition of the principles upon which the American Fourth Estate was founded. The remaining chapters examine modern journalism -- including newspapers, radio, television, magazines, and news-gathering organizations -- and its role in an increasingly complex society. It is this latter section which has been reorganized in the new edition." Contains an annotated bibliography at the end of each chapter and an index.

462. The European Press Today. Washington, D.C.:
     Library of Congress, European Affairs Division,
     1949.
          A selective list of newspapers and period-
     icals in 25 European countries (with a supple-
     ment for Turkey), briefly describing the
     characteristics and political affiliations or
     leanings of each paper.

463. Feureisen, Fritz, and Ernst Schmacke. Die Presse
     in Afrika. Die Presse in Asien. Die Presse in
     Lateinamerika. München-Pullach, Germany: Verlag
     Dokumentation, 1968. (Distributed by Bowker)
          Three separate bilingual (German-English)
     manuals, similar in format and intended to give
     users in business and advertising information
     about newspapers in the various countries of
     the three continents covered. Facts, which are
     in tabular form, include name, address, circu-
     lation, political trend, language, frequency,
     kind of reader, size of paper, method of print-
     ing, and closing date of advertising. There is
     also a general listing of international publica-
     tions, and alphabetical and geographical indices
     of all publications.

     First National Directory of "Rightist" Groups,
     Publications and Some Individuals in the United
     States (and Some Foreign Countries). (See No.
     418.)

464. Frank, Joseph. The Beginnings of the English News-
     paper: 1620-1660. Cambridge, Mass.: Harvard
     University Press, 1961.
          Reflects the beginnings of the English news-
     paper against the political, social, and literary
     climate of the time. Contains an index of the
     newspapers discussed, an extensive bibliography,
     and bibliographical references.

465. Glessing, Robert J. The Underground Press in
     America. Bloomington: Indiana University Press,
     1970.
          The author covers 15 years of underground
     publishing in the United States. He deals
     systematically with its beginnings and its
     present status, showing how it has affected the
     American style of life by effecting changes in
     clothing, music, hair styles, sexual mores,
     politics, advertising, and similar aspects.
     There are a number of illustrations of writings
     from the press, a bibliography of sources used,

a directory of underground newspapers, and an index.

Gorokhoff, Boris I. Publishing in the U.S.S.R. (See No. 137.)

466. Great Britain. The British Press. New York 10022: British Information Services, 845 Third Ave., 1963.
A 50-page pamphlet giving succinct information on the following aspects: historical background; newspapers today, including ownership and policy; news agencies; broadcast news services; government information services and the press; production of a newspaper; pay and training of journalists; press institutions; the press and the law; list of press organizations. Contains a bibliography.

467. Great Britain. Royal Commission on the Press. Documentary Evidence. Presented to Parliament by the Prime Minister by Command of Her Majesty, September, 1962. 6 vols. London: Her Majesty's Stationery Office, 1962.
Documentary evidence given during the extensive examination of the workings of the British press and its allied industries and professions. Vol. I: national newspaper undertakings; Vol. II: provincial daily and Sunday newspaper undertakings in Scotland, Wales, and Northern Ireland; Vol. III: weekly newspaper, magazine, and periodical undertakings; Vol. IV: associations of various kinds and trade unions; Vol. V: advertising agents and associations, paper manufacturers and import agents, other organizations, etc., individuals; Vol. VI: miscellaneous. Sometimes known as the Shawcross Report after the Right Honorable Lord Shawcross.

468. Great Britain. Royal Commission on the Press. Minutes of Oral Evidence Taken before the Royal Commission of the Press. Presented to Parliament by the Prime Minister by Command of Her Majesty. 3 vols. London: Her Majesty's Stationery Office, 1962.
An examination of the British press and the professions and industries and associations connected with it, such as advertising, paper manufacturing, and so on. These three volumes are

are concerned with the oral evidence. It is
sometimes known as the Shawcross Report.
  Vol. I contains the minutes of oral evidence
taken by the Royal Commission from certain individuals, associations of various kinds, and
newspaper and periodical proprietors; Vol. II,
trade unions and associations, paper manufacturers and import agents, advertising agents and
institutes of practitioners in advertising;
Vol. III, National Union of Printing, Bookbinding and Paper Workers, Scannews (London) Ltd.,
the Right Honorable Lord Beaverbrook, Mr. N.
Kaldor, and Mr. R. R. Neild. Indexed.

469. Greece. Ministry to the Prime Minister's Office.
Press and Local Information Department. Local
Press Division. Yearbook of the Greek Press,
annual.
  Directory of newspapers published in Greece.
Includes for each title the city of publication,
frequency, and names of owners and editors.
Also gives a 21-page history of the Greek press.
In both French and English languages.

470. Hale, Oran J. The Captive Press in the Third
Reich. Princeton, N.J.: Princeton University
Press, 1964.
  A thoroughgoing examination of the way in
which the Nazis gained possession of the German
press and the way in which they maintained it
and used it for their own purposes. There are
charts on the organization of the Reich Press
Chamber and the organization of the Eher Verlag
in 1944. Contains notes on records, interviews,
and books, a bibliography, and an index.

Hall, Max, ed. Made in New York: Case Studies
in Metropolitan Manufacturing. (See No. 142.)

471. Hathorn's Suburban Press Directory: The Nation's
Guide to Suburban Markets. Chicago 60602:
Associated Release Service Co., 173 West Madison,
1971.
  This directory, the first of its kind, includes
2,591 suburban newspapers with combined circulation in excess of 30 million suburban families,
along with 262 inner-city community newspapers
and 179 shoppers. The main portion of the directory is a geographical listing of suburban
papers, with address, population of their community, circulation, frequency, whether printed
in letterpress or offset, and type (whether

suburban, neighborhood, or shopper). If the
paper is part of a chain, this is also indicated.

472. Hill, Roy L. <u>Who's Who in the American Negro
Press</u>. Dallas, Tex. 57217: Royal Publishing Co.,
7918 Maxwell Ave., 1960.
About half of this book is taken up with
biographical information. The author has
attempted to make his data as complete as possible by polling all Negro newspapers listed
in <u>Editor & Publisher Yearbook</u> at the time of
writing. For those polled who replied, extensive information of the "who's who" variety
is given; for those who did not, only names
and affiliations are listed. In another section Mr. Hill has analyzed his biographical
data, breaking them down by such factors as
political and religious affiliations and so
on.
There are other chapters on the contemporary
Negro press -- its leading figures and their
criticisms of existing conditions; the factor
of sensationalism, which was a major criticism;
and suggestions for improvement. Contains a
bibliography and a directory of Negro newspapers.

473. Holden, W. Sprague. <u>Australia Goes to Press</u>.
Detroit, Mich.: Wayne State University Press,
1961.
An overview of Australian newspaper journalism -- how it works, press law, the Australian
Journalists' Association, training for journalism, advertising, circulation, and promotion.
Appendices give brief historical sketches of
15 leading newspapers; a very brief survey of
radio and television structure; a discussion of
professional associations, trade services and
publications, and the authorized news agent
system. There is a selected bibliography and
an index.

474. Hopkins, Mark W. <u>Mass Media in the Soviet Union</u>.
New York: Pegasus, 1970.
"The focus of this book is on the Soviet
newspaper press, which has throughout Soviet
history been dominant in the mass media. Most
of what is said about newspapers and the work
of Soviet newspaper journalists applies also to
the Soviet magazine press and to radio and television. Yet the latter especially deserve increasing separate attention for the changes they
are effecting in Soviet society." - Preface.

As the Milwaukee Journal's Soviet affairs
specialist since 1964, the author has spent much
time in Russia and has attended Leningrad University. He possesses insight into what are in
his opinion the good and bad elements of the
Soviet system, which he frequently compares with
the good and bad elements of our own. Contains
detailed footnotes and an excellent bibliography
as well as maps, lists, tables, and an index.

475. Hudson's Washington News Media Contacts Directory.
Ed. by Howard Penn Hudson and Mary Elizabeth
Hudson. Arlington, Va.: Hudson Associates,
annual.
The editors call this "the first effort to
provide a breakdown of the Washington Press
Corps by functions." They have divided the
news media into various categories -- general
news services, newspapers, radio-TV, periodicals,
newsletters, and free-lance writers, and have
provided an alphabetical index as a key to
individuals, organizations, magazines, newspapers, and broadcasting stations. Over 1,300
publications, broadcasting stations, and networks are listed, as well as over 1,500 correspondents and editors who write for them.

476. Husain, Asad. Bibliography of a Century of Indian
Journalism 1858-1958. Minneapolis: University
of Minnesota, School of Journalism, 1959.
A 29-page unannotated list of periodicals,
books, and unpublished theses on India, written
in the English language. The author in his
preface says that the list is by no means
inclusive, but it is nevertheless valuable because all of the entries are available in libraries in the United States.

477. Iben, Icko. The Germanic Press of Europe: An
Aid to Research. Münster in Westfalen, Germany:
Verlag C. J. Fahle, 1965.
"The author has set himself the goal of pro-
ducing lists of newspapers for the Germanic
countries of Europe which 'would be indispensable' in the writing of the history of each
country and, consequently, of Europe as a
whole." - Introduction. As he has stated, the
list is selective rather than inclusive. Countries covered are Belgium, Luxembourg, the
Netherlands, Denmark, Finland, Norway, and
Sweden.

ILPA Directory of Member Publications. (See No. 424.)

478. The Japanese Press. Tokyo: Nihon Shinbun Kyokai (Japan Newspaper Publishers and Editors Association), Shisei Kaikan, Hibiya Park, Chiyoda-Ku, annual.

Devoted mainly to the newspaper press, although broadcasting, advertising, and mass communications research are dealt with briefly in one article each.

The annual issues differ slightly in content; the latest contains the following: canons, trends, editorial problems, management, circulation, advertising, newsprint, labor, newspaper techniques, news agencies, broadcasting, studies in mass communications, history, international activities of Japanese newspapers and the Asian program, organization and activities of the Press Association, and a directory, which, in addition to broadcasting stations and television newsreel agencies, lists newspapers, news agencies, and Japanese overseas correspondents. There is an index of statistical data.

479. Khurshid, Abdus Salem. Journalism in Pakistan: First Phase, 1845 to 1857. Lahore, West Pakistan: Publishers United Ltd., 176 Anarkali, 1964.

Traces the origins of journalism in Pakistan. Contains a bibliography, a list of newspapers, a glossary, and an index.

480. King, Frank H. H., and Prescott Clarke, eds. A Research Guide to China-Coast Newspapers, 1822-1911. Cambridge, Mass.: Harvard University, East Asian Research Center, Harvard East Asian Monographs No. 18, 1965. (Distributed by Harvard University Press)

"This research guide is designed primarily to facilitate the use of Western-language newspapers published in China, including Hong Kong and Macao, during the late Ch'ing period. It contains information on several related topics, including those newspapers published in London concerned with news of China, and certain Chinese-language sheets published as an integral part of or in close connection with the Western-language newspapers. There is also an appendix listing Japanese-language newspapers published in China during the period through 1911." - Introduction. Contains a bibliography.

481. Kitchen, Helen, ed. The Press in Africa. Washington, D.C.: Ruth Sloan Associates, 1956.
Tabular and descriptive information about
daily and weekly newspapers in 23 African
countries. Gives leading papers, their frequency, language, estimated circulation, editor,
publisher, and political orientation or influence. Discussions preceding each country
summarize the situation of the press as a whole,
placing it briefly in its socioeconomic context.
Egypt is omitted on grounds that it belongs to
the Near Eastern journalistic tradition.

482. Kobre, Sidney. Development of American Journalism.
Dubuque, Iowa: William C. Brown, 1969.
Chronological history, telling about certain
newspapers and personalities connected with
them. In five sections: colonial and Revolutionary press, young nation's newspaper press,
popular penny press, Gilded Age journalism,
chain and syndicate journalism. A list of
references follows each part. Indexed.

483. Kobre, Sidney. The Development of the Colonial
Newspaper. Pittsburgh, Pa. 13191: Colonial Press,
620 Second Ave., 1944.
Takes the American newspaper from 1690
through 1783, tracing its social development
and discussing various newspapers. Contains a
number of charts and tables, an appendix giving
a chronological account of newspapers in other
colonies, a list of newspapers within the
period, and a bibliography.

484. La Brie, Henry G. III. The Black Press in America:
A Guide. Iowa City: University of Iowa, Institute of Communication Studies, 1970.
Directory of practically every black newspaper being currently printed in the country,
with name, address, publisher, editor, method of
printing, circulation, date of publication, date
of founding, and size of labor force broken
down by race. An introduction tells how the
information was obtained, draws conclusions,
and suggests other areas of research needed.
There is also a list of newspapers no longer
published.

485. Lee, Alfred McClung. The Daily Newspaper in America: The Evolution of a Social Instrument. New
York: Macmillan, 1937.

The author, a sociologist, calls this a
natural history of the daily newspaper in this
country and has brought together many of the
interrelated factors which have formed it.
Organization is topical, with such headings
as: the newspaper in society; the pre-daily
paper; the physical basis of the newspaper;
labor, ownership, and management; chains and
associations; advertising; weekly and Sunday
issues; propaganda and public relations tie-
ins; the gathering of world news; feature syndicates; the editorial staff; crusades; invasion of privacy; and other important aspects.

486. Lent, John A., ed. The Asian Newspapers' Re-
luctant Revolution. Ames: Iowa State University
Press, 1971.
    Eighteen authors, including practicing
journalists, teachers, directors of press
associations, the director of the Press Foundation of Asia, an ex-ambassador, and ex-govern-
mental information directors, have written a
history and contemporary description of the
patterns of newspaper press development within
15 Asian nations. Included are China (both
present and prior to 1949), Hong Kong, Japan,
Korea, Taiwan, Burma, Indonesia, Malaysia,
Singapore, the Philippines, Thailand, South
Vietnam, Ceylon, India, and Pakistan. There is
also a section on Australia. Contains a bibliography.

487. Liu, Alan P. L. The Press and Journals in Communist China. Cambridge, Mass.: Massachusetts
Institute of Technology, Center for International
Studies, Research Program on Problems of International Security, 1966. (Distributed by Clearinghouse of Federal Scientific and Technical
Information, U.S. Dept. of Commerce, National
Bureau of Standards, Institute for Applied Technology)
    Succinct analysis of the background, structure,
function, and content of news and news reporting,
newspaper reading patterns, and periodicals,
with a concluding chapter on the effectiveness
of the press. The author has documented his
study (necessarily from secondhand sources) with
extensive footnotes and a bibliography.

Marty, Martin E., and others. The Religious Press
in America. (See No. 426.)

488. <u>Mason's Publishers</u>. 3d ed. Hampshire, England:
Kenneth Mason Publications Ltd., 1969.
Alphabetical listing of Britain's 3,000 publishers of newspapers, magazines, books, and
greeting cards, intended as "a complete guide
to all firms, associations and private presses
who publish for gain rather than for prestige,
propaganda or other non-remunerative purposes."
Gives a profile sketch of each entry which includes telephone numbers; cable addresses; names
of directors, print buyers, or production managers; subsidiary companies; number of books
published during the year, with type of publication (books, annuals, directories, journals,
newspapers, music, greeting cards, prints, or
diaries). There are also classified listings
by type of publication issued by each firm and
a geographical listing.

489. Mayer, Henry. <u>The Press in Australia</u>. Melbourne:
Lansdowne, 1964.
"This book attempts three main tasks: <u>First</u>,
to give the basic facts about the history,
structure and content of the Australian press;
<u>second</u>, to argue that newspapers, given the
technical and business conditions under which
they work, and granted my view about why they
are read, are bound to be much as they are;
<u>third</u> -- and this is my major interest -- to
analyze common attitudes toward the Press and
criticize the assumptions made both by its
critics and its defenders." - Preface.
The author further states that he is not
aiming to bring out the special flavor of the
Australian press or to compare it with the
press of other countries. He deals only with
capital-city dailies and gives considerable
information about content and readership.
Although there is no bibliography, there are
detailed footnotes at the end of each chapter.
Indexed.

<u>Media Records: Newspapers and Newspaper Advertis-
ers</u>. (<u>See</u> No. 574.)

490. Merrill, John C. <u>The Elite Press: Great Newspapers of the World</u>. New York: Pitman, 1968.
The author has skillfully made qualitative
evaluations of newspapers throughout the world
in an analysis, brief but in depth, of each of
the 40 papers he considers the finest. Defining his criteria, he gives thumbnail sketches

of their histories, their social responsibility,
their relationship with their governments, their
ability to withstand pressure, their styles, and
other elements. Contains a bibliography and an
index.

491. Merrill, John C., Carter E. Bryan, and Marvin
Alisky. The Foreign Press: A Survey of the
World's Journalism. 2d rev. and enl. ed. Baton
Rouge: Louisiana State University Press, 1970.
    The authors' aim is "to present a panoramic
picture of the world's press systems with a
minimum of distortion and to bring to the student who desires a more intensive study many
excellent sources for further investigation."
They give a general overview which consists of
thumbnail (longer for large countries) sketches
of national press systems in European countries,
including the Communist bloc, Latin America,
Far East and South East Asia, Africa, Canada,
Australia, and New Zealand. There is also a
lengthy and excellent bibliographical section
which contains notes and selected readings.
Part of this latter section is broken down by
country.
    Revision has been extensive. The handbook
now contains an overview of the U.S. press as a
point of departure and a great deal more information about various African countries. As in
the earlier editions, it deals chiefly with the
newspaper press of the principal nations, with
some emphasis on the magazine press and briefer
data on radio and television, some of which are
new. The user must remember, however, that the
more comprehensive a reference book of this sort
is, the more it must of necessity rely upon a
great deal of secondary data, which are likely
to vary in reliability from country to country
according to the source of supply.

492. Mott, Frank Luther. American Journalism: A
History: 1690-1960. 3d ed. New York: Macmillan,
1962.
    The definitive history in its field to date.
The author states that his purpose is "to provide a comprehensive work in which historical
narrative is combined with some of the characteristics of a reference book." Arrangement is
chronological, with much attention to individual
newspapers as well as to such broad trends as
the party press of the pre-Civil War period,
yellow journalism, and so on.

157

493. Munter, Robert. The History of the Irish Newspaper 1685-1760. Cambridge: Cambridge University
Press, 1967.
    Discusses structure, organization, and con-
tent. An appendix contains information on the
government and press prosecutions, and there
is a bibliography and 16 facsimiles of Irish
papers. Indexed.

494. Murthy, Nadig Krishna. Indian Journalism: Origin,
Growth and Development of Indian Journalism from
Asoka to Nehru. Mysore, India: "Presaranga,"
University of Mysore, 1966.
    Traces the development of India's press
against the background of her history, with
special emphasis upon the problem of the country's various languages and its struggle for
independence from England. Contents include an
overall introduction; the history of English
daily newspapers; journalism in Indian languages;
periodicals; and a general section including
government publicity, news agencies and syndicates, newsprint and technical problems, teaching of journalism, professional organizations,
press laws, and the Indian Press Commission.
Has a bibliography and appendices which give
tables of facts and figures.

495. N. W. Ayer & Son. Directory of Newspapers and
Periodicals. Philadelphia: N. W. Ayer & Son,
annual.
    This is the one single source which lists
daily newspapers, weekly newspapers, and periodicals published in the U.S., Canada, Bermuda,
Panama, and the Philippines. For each it gives
frequency, political leanings, founding date,
subscription rate, and circulation. Many of
the publications are difficult to find elsewhere. Those omitted are generally small subsidized ones which carry little or no advertising.
    The main portion is arranged geographically,
with gazetteer information for each community.
Another section groups titles into: college,
Negro, foreign language, religious, labor,
fraternal, agricultural and trade, technical,
and subject classification. Contains a title
index of publications.

496. Natarajan, Swaminath. A History of the Press in
India. New York: Asia Publishing House, 1962.

A social history, sponsored by the Audit
Bureau of Circulation, designed to show the
press as a medium both for news dissemination
and for advertising. Appendices include press
legislation, the press and the Registration of
Books Act, leading newspapers, and wages of
journalists. There is a bibliography and an
index.

National Advertising Investments: Magazines.
Newspaper Supplements. Network TV. Spot TV.
(See No. 575.)

497. National Directory of Weekly Newspapers. New
York 10017: American Newspaper Representatives,
Inc., 347 Madison Ave., annual.
    Weekly, semiweekly, and triweekly newspapers
in the United States, listed alphabetically by
state and city. For each paper is given circulation, name of publisher, facts about advertising rates, and industrial characteristics of its
area -- whether agricultural, suburban, industrial, resort, mining, fishing, oil, or lumber.

498. News Agencies in Developing Countries. Strasbourg:
International Centre for Higher Education in
Journalism, 10 Rue Schiller, 1966. (No. 25 or
Journalism; Journalisme)
    The entire issue of this bilingual (English-
French) journal is devoted to a discussion of
news agencies by various experts from a number
of countries. Part I deals with general problems; Part II contains monographs on the situation in Afghanistan, Cambodia, Congo-Brazza-
ville, Gabon, the Ivory Coast, Jordan, Madagascar,
Morocco, Nepal, Nigeria, Senegal, Somalia,
Tanzania, Thailand, and Togo; Part III is a
commentary.

499. News Agencies: Their Structure and Operation.
New York: UNESCO Publications Center, 1953.
    A detailed and thorough analysis of news
agencies throughout the world. Gives a historical review, discusses legal organization
and international regulation, and describes
their relationship with radio newscasting and
their use of telegraph and telecommunication.
Also contains an alphabetical list of tele-
graphic news agencies.

Newspaper Circulation Analysis. (See No. 577.)

Newspaper Circulation & Rate Trends (1946-1968).
(See No. 578.)

Newspaper International: Basic Newspaper Data on
Major Newspapers and Markets in 79 Countries Excluding U.S.A. and Canada. (See No. 579.)

500. The Newspaper Press Directory and Advertisers'
Guide. London: Benn Brothers Ltd., annual.
An extensive listing of newspapers and magazines throughout the British Commonwealth and
a listing of the most prominent ones in other
foreign countries. Information for each entry
includes date of establishment, group (if any)
to which it belongs, circulation and its area,
head office, publisher, key personnel, and
advertising rates. Political leaning, too, is
sometimes given. For most countries trade,
technical, and other specialized newspapers and
periodicals are included along with the general
ones. A special section is devoted to house
magazines in the United Kingdom. Lists press,
advertising, printing, and kindred organizations
for the United Kingdom.

Newspaper Rates and Data. (See No. 580.)

501. Oak, Vishnu V. The Negro Newspaper. Yellow
Springs, Ohio: Antioch Press, 1948. (Vol. I of
The Negro Entrepreneur Series)
Critical appraisal of the Negro press. Contents include: favorable and unfavorable evaluations; function in relation to such factors as
circulation, publishing establishments, wage
and labor policies, and so on; news coverage
and general makeup; news-gathering agencies;
advertising; a brief history; suggestions for
improvement. Appendices contain an extensive
bibliography, a directory of Negro newspapers
and one of college campus publications, and a
subject index.

Ogilvy & Mather Pocket Guide to Media. (See No.
582.)

502. Olson, Kenneth E. The History Makers: The Press
of Europe from Its Beginnings through 1965. Baton
Rouge: Louisiana State University Press, 1966.
The growth of the press in 24 nations of
Europe, with an evaluation of the European
press today. Contains a list of papers for each
country and a comprehensive bibliography.

503. One Hundred Years of the Yiddish Press in America, 1870-1970. Comp. by Z. Szajkowski. Catalogue of the Exhibition. New York 10028: YIVO Institute for Jewish Research, 1048 Fifth Ave., 1970.
    This listing of items, with notes about each, forms an outline history of the Yiddish press in the U.S. -- its weeklies and dailies, including the labor press, its writers, compositors, newsdealers, readers, advertisements, and its social role. It is not limited to the past; one section gives dailies appearing in 1970. There is also a section on the Yiddish press of various cities and various groups. All items are available at the YIVO Institute.

504. P&D Overseas Newspaper and Periodicals Guide Book. 2 vols. 8th ed. London: Publishing and Distributing Co. Ltd., 1964-65.
    Vol. I is entitled Markets in Europe, Vol. II, Markets outside Europe. The first volume lists a large number of newspapers and of trade and consumer magazines in western and eastern European countries, giving for each the circulation, typographical data, advertising rates, and, for some, a descriptive annotation. Vol. II gives similar data for over 100 countries in other parts of the world. For each country there is some gazetteer information. There are also small sections on radio and television.

505. Penn, I. Garland. The Afro-American Press and Its Editors. New York: Arno Press/New York Times, c1891, 1969.
    Reprint of a book originally published in 1891. To quote from the introduction to the new edition: "The first part takes all of the Afro-American newspapers and magazines, from Freedom's Journal (1827) to 1891. The second part, which is very long, consists of many sketches of editors and newspapers, opinions of eminent Negro men on the Afro-American press, its editors' mission, and other chapters on the relation of the Negro press to the white press (including Negroes who write for white newspapers and magazines), the Afro-American League, and the Associated Correspondents of Race Newspapers. There are scores of photographs." Magazines as well as newspapers are included. The author was for years a principal in Lynchburg, Virginia, schools and ex-editor of the Lynchburg Laborer. Indexed.

506. Press and Advertisers Year Book. New Delhi: INFA
Publications, Jeevah Deep, Parliament St., annual.
Subtitled "India's Leading Press and Media
Guide," this yearbook emphasizes newspapers,
magazines, and advertising. One of its most
useful features is a listing of newspapers and
magazines which carry advertising, with address,
telephone number, circulation, and details
about rates. A substantial portion is devoted
to government information services and press
law. Among other features, it lists trade and
professional associations, journalism courses,
press correspondents, news agencies, a "who's
who" in the press and another in advertising
and public relations, and statistics on the
cinema.

507. Press Councils and Press Codes. 4th ed. Zurich
8001: International Press Institute, Munster-
gasse 9, 1966.
Summary prepared by the IPI Research Service
on the basis of texts published in IPI Report
and other documents. Part I gives 88 pages of
background information on press codes and
councils in Austria, Belgium, Canada, Denmark,
Germany, India, Israel, Italy, the Netherlands,
Norway, Pakistan, the Philippines, South Africa,
South Korea, Sweden, Switzerland, Turkey, the
United Kingdom, and the United States. Part II
gives texts of international codes for the
United Nations and the Inter-American Press
Association, and texts of national codes for
Australia, Belgium, Canada, Chile, Denmark,
France, Germany, India, Israel, Italy, Nigeria,
Norway, Pakistan, South Africa, South Korea,
Sweden, Turkey, the United Kingdom, and the
United States.

508. Price, Warren C. The Literature of Journalism:
An Annotated Bibliography. Minneapolis: University of Minnesota Press, 1959.
An invaluable bibliography of 3,147 books.
Emphasis is on newspapers and magazines rather
than advertising and broadcasting, although
these receive brief attention. Deals at considerable length with history, biography,
anthologies, freedom and ethics of the press,
public opinion, and propaganda. The late Professor Price had been working on a supplement
which Calder Pickett has completed, entitled
An Annotated Journalism Bibliography, 1958-
1968. (See No. 509.)

509. Price, Warren C., and Calder M. Pickett. <u>An</u>
     <u>Annotated Journalism Bibliography 1958-1968.</u>
     Minneapolis: University of Minnesota Press,
     1970.
          Updates the late Warren Price's <u>The Liter-</u>
     <u>ature of Journalism: An Annotated Bibliography</u>.
     (See No. 508.) The scope is broadened to
     include new developments in the field. Cate-
     gories are: histories; biographies; anthol-
     ogies, columns, general news and features,
     photography, and cartooning; appraisals,
     ethics, and law and freedom of the press both
     in the U.S. and Great Britain; techniques,
     including texts; journalism education and
     vocational guidance; magazines; press manage-
     ment; advertising and marketing; public opinion,
     propaganda, and public relations; radio and
     television; foreign press and international
     communication facilities; bibliographies and
     directories. Only books are included, and
     practically all are briefly annotated. Entries
     total 2,172. Unlike the earlier edition, which
     was arranged by categories, this is alphabetical
     with a subject index.

510. Rajan, S. P. Thiaga. <u>History of Indian Journal-</u>
     <u>ism</u>. Thanjavur, India: Columbia House, Gandhigi
     Road, 1966.
          Collection of talks by the author in which
     he discusses aspects of the Indian newspaper
     press. Among his topics are the Press Commis-
     sion, the Press Council, Reuters and India, a
     free press, parliamentary immunities, the press
     in developing countries, and training for
     journalism.

511. Rosengarten, Frank. <u>The Italian Anti-Fascist</u>
     <u>Press (1919-1945)</u>. Cleveland, Ohio: Press of
     Case-Western Reserve University, 1968.
          Traces the development from the legal
     opposition press to the underground newspapers
     of World War II, which were carried on with con-
     siderable success by the resistance forces. An
     appendix gives some key aspects of the laws and
     principles governing the exercise of freedom of
     the press in Italy after fascism, and there is
     a detailed bibliography, most of which is in
     Italian. Indexed.

512. Rucker, Bryce W. <u>The First Freedom</u>. Carbondale:
     Southern Illinois University Press, 1968.

163

In 1946 Morris Ernst, the author-lawyer,
published a study about monopoly in the newspaper, radio, and motion picture industries,
The First Freedom (No. 24). The present book
by the same title is an updating, done by Mr.
Rucker at Mr. Ernst's request, with emphasis
on newspapers and broadcasting.

An appendix illustrates the text with
tables and charts. For example: "Chains hold-
ing interest in ten or more dailies in 1967,"
"AM and AM-FM financial data in millions of
dollars, 1935-66," "A thirteen-year record of
station trading, 1954-66," "Eighty-five communities with one AM radio station and one
daily newspaper, with newspaper having ownership in station." Sources of information are
cited. Numerous footnotes compensate somewhat
for lack of a bibliography. Indexed.

513. Sarkar, Chanchal. Challenge and Stagnation: The
Indian Mass Media. New Delhi, India: Vikas
Publications, 1969.
The author, director of the Press Institute
of India, surveys his country's mass media and
that of other parts of Asia as well. He discusses critically both the government-owned and
private sectors. Much emphasis is on newspapers,
perhaps because they play a major role. Among
chapter headings: "Relevance of Indian Newspapers," "An Apologia for Communication," "What
Ails the Indian Press?," "The Government and
the Press," "Here Is the News . . ." (All-
India Radio Service), "Communication in Asia,"
"Distorting Asia," "The Role of Mass Communications in India," "Social Welfare for Journalists." Contains a bibliography, only a small
portion of which concerns India, and an index.

514. Schulte, Henry F. The Spanish Press 1470-1966:
Print, Power, and Politics. Urbana: University
of Illinois Press, 1968.
An analysis of the Spanish newspaper press,
especially with relation to censorship, which
places it in historical perspective. Contains
an extensive bibliography and an index.

Shawcross Report. See Great Britain. Royal Commission on the Press. Documentary Evidence and
Minutes of Oral Evidence (Nos. 467 and 468).

164

515. Somerland, Ernest Lloyd. The Press in Developing
     Countries. Sidney, Australia: Sidney University
     Press, 1966. (Available also through Pennsylvania
     State University Press)
          A broad survey, devoted entirely to news-
     papers. Arrangement is by broad topics -- pat-
     terns of development, role, problems, training,
     production, news agencies, and so on -- rather
     than by specific countries. Contains a bibliog-
     raphy, footnotes, and an index.

516. Soviet and Russian Newspapers at the Hoover Insti-
     tution: A Catalog. Comp. by Karol Maichel.
     Stanford, Calif.: Hoover Institution and Library
     on War, Revolution and Peace, Stanford University,
     1966. (Hoover Institution and Library Biblio-
     graphical Series XXIV)
          Catalog of the 1,108 titles of Russian-
     language newspapers -- Imperial Russian, Soviet,
     and emigré -- held by the Hoover Institution
     as of January 1966. Also gives references to
     other catalogs of institutions with large hold-
     ings, such as Columbia University, the Library
     of Congress, and the New York Public Library.

517. Statistics of Newspapers and Other Periodicals.
     New York: UNESCO Publications Center, 1959.
     (Statistical Reports and Studies)
          Contains various types of data about news-
     papers and periodicals throughout the world.
     Arrangement is by country, and all information
     is statistical and tabular under broad headings
     rather than by individual countries. UN Sta-
     tistical Yearbook helps keep statistics up to
     date.

518. Stewart, Kenneth, and John Tebbel. Makers of
     Modern Journalism. Englewood Cliffs, N.J.:
     Prentice-Hall, 1952.
          "This book is a history of American journal-
     ism told in terms of men and motives. It is
     a biographical history, intended to encompass
     the story of newspapers in America (and a few
     of the significant magazine, radio, and tele-
     vision leaders) by means of the interconnected
     lives and times of the men who have made, and
     are making, the free press in this country." -
     Foreword.

519. Taylor, Henry A. The British Press -- A Critical
     Survey. London: Arthur Barker Ltd., 1961.

165

Survey of English journalism, reviewing its
history but dwelling chiefly on the report of
the Royal Commission on the Press in 1949.

520. Tebbel, John. The Compact History of the American
Newspaper. New York: Hawthorn Press, 1963.
Survey of some 275 pages, extending from
colonial times to the present and examining the
role of the newspaper -- first as propaganda,
next as a personal instrument, and currently as
a business institution. Contains a list of
suggested readings.

521. Udell, Jon D. Economic Trends in the Daily Newspaper Business 1946 to 1970. New York 10017:
American Newspaper Publishers Foundation, 750
Third Ave., 1970. (Wisconsin Project Reports
IV:6)
In chart and tabular form accompanied by
commentary, this 19-page pamphlet about the
economic progress of the daily newspaper since
the end of World War II contains useful facts
and figures. There are data over the past 30
years, as well as projections, a discussion of
employment, advertising, size, number, circulation, and various other aspects, and six appendices. No. I gives indices of employment in
the newspaper business compared with all manufacturing industries and the total U.S. economy
from 1947 to 1970; II lists average number of
pages in the nation's large daily papers; III,
growth of newspaper advertising and the U.S.
economy 1946-69; IV, circulation and adult
population 1946-69; V, newspaper growth and
national economic growth 1946-69; VI, growth
of newspapers of various sizes 1953-69. A useful feature is the citations with sources of
data.

522. Underground Press Directory. Comp. by William D.
Lutz. 5th ed. Stevens Point, Wis. 54481: P.O.
Box 549, 1970.
Alphabetical list with addresses, but no
descriptions, of about 800 publications which
originate and are a part of the alternative or
counter culture that exists within the United
States and around the world. Titles range from
"establishment" underground like the Berkeley
Barb and East Village Other to the lesser known,
more ephemeral, and more highly specialized
(Marijuana Review). Obviously, the latter type
predominates. The editor says that the task of

keeping the publication going is too much for his limited resources and that if it is continued past 1970, it must be through other means.

523. U.S. Library of Congress. Slavic and Central European Division. Reference Department. Newspapers of East Central and Southeastern Europe in the Library of Congress. Ed. by Robert G. Carlton. Washington, D.C.: Government Printing Office, 1965.

Lists holdings of newspapers issued during the period from 1918 to 1965 within the territorial boundaries of Albania, Bulgaria, and Czechoslovakia, and those issued in Estonia, Latvia, and Lithuania from 1917 to 1940. Contains a language index and an index to titles.

524. U.S. Library of Congress. Slavic and Central European Division and Serial Division. Reference Department. Newspapers of the Soviet Union in the Library of Congress (Slavic, 1954-1960; Non-Slavic, 1917-1960). Prepared by Paul L. Horecky with the assistance of John P. Balys and Robert G. Carlton. Washington, D.C.: Government Printing Office, 1962.

Lists holdings in the Library of Congress of (1) newspapers in Slavic languages of the USSR for 1954-60, as well as some of the pre-1954 titles added to the Library of Congress collections since 1954 and therefore not included in the previous lists; (2) Baltic newspapers from the date of the initial occupation of the Baltic countries by the Soviet Union in June 1940 until the end of 1960; and (3) newspapers in other languages published within the boundaries of the USSR from 1917 to the end of 1960. Covers both printed newspapers and microfilm.

525. U.S. Library of Congress. Slavic and Central European Division. Reference Department. Russian, Ukrainian, and Belorussian Newspapers 1917-1953: A Union List. Comp. by Paul L. Horecky. Washington, D.C.: Government Printing Office, 1953.

Records 859 Russian, Ukrainian, and Belorussian newspapers issued since 1 January 1917 within the territory of the present USSR and which were in possession of libraries in the U.S. as of May 1953.

526. U.S. Negro World. Ed. and published by Frank B.
Sawyer. New York 10005: Amalgamated Publishers,
79 Wall St., annual.
  The latest issue at this time, "Communications
Edition," contains a rate and data listing of
black-oriented newspapers represented by Amalgamated Publishers, the agency representative for
70 such papers in 28 states. For each, gives
publisher, advertising manager, address, time
of publication, mechanical measurements, color
availability, open rate, circulation, volume
discounts, combination rates, and color costs.

Weekly Newspaper Rates and Data. (See No. 599.)

527. Whatmore, Geoffrey. News Information: The
Organisation of Press Cuttings in the Libraries
of Newspapers and Broadcasting Services. Hamden,
Conn.: Shoe String Press, 1964.
  Detailed techniques on the operation of
news clipping files. Contains bibliographical
notes and an index.

Who's Who in Journalism 1969. (See No. 436.)

528. Wilcox, Dennis L. English Language Dailies Abroad:
A Guide to Daily Newspapers in Non-English-Speak-
ing Countries. Detroit, Mich.: Gale Research
Co., 1967.
  For 59 countries -- Aden through Zambia --
gives names of newspaper, circulation, founding
date, readership, circulation patterns, advertising ratio, news emphasis, wire services,
editorial policy, other languages used, and a
brief description of physical appearance. Also
contains a short bibliography of articles,
books, and reports and a newspaper microfilm
list.

529. Williams, Francis. Dangerous Estate: The Anatomy
of Newspapers. London: Longmans, 1957.
  An account of the English press, showing its
social role in the past and in the present.
The author weaves his history around the issues
of society as it affects and is affected by the
papers of the time and by the men who made them.
There are no references and no index.

530. Williams, Francis. The Right to Know: The Rise
of the World Press. London: Longmans, 1969.
  Treating the press media -- with special
emphasis on newspapers -- as barometers of time

168

and geography, the author discusses the shape
it has taken in various countries. Among
other topics, he deals with its switch from
political control to business orientation in
certain parts of the world; the growth of
radio; the place of television; the press in
Europe, America, and the new nations; public
interest and commercial ownership. There is
a brief bibliography of sources and an index.

531. Williams, Francis. Transmitting World News: A
Study of Telecommunications and the Press. Paris:
UNESCO, 1953.
    An investigation of the system of rates and
priorities and other factors affecting the
dispatch of press messages. Although the author
discusses the technical means of news transmission, he goes beyond these to show the human
elements: the competence, integrity, and good
judgment of those who collect and distribute
news; the readiness of governments and peoples
to allow or forbid objective reporting; and so
on. He takes cost factors and availability of
newsprint into account also.
    Part I consists of historical background;
Part II, the various news agencies and their
problems; Part III, conclusions and recommendations. A map shows major ocean cable systems;
pictographs show locations of transmitters and
other features. There is a bibliography and
an index.

532. Willing's European Press Guide. 2d ed. New York:
Bowker, 1968.
    Companion volume to Willing's Press Guide
(No. 533), listing the daily newspapers,
periodicals, magazines, reviews, and trade,
technical, religious, and specialized journals
and annals of 12 European countries -- Austria,
Belgium, Denmark, France, Germany, Great Britain,
Italy, the Netherlands, Norway, Portugal, Sweden,
and Switzerland.
    Contains over 50,000 entries, classified
under their relevant subject headings. Information consists of name and address, name of
publisher, frequency of publication, and price
per issue or per annum. There are also tables
enabling conversion of differing physical standards and currencies, and a list of towns and
districts where names are rendered differently
in different languages. Although the volume is
generally printed in English, all references and

headings are in English, French, German, and
Italian. It is issued at irregular intervals.

533. Willing's Press Guide. London: James Willing
     Ltd., annual.
          Subtitled "A Comprehensive Index and Hand-
     book of the Press of the United Kingdom of
     Great Britain, Northern Ireland and the Irish
     Republic; Together with the Principal British
     Commonwealth, Dominion, Colonial and Foreign
     Publications." Newspapers and periodicals
     published in Great Britain and Ireland are
     listed alphabetically, with year of establish-
     ment, when published, price, and publisher's
     name and address. Titles are then arranged by
     subject and again by geographic location.
     There are also geographic listings of Dominion
     and Commonwealth publications and selected pub-
     lications from countries with no British con-
     nections. Useful features are lists of pub-
     lishers and some of their leading journals,
     group advertisers, reporting and news agencies,
     and three cinema newsreel companies.

534. Wittke, Carl. The German-Language Press in Amer-
     ica. Lexington: University of Kentucky Press,
     1957.
          A history of America's German-language press,
     from 1732 to the present, with emphasis pri-
     marily upon the role it played in American
     social, political, and economic history rather
     than upon individual papers. Footnotes, but
     no bibliography. Indexed.

535. Wolseley, Roland E. The Black Press, U.S.A.
     Ames: Iowa State University Press, 1971.
          Survey of the journalism of the black race
     in this country -- its origin, history, nature,
     viewpoints, problems, and many of the journal-
     ists and publishers who have participated in
     it, past and present. Contains a bibliography
     and an index.

536. Wolseley, Roland E., ed. Journalism in Modern
     India. 2d rev. ed. New York: Asia Publishing
     House, 1964.
          Surveys of the English-language newspapers and
     those in the vernacular, news agencies, public
     relations and publicity, radio, law, education,
     and the future of Indian journalism. Indexed.

537. Wolseley, Roland E. The Journalist's Bookshelf:
An Annotated & Selected Bibliography of United
States Journalism. Rev. ed. Philadelphia:
Chilton, 1961.
First issued in 1930 and revised six times
since, this present edition carries titles
under 29 classifications. The most extensive
are the biographical and historical sections.
Contains an index to authors and titles.

538. The Working Press of the Nation. Newspapers and
Allied Services. Vol. 1. Chicago 60601: National Research Bureau, Inc., 221 North LaSalle
St., annual.
The primary purpose of this volume is to
give public relations officials detailed personnel for large newspapers and news services in
the U.S. and Canada and to list various types
of newspapers and services -- special interests
such as college, agriculture, apparel, building,
labor, and principal foreign-language newspapers published in the U.S.; daily newspapers
with a weekend TV supplement or section; Sunday
magazine newspaper supplements and their personnel; news services, newsreel companies, and news
picture services with their personnel; and the
principal Negro publications in the U.S.
There is also a section on daily newspapers
of Great Britain, Northern Ireland, and the
Republic of Ireland, and daily newspapers of
certain principal foreign countries. This
section does little with personnel.

539. World Press: Newspapers and News Agencies. New
York: UNESCO Publications Center, 1964.
Describes existing newspaper and news agency
facilities in nearly 200 countries. Material
is drawn from UNESCO's more comprehensive World
Communications. Contains a brief bibliography.

Advertising and Public Relations

540. <u>Advertiser's Annual</u>. London E.C. 4: Admark
Directories, 180 Fleet St., annual.
A 1,250-page directory containing a miscellany of information about Great Britain's
advertising media. Specifically, it includes:
a listing of British daily, weekly, and Sunday
newspapers and consumer and trade magazines
(trade magazines are arranged in subject classifications); outdoor publicity and poster
advertising; television, radio, and cinema;
advertising agents and their clients; public
relations firms and their clients; direct mail,
marketing research, and other specialized services; graphic arts, design, and photography
firms; display, exhibition, and sign writers;
printers; gifts and premium promotions; and
leading British advertisers. An "Overseas Section" deals rather spottily with media and
agencies in foreign countries.

<u>An Advertiser's Guide to Scholarly Periodicals</u>.
(<u>See</u> No. 408.)

541. <u>The Advertising Agency Business around the World:
Reports from Advertising Agency Associations and
Agency Leaders in 40 Countries</u>. 5th ed. New
York 10021: American Association of Advertising
Agencies, 200 Park Ave., 1967.
Information for each country varies, concen-
trating on expenditure by media and giving a
list of agencies and advertising associations.
Facts pertinent to advertising in each country
are also included.

172

Countries are: Angola, Argentina, Aruba,
Australia, Austria, Brazil, Canada, Ceylon,
Chile, Colombia, Costa Rica, Curaçao, Denmark,
Finland, Germany (Federal Republic), Ghana,
Greece, Iraq, Ireland (Republic), Israel,
Italy, Japan, Lebanon, Mexico, New Zealand,
Norway, Panama, Peru, Philippines, Portugal,
Rhodesia/Zambia/Malawi, South Africa (Republic),
Surinam, Sweden, Switzerland, United Arab Re-
public, United Kingdom, United States, and
Uruguay.

542. Advertising and Press Annual of Africa. London,
Capetown, Johannesburg: National Publishing Co.,
White-Ray House, 51 Wale St., Box 335 (Capetown);
405-10 S.A. Centre, 253 Bree St., Box 2735
(Johannesburg), annual.
Detailed guide to advertising and press
information for South Africa, Rhodesia, and
Central, East, and West Africa. North Africa
is omitted.
Includes data about advertisers and agencies,
names of associations, regulations, codes and
laws, and advertising rates and data for newspapers, magazines, exhibitions, radio, movies,
television, billboards, car cards, and direct
mail.

543. Advertising Directory: Agencies and Advertisers.
Pt. 2. London E.C. 4: Legion Information Services Ltd., 25 Bream's Bldgs., annual.
The main feature of this two-part annual
(begun in 1968) is a list of British advertising
agencies, with accounts carried. An introductory section gives numerous advertising statistics and the account charges of individual
advertisers grouped according to product.
Advertising Directory: Products and Promotion.
Pt. 2. London E.C. 4: Legion Information Services Ltd., 25 Bream's Bldgs., annual.
Among other features, it lists for practically all major British brands their press
and television advertising in 1966 and 1967.
It also gives advertising expenditures for
products by groups (disinfectants, typewriters,
and so on) broken down by press and television.
Kept up to date by The Statistical Review of
Press and TV Advertising.

544. Advertising Expenditure. London W.C. 2: Advertising Association, 1 Bell Yard, 1948.

173

Detailed analysis of British advertising statistics, begun in 1948 (<u>Advertising Expenditure
in 1948</u> by Roddy Silverman) and continuing at
intervals of approximately four years. The
latest of the series, <u>Advertising Expenditure
1960-65</u>, is reprinted from <u>Advertising Quarterly</u>,
Issue No. 8, Summer 1966.

<u>Advertising Expenditures around the World</u>. See
<u>World Advertising Expenditures</u> (No. 602).

545. <u>Advertising in Africa: A Survey of Media South
of the Sahara</u>. Melbourne, Australia: Overseas
Trading, Department of Trade, 83a Queens Road,
1961. (Supplement to <u>Overseas Trading</u>, 15
Dec. 1961)
Country-by-country survey of 17 African
nations, giving for each information about population, currency, exports, codes and regulations,
major newspapers, national magazines, radio,
television, cinema, outdoor advertising, and
advertising agencies.

546. <u>American Newspaper Markets' Circulation</u>. North-
field, Ill. 60093: American Newspaper Markets,
Inc., P.O. Box 182, annual.
Detailed analysis of the circulation of all
U.S. dailies and Sunday newspapers, and of
seven national supplements and 23 national magazines (1968 edition). Breaks down circulation
figures by county and metropolitan area and by
individual newspapers.

The Associated Church Press. <u>Directory</u>. (<u>See</u>
No. 409.)

547. <u>Average Circulation and Rate Trends of Leading
Magazines, 1946-1966</u>. New York 10017: Association of National Advertisers, 155 East 44th St.,
1967.
Trend analysis of circulations, rates,
costs per thousand, and single-copy prices for
audited consumer and farm magazines from 1946
through 1966. Gives statistics in the form of
averages for the 51 publications totaled and
for each of the 11 categories of magazines,
grouped by editorial interests.
Updated by a cumulative volume at various
intervals. (See also <u>Magazine Circulation and
Rate Trends 1940-1967</u> (No. 573).)

174

548. Bacon's Publicity Checker: Magazines, Newspapers.
Chicago 60604: Bacon's Clipping Bureau, 14 East
Jackson Blvd., annual.
   The major purpose of this reference book is
to aid in the preparation of news releases by
listing publications which are known to use
publicity materials and are read by Bacon's
Clipping Bureau.
   It is in two main sections: magazines and
newspapers. Each lists and analyzes publicity
requirements of a large number of trade, farm,
and consumer magazines and of daily newspapers
in the United States and Canada. In addition
it gives address, editor, time and frequency of
publication, circulation, and telephone. Finally, there is a section on news services and
syndicates and a listing of multiple magazine
publishers and their publications.

549. Borden, Neil H. The Economic Effects of Advertising. Homewood, Ill.: Richard D. Irwin, 1944.
   Although old, this study -- a joint project
of Harvard Business School and the Advertising
Research Foundation -- remains one of the most
thorough factual analyses on the subject in the
English language. Contains background information about the development and use of advertising by businessmen; gives its relation to price
and pricing practices; and discusses its effect
on the range and quality of products and on
investment and volume of income. There is also
a chapter on the ethical aspects of advertising.
Has appendices and an index.

550. Bradford's Directory of Marketing Research Agencies and Management Consultants in the United
States, Canada, and the World. Middleburg, Va.
22117: Ernest A. Bradford, P.O. Box 207, biennial.
   Contains names and addresses of over 350
marketing research agencies. Service offered
by each agency is shown, along with other
pertinent data about the firm. Also contains
an index of personnel and a classified service
guide index.

Brandsberg, George. The Free Papers: A Comprehensive Study of America's Shopping Guide and
Free Circulation Newspaper Industry. (See No.
447.)

551. British Rate & Data: The National Guide to Media
Selection. London W. 1: British Rate & Data,
30 Old Burlington St., monthly. (Obtain in U.S.
through Standard Rate & Data Service, Inc.)
     Gives advertising rates in the British Isles
for daily, Sunday, and weekly newspapers; consumer, trade, technical, and professional magazines; television, radio, and cinema; outdoor
advertising; and such other media as the telephone directory, exhibitions, and so on. Also
contains a list of associations, societies,
clubs, and advertising agencies.

552. Business Publications Rates and Data. Skokie,
Ill. 60076: Standard Rate & Data Service, Inc.,
5201 Old Orchard Road, monthly.
     A comprehensive list of U.S. business publica-
tions classified by subject and giving address,
key personnel, circulation, and detailed advertising rates. For certain of the large magazines, summaries of readership surveys inserted
as advertisements provide further information
about specific titles. The subject classification of trade magazines can be a useful guide
in marketing articles.

553. Canadian Advertising Rates and Data: The Media
Authority. Toronto 2: Maclean-Hunter Ltd. and
Standard Rate & Data Service, Inc., 481 University Ave., monthly.
     Emphasis is primarily on advertising rates,
which are given in detail, but much other
information is also included. Media covered
are English and French radio and television
stations and networks, daily and weekly newspapers, weekend newspapers and supplements,
consumer magazines, religious publications,
farm publications, business publications, and
transit advertising. There is a special section on advertising agency personnel and
media representatives. Was formerly Canadian
Media Rates and Data, published solely by SRDS.

Catholic Press Directory. (See No. 413.)

554. Comprehensive Media Guide. Korea. Seoul: International Advertising Association, Korea Chapter,
I.P.O. Box 3562, annual.
     Intended as a directory for the overseas
practitioner seeking information on advertising
media. Includes daily newspapers, broadcasting
stations, and weekly, monthly, quarterly, and

annual publications. Data is given on personnel, address, rates, commissions, and mechanical
information, but not on circulation because
Korea has no official audit bureau. The association suggests that this information can best
be obtained through the established advertising
agencies in Korea.

555. Concise Guide to International Markets. Ed. by
Leslie Stinton. 2d ed. London W. 1: International Advertising Association, United Kingdom
Chapter, 15-19 Great Chapel St., 1969.
Gives selected facts and figures for over
90 countries. Information varies in quantity
and quality according to the size of the country (obviously, the larger the country, the
more the media and the greater the amount of
data), and also because material is compiled by
various agencies within the country rather than
by a single source. An example of the data for
a large country (Brazil): demographic breakdown by urban and rural dwellers, race, religion,
literacy; gazetteer information; brief data on
incomes; number of advertising agencies; commission structure; associations and/or official
bodies concerned with the advertising industry;
advertising controls, restrictions, and expenditures; media available; number of market
research facilities.
None of the data are detailed; the information is by its nature outdated almost as soon
as it is recorded. Nevertheless, the book
gives an excellent overview of advertising
conditions in most of the major and many of
the minor countries of the world.

556. Consumer Magazine and Farm Publication Rates and
Data. Skokie, Ill. 60076: Standard Rate & Data
Service, Inc., 5201 Old Orchard Road, monthly.
A subject listing, with addresses, key personnel, circulation, and advertising rates, of
consumer and farm magazines in the U.S., including those distributed through newspapers,
and international consumer magazines. Tables
preceding the subject listings give the territorial distribution for each magazine, as well
as a breakdown of subscription and single-copy
sales. A few of the larger magazines have
summarized the results of readership studies to
accompany their listings. A useful feature is
the list of publications with one million or
more circulation.

Since the primary purpose of this publication
is to guide advertisers in placing their material
advantageously, no magazines are included unless
they accept advertising. Therefore, information
about scholarly publications, college publications, small literary weeklies, and similar
periodicals is not found here.

Consumer Magazine Report. See Demographics Report
(No. 558).

557. Cutlipp, Scott M., comp. A Public Relations
Bibliography. 2d ed. Madison: University of
Wisconsin Press, 1965.
"A new edition of a comprehensive, annotated
bibliography. More than 2,000 new entries are
included, bringing the total to over 5,900
items. Books, articles and other related material written about public relations since it
first emerged as an identifiable vocation in
the early 1900's are classified under 74 subject
categories." - Marketing Information Guide.
Public relations is interpreted broadly in
both editions to include theory as well as
practice and such allied fields as communications and opinion change. In the new edition
changes in entries reflect changes in attitude
toward the profession, with more attention paid
to substantive issues and to self-justification,
tools, and research.

558. Demographics Report. Mamaroneck, N.Y. 10543:
Daniel Starch & Staff, Inc., Boston Post Road and
Beach Ave., annual.
Popularly called the Starch Report, this
readership analysis of about 60 widely distributed consumer magazines gives in tabular
form data derived from a probability sample of
over 30,000 households. Among data included
are: readers per copy by age, sex, marital
status, education, occupation, income, size of
household, and metro versus non-metro markets.
Although intended primarily as an aid for advertisers and marketers, it provides social scientists with valuable information also. Until
1969 its title was Consumer Magazine Report.

559. Deschampsneufs, Henry. Selling in Europe: An
Introduction to the European Markets. London:
Business Publications, 1963.
The main object of this book is to help
manufacturers who are planning to enter the

European market for the first time, as well as
students of foreign trade. Since communications
media and advertising constitute major factors,
these are discussed for each of the 14 countries
covered: Belgium, Holland, Norway, Sweden,
Denmark, Finland, West Germany, Austria, France,
Switzerland, Italy, Spain, Portugal, and Ireland.

560. Directory of Advertising, Marketing and Public
Relations Education in the United States. Comp.
and ed. by Elon G. Borton. Washington, D.C.
20036: American Advertising Federation, 1225
Connecticut Ave., NW, 1960.
Detailed list of the nation's college and
university "degree-credit" courses in advertising, marketing, selling, retailing, public
relations, and related subjects. The federation says that a revision is being planned but
no date has been set.

561. Dunn, S. Watson, ed. International Handbook of
Advertising. New York: McGraw-Hill, 1964.
A 450-page section, Part II, deals with the
structure of advertising in about 50 countries.
Appendices contain useful information on the
International Advertising Association, a partial
list of the largest advertising agencies and
their addresses in 54 countries, a list of
audience measurement services, and information
about advertising expenditures. Indexed.

562. Editor & Publisher Market Guide. New York 10022:
Editor & Publisher Co., 850 Third Ave., annual.
Intended as a guide to help advertisers
place newspaper copy. Gives state-by-state
market analysis of communities throughout the
country, including transportation facilities,
population, housing, number of automobiles,
savings banks, telephones, gas and electric
meters, principal industries, climate, retail
sales, and so on. Marketing maps locate newspapers within each state.

563. Elliott, Blanche B. A History of English Advertising. London: Business Publications Ltd.,
1962.
The author traces advertising from its
beginning in the late 16th century to the
present, with most of the emphasis on pre-20th
century. Her concern is basically with facts
rather than ethical pros and cons. Much of
her information comes from original sources,

notably the Burney collection and the Thomason
Tracts in the British Museum. Contains a brief
bibliography of monographs and an index.

564. Expenditures of National Advertisers in Newspapers. New York 10017: American Newspaper Publishers Association, Bureau of Advertising, 485
Lexington Ave., annual.
    List of national advertisers who invested
    $25,000 or more in newspapers measured by Media
    Records, Inc. (No. 574). The dollar estimates
    include newspaper supplements and color adver-
    tising. Most of the advertisers give a break-
    down on the amount spent on the various products
    under their aegis.

Feureisen, Fritz, and Ernst Schmacke. Die Presse
in Afrika. Die Presse in Asien. Die Presse in
Lateinamerika. (See No. 463.)

565. Graham, Irvin. Encyclopedia of Advertising. 2d
ed. New York: Fairchild, 1969.
    Defines more than 1,100 entries relating to
    advertising, marketing, publishing, law, re-
    search, public relations, publicity, and the
    graphic arts. Section I, which is the main body
    of the book, is devoted to terminology; Section
    II groups the terms according to subject matter
    to form a sort of index; Section III is a di-
    rectory of associations.

Hathorn's Suburban Press Directory: The Nation's
Guide to Suburban Markets. (See No. 471.)

566. Hill and Knowlton International. Handbook on
International Public Relations. 2 vols. New
York: Praeger, 1967, 1968.
    Although concerned with the "how to" aspect
    of public relations, this handbook also contains
    a country-by-country discussion of such facts
    as media, audience, and government regulations.
    Specialists in each country contribute articles,
    each covering slightly different aspects. Vol.
    I treats Belgium, France, Italy, the Netherlands,
    Scandinavia, Spain, Switzerland, the United
    Kingdom, and West Germany. Vol. II treats
    Australia, Hong Kong, India, Japan, Latin Amer-
    ica, Malaysia, New Zealand, and Singapore.

567. IAA World Directory of Marketing Communications
Periodicals. New York 10017: International Advertising Association, 475 Fifth Ave., 1968.

180

Multilingual (English, French, German,
Spanish) guide intended for the practitioner
seeking information on marketing publications
other than his own. Interrelated fields
covered are advertising; sales management and
promotion; market, media, and creative research; merchandising and point-of-sale;
exhibits and fairs; packaging; public relations and publicity; the commercial graphic
arts. Information about each entry includes
field of interest, year established, editions
in other languages, name and address of advertising manager or representative, frequency,
reproduction process, address of source of
data on reproduction requirements, cost in local
currency, method of circulation. Forty-three
countries are covered, of which ten report that
no periodical exists in these areas. All Communist countries are omitted.

International Advertising Association. See <u>World
Advertising Expenditures</u> (No. 602).

568. <u>International Directory of Marketing Research
Houses and Services</u>. Green Book. New York 10022:
American Marketing Association, New York Chapter,
527 Madison Ave., annual.
    Part I is an alphabetical listing by name
of various research agencies, with address,
telephone number, top personnel, and types of
research performed; Part II is a geographical
telephone listing.

569. <u>Leading Advertisers in Business Publications</u>. New
York 10017: American Business Press, Inc.,
Business Press Advertising Bureau, Information
Division, 205 East 52d St., annual.
    Ranks by expenditures those advertisers
investing $175,000 or more in business publica-
tions; lists alphabetically about 2,500 advertisers investing $35,000 or more in business
publications; gives SIC (Standard Industrial
Classifications) analysis of advertiser expenditures; analyzes advertisers geographically
by state.

570. Leading National Advertisers, Inc. <u>LNA Television Service</u>. Norwalk, Conn. 06856: Miller
Associates, P.O. Box 104, weekly with quarterly
cumulation.
    Product-by-product analysis of advertising
time and expenditures on the three national

networks -- ABC, CBS, and NBC. Comes in seven separate sections according to product: foods, beverages; business, financial; apparel; homes, building; drugs, toiletries; transportation, agriculture; general. The December cumulative issue covers the entire year and can be bought separately. Contains a classification and a product index.

571. Leading National Advertisers, Inc. P.I.B. Magazine Service. New York 10022: Publishers Information Bureau, 575 Lexington Ave., monthly with annual cumulation.

Product-by-product analysis of advertising space and revenue in about 100 large-circulation magazines (including farm magazines) and Sunday magazine sections. The December cumulative issue covers the entire year and can be bought separately. Comes in seven different sections according to type of product: foods, beverages; business, financial; apparel; homes, building; drugs, toiletries; transportation, agriculture; general. Contains a general brand index and an index to product classifications.

572. Leading National Advertisers, Inc. Rorabaugh Spot TV. Norwalk, Conn. 06856: N. C. Rorabaugh Co., P.O. Box 81, quarterly with annual summary issued in December.

Subtitled "A Continuing Analysis of Spot Television Activity in 400 TV Stations in 240 Cities 365 Days a Year," this service gives a product-by-product analysis of advertising time and expenditures on spot television. Comes in seven separate sections according to product: foods, beverages; business, financial; apparel; homes, building; drugs, toiletries; transportation, agriculture; general. There is, in addition, a summary section of all seven parts. The December summary covers the entire year and can be bought separately. Contains a classification index, a product index, and a station activity index.

573. Magazine Circulation and Rate Trends 1940-1967. New York 10017: Association of National Advertisers, 155 East 44th St., 1969.

Trend compilation of circulation data, rates, and costs per thousand for 62 audited consumer and farm magazines, broken down into detailed data.

Cumulative editions have appeared since 1937 at irregular intervals. With each edition the list of magazines changes because of additions, discontinuations, mergers, and so on. Supplements frequently appear between editions. This one has a supplement for 1968.

574. Media Records: Newspapers and Newspaper Advertisers. New York 10001: Media Records, Inc., 370 Seventh Ave., quarterly with annual cumulation.

The basic purpose of Media Records is to give a detailed report of newspaper advertising volume in terms of linage in approximately 400 daily papers published in about 150 cities. The choice of cities varies from year to year.

Part I gives linage records of selected daily and Sunday newspapers, showing totals on approximately 170 classifications and subclassifications of advertising for each paper, with papers arranged alphabetically by city. Part II contains an alphabetical listing by individual name of all general and automotive advertisers, and the individual linage record of over 5,000 automotive and general advertisers in the papers represented. Expenditures of National Advertisers in Newspapers (No. 564) is based on information from Media Records in condensed form.

N. W. Ayer & Son. Directory of Newspapers and Periodicals. (See No. 495.)

Natarajan, Swaminath. A History of the Press in India. (See No. 496.)

575. National Advertising Investments: Magazines. Newspaper Supplements. Network TV. Spot TV. Norwalk, Conn. 06856: Leading National Advertisers, Inc., P.O. Box 525, semiannual with annual cumulation.

A record of the overall advertising expenditures of national advertisers as reported in P.I.B. Magazine Advertising Analysis (No. 571) in magazines and newspaper supplements, by Leading National Advertisers in network television (No. 570), and by the Rorabaugh Report (No. 572) in spot television. Companies listed are those which invest $20,000 or more in advertising in the first six months and $25,000 or more in the 12-month period.

An introductory "Highlights" section gives expenditures of the ten top-ranking magazine, newspaper supplement, and network and spot television advertisers; the 50 top network radio advertisers, outdoor advertisers, and transit advertisers; and the 50 top-ranking advertisers in magazines, newspaper supplements, and spot and network television. For newspaper expenditures see Expenditures of National Advertisers in Newspapers (No. 564).

National Directory of Weekly Newspapers. (See No. 497.)

576. Network Rates and Data. Skokie, Ill. 60076: Standard Rate & Data Service, Inc., 5201 Old Orchard Road, monthly.
      Lists the various national and regional radio and television networks, giving the stations they serve, advertising rates, and pertinent technical information such as frequency for radio, channel for television, and so on.

577. Newspaper Circulation Analysis. Skokie, Ill. 60076: Standard Rate & Data Service, Inc., 5201 Old Orchard Road, annual.
      Breaks down newspaper circulation data in two basic analyses: (1) geographic county-by-county/metro area analysis, giving degree of penetration by county and metropolitan area; (2) circulation by city zone, county, and metropolitan areas. Also contains ranking tables for daily newspaper market area, city zone, and total circulation.

578. Newspaper Circulation & Rate Trends (1946-1968). New York 10017: Association of National Advertisers, Inc., 155 East 44th St., 1969.
      Presents data on the aggregate circulation and rate trends of all U.S. English-language daily and Sunday newspapers and individual papers with 50,000 circulation and over. Figures for Sunday magazine sections and comic groups are also included. Every few years a new edition appears which updates and cumulates figures.

579. Newspaper International: Basic Newspaper Data on Major Newspapers and Markets in 79 Countries Excluding U.S.A. and Canada. Skokie, Ill. 60076: National Register Publishing Co., 5201 Old Orchard Road, annual.

New publication (1969), intended to assist the international advertiser. Gives concise sketches of the structure of newspaper advertising in specific countries and then lists principal dailies, telling their rates, circulation, and mechanical requirements.

Information, which varies for each country, is pertinent and pinpointed. The entry on India, for example, deals with the language situation, the surcharge on advertising, the use of the Audit Bureau of Circulation, the names of the most influential newspapers, the fact that cows cannot be used in any advertising or bacon and ham in Muslim advertising, and the conversion basis of the rupee. Communist countries are not included.

The Newspaper Press Directory and Advertiser's Guide. (See No. 500.)

580. Newspaper Rates and Data. Skokie, Ill. 60076: Standard Rate & Data Service, Inc., 5201 Old Orchard Road, monthly.

Like all other SRDS publications, the main function of this one is to give advertising rates for those dailies audited by the Audit Bureau of Circulation. This includes the main body of daily newspapers and certain special newspaper publications -- not all of them daily -- such as comic groups, newspaper-distributed magazines, weeklies (only a few are audited; for a fuller list see National Directory of Weekly Newspapers, No. 497), Negro newspapers, and religious weeklies. For each paper, gives addresses, circulation, a few top personnel, and advertising rates.

Preceding the listings of specific titles is a breakdown of daily newspapers by circulation and by population and marketing data for the U.S. as a whole, including definitions of major metropolitan areas and figures about consumer spendable income, farm income, and total retail sales by household and by broad product grouping. Much of this data is also given for larger cities. Similar information is listed for each state, and state maps indicate the types and overlapping of media within communities.

There is, in addition, a summary tabulation section, with newspaper groups, the types of advertising (comic strip, split-run, and so on) which specific papers will accept, contract and copy regulations, and other detailed data of this sort.

581. Nielander, William A. <u>Selected and Annotated Bibliography of Public Relations</u>. 3d rev. ed. Austin: University of Texas, Bureau of Business Research, 1967. (Bibliography Series No. 3)
Over 600 titles listed under general works, specialized works, and periodicals and directories. Titles in the specialized works section are broken down into 30 headings. Annotations are succinct and evaluative.

582. <u>Ogilvy & Mather Pocket Guide to Media</u>. 4th ed. New York 10017: Ogilvy & Mather Inc., 2 East 48th St., 1971.
Pocket guide containing quick estimates of the dimensions, audience, and costs of major media. For television it gives ownership, audience composition, reach and frequency estimates, cost and efficiency, top 100 markets, and the NAB Code. For radio: ownership, audience, cost. For consumer magazines: circulation and costs, on-sale and closing dates, demographic editions, total audience composition, coupon redemption data. For newspapers: supplements, comics, color in newspapers, readership. There is also information on outdoor, transit, and direct mail media; a glossary; and a list of syndicated services.

583. <u>Outdoor Advertising Circulation and Rate Trends (1959-66)</u>. New York 10017: Association of National Advertisers, Inc., 155 East 44th St., 1967.
Presents current rate information on population, allotment, advertising rate, and cost-per-thousand circulation of each illuminated outdoor plant in the U.S. Frequently updated.

<u>P&D Overseas Newspaper and Periodicals Guide Book</u>. (<u>See</u> No. 504.)

584. Presbrey, Frank. <u>The History and Development of Advertising</u>. Garden City, N.Y.: Doubleday, 1929.
One of the best and fullest sources available for the history of advertising from ancient days to the Depression. Over 100 of its more than 600 pages are devoted to early advertising outside the American colonies, and throughout the book social and economic implications are

stressed. An appendix contains an address by
President Coolidge on the economic aspects of
advertising. Indexed.

Press and Advertisers Year Book. (See No. 506.)

585. "The Profitable Difference": A Study of the Magazine Market . . . Its Size, Quality and Buying.
New York 10022: Magazine Advertising Bureau of
Magazine Publishers Association, Inc., 575 Lexington Ave., 1960.
     A marketing and media study which gives
demographic data about the magazine audience
as well as information about its purchases of
both rapid-turnover products and durable goods.
Although dated, this is the latest available
data of its sort. In 1948 and 1949 the Magazine Advertising Bureau also issued several
demographic studies of the nationwide magazine
audience. Few such studies have ever been done.

586. The Rome Report of Business Publication Advertising. New York 10033: Rome Research, Inc., 1960
Broadway, semiannual with annual cumulation.
     Compilation of the advertising appearing in
over 600 business publications representing 94
publishing classifications. Designed to provide
advertisers, agencies, and publishers with a
standard source of competitive media information. Replaces Brad-Vern Reports: The Blue
Book of Business Paper Advertisers.

587. Ross, Billy I. Advertising Education: Programs
in Four-Year American Colleges and Universities.
New York 10021: American Association of Advertising Agencies, 200 Park Ave., 1965.
     Includes virtually all of the advertising
programs designed for undergraduates in the 77
institutions, located in 37 states, which
offered such a program at the time this work
was written. Also contains an early history of
advertising education, information on various
advertising organizations, current trends, and
future projections. Bibliography.

588. Sandage, Charles H., and Vernon Fryburger. Advertising Theory and Practice. 8th ed. Homewood,
Ill.: Richard D. Irwin, 1971.
     Although much of this book is concerned with
market analysis and research and with the writing and placing of advertising, the first section
is devoted to certain broad trends of general

187

interest, as, for example, advertising's definition and function, its history, some of its
appeals, its social and economic aspects, and
its ethics. Contains a bibliography and an
index.

589. Sandage, Charles H., and Vernon Fryburger, eds.
The Role of Advertising: A Book of Readings.
Homewood, Ill.: Richard D. Irwin, 1960.
Discusses many pertinent facts and theories,
such as advertising's place in society, its
responsibility, its appeals, its function, and
its impact. Includes a bibliography at the
end of each section and gives "Standards of
Practice of the American Association of Advertising Agencies" and the Television Code.

590. Simon, Morton J. Public Relations Law. New York:
Appleton-Century-Crofts, 1969.
"We have sought to produce for the PR
practitioner a basic book which will also guide
the lawyer when he ventures into the legal
sectors of public relations," says the author,
a lawyer who specializes in the legal aspects
of business communications. Gives legal basics
of such areas as copyright, privacy, libel,
trademarks, photography, deception, contests,
industrial espionage, government relations,
lobbying, employee-employer relations, and
similar aspects.

591. Spot Radio Rates and Data. Skokie, Ill. 60076:
Standard Rate & Data Service, Inc., 5201 Old
Orchard Road, monthly.
The main part of this publication consists
of a geographical listing by state of approximately 5,000 AM and all FM radio stations in
the U.S., with addresses, key personnel,
facilities, and time rates. Preceding this is
a great deal of information about radio, including the number of radio households by state;
radio networks and groups; and stations regularly scheduling farm programs, foreign-language programs, and programs for blacks. Also
contains general marketing data and state maps
indicating the types and overlapping of media
within specific communities.

592. Spot Television Rates and Data. Skokie, Ill.
60076: Standard Rate & Data Service, Inc., 5201
Old Orchard Road, monthly.

A geographical listing by state of all television stations in the U.S., with addresses,
key personnel, facilities, time rates, and network affiliates. Preceding the station listings is information about the number of TV households by states, estimates as to the number of
black-and-white and color sets within the larger
cities, a list of regional TV networks and
groups, a map of television cities and time
zones, and much of the same marketing data as
in Spot Radio Rates and Data (No. 591). Also
contains similar state maps giving types and
overlapping of media within specific communities.

593. Standard Directory of Advertising. Skokie, Ill.
60076: National Register Publishing Co., 5201
Old Orchard Road, annual with monthly supplements.
For about 17,000 corporations doing national
or regional advertising gives address, telephone number, products or services, agency
handling the account, account executives, media
used, distribution, and occasionally appropria-
tion. There is a geographical index, published
separately in a pocketbook edition, which breaks
down advertisers by city and state. This is a
subsidiary service of Standard Rate & Data.

594. Standard Directory of Advertising Agencies.
Skokie, Ill. 60076: National Register Publishing
Co., 5201 Old Orchard Road, three times yearly
with monthly supplements.
An alphabetical list of advertising agencies
in the U.S., with addresses, personnel, and
accounts carried. This is a subsidiary service
of Standard Rate & Data.

595. Standard Rate & Data Service, Inc. Foreign Editions. Skokie, Ill. 60076: Standard Rate &
Data Service, Inc., 5201 Old Orchard Road, frequency varies with publication.
SRDS has foreign editions covering rates for
major media in France, Germany, Italy, Mexico,
and West Germany. These are, respectively,
Tarif Media: Le Guide des Supports Publi-
citaires de France; Dati & Tariffe Pubblicitarie:
Pronturrio dei Mezzi Pubblicitari Italiani;
Directorio de Medios: Información y Tarifas;
and Media Daten. SRDS also publishes British
Rate & Data (No. 551).

596. Stanley, Alexander O. Handbook of International
Marketing: How to Export, Import, and Invest
Overseas. New York: McGraw-Hill, 1963.
    Technical manual, giving facts on credits,
sales, advertising, financing, licensing,
trademarks and industrial property protection,
subsidiary and branch investments overseas,
and other aspects. Indexed.

Starch Report. See Demographics Report (No.
558).

597. Television Circulation and Rate Trends (1962-
1968). New York 10017: Association of National
Advertisers, Inc., 155 East 44th St., 1967.
    Trend information on network and spot rates,
estimated homes reached, and cost per thousand
homes reached for approximately 500 U.S. commercial television stations for which American
Research Bureau estimates are available.
Audience measurement data are secured through
sampling; stations included are those in the
larger urban areas.

U.S. Negro World. (See No. 526.)

598. Vigrolio, Tom, and Jack Vahler. Marketing and
Communications Media Dictionary. Norfolk, Mass.
02056: NBS Co., Box 246, 1969.
    Brief, pointed definitions of terms, often
technical, used in advertising, marketing,
public relations, and graphics. Also contains
a list of publications for publicity use and
sections on postal, copyright, and other types
of information, as well as numerous illustrations such as typefaces, proofreading symbols,
and so on. The orientation is highly practical.

599. Weekly Newspaper Rates and Data. Skokie, Ill.
60076: Standard Rate & Data Service, Inc., 5201
Old Orchard Road, semiannual.
    Lists audited weekly newspapers that are
members of or subscribers to one of the three
audit bureaus; weekly newspapers not members
of or subscribers to an audit bureau but whose
reporting of circulation is formalized and
notarized on a sworn statement form; and weekly
shopping guides, broadly defined as publications
containing either less than 25 percent editorial
content, consisting primarily of general interest
news, or 100 percent advertising content. In
this latter section listees have either reported

190

circulation data on a sworn statement form or
through membership in or subscription to an
audit bureau. Section I contains a list of
religious weekly newspapers which are members
of the Audit Bureau of Circulation.

600. Wilson, Alexander, ed. Advertising and the Community. Manchester, England: Manchester University Press, 1968.
  Essays about the social and economic effects
of advertising on British society, centering
around the question of advertising's present
quality. Articles discuss the need, if it
exists, for advertising; the public confidence
in it; forms of control; responsibility toward
the consumer; and consumer safeguards. Contributors, who number both detractors and
defenders, represent a variety of viewpoints --
the media, consumer organizations, the law,
the advertising business, the university professor. Appendices give the Independent Television Authority's Advertising Code, a summary
of recommendations of the Advertising Inquiry
Council, and advertising expenditures and other
statistics for selected years from 1938 through
1966. Contains a bibliography and an index.

Wolseley, Roland E., ed. Journalism in Modern
India. (See No. 536.)

601. Wood, James Playsted. The Story of Advertising.
New York: Ronald Press, 1958.
  Five-hundred-page history in which the
author discusses the good and bad points of
advertising. Includes a bibliography and an
index.

The Working Press of the Nation. Feature Writer and
Syndicate Directory. Vol. 4. (See No. 439.)

The Working Press of the Nation. Magazine and
Editorial Directory. Vol. 2. (See No. 440.)

The Working Press of the Nation. Newspapers and
Allied Services. Vol. 1. (See No. 538.)

The Working Press of the Nation. Radio and TV
Directory. Vol. 3. (See No. 296.)

602. World Advertising Expenditures (1968). New York
10017: International Advertising Association,
475 Fifth Ave., biennial.

191

This is the ninth in a series of biennial
worldwide surveys of advertising expenditures
providing estimates of expenditure data in
various media categories by country. It is
designed to enable comparisons to be made between countries and broad geographical regions.
Estimates have been obtained for 64 countries,
distribution of expenditures by media for 46.
Has had various titles -- Advertising Expenditures around the World and International
Advertising Expenditures.

603. The World of Advertising. Chicago 60611: Advertising Age, 740 Rush St., 1963.
This, the 15 January 1963 issue of the
periodical Advertising Age, is designed, so the
editors say, to broaden the knowledge of both
practitioners and the general public about
advertising. Although now somewhat out of
date, it still contains valuable factual information of which the following is part: introductory statement defining advertising and discussing its place in the nation's economy; a
description of how the agency business works,
including the operations of the media themselves; a listing of more than 65 associations
serving the advertising business, with descriptions of their memberships, basic functions,
and services; detailed reports on regulatory
controls from self-regulation to state, local,
federal, and private testing organizations; the
social, political, and educational roles of
advertising; international advertising; and,
finally, the pros and cons, in which contributors such as Neil Borden, John K. Galbraith,
Arnold Toynbee, Walter Taplin, and others argue
its virtues and defects.

Periodical, Dissertation, and Newspaper Indexes

604. <u>Business Periodicals Index</u>. New York: Wilson, cumulative.

     Begun in 1958 to succeed <u>The Industrial Arts Index</u> (No. 605), this analyzes by subject a number of trade and scholarly periodicals in business and allied fields such as advertising and the mass media. Among periodicals specializing in the mass media which it indexes are <u>Advertising Age</u>, <u>Broadcasting</u>, <u>Columbia Journalism Review</u>, <u>International Advertiser</u>, <u>Journal of Advertising Research</u>, <u>Journal of Marketing</u>, <u>Marketing/Communications</u> (formerly <u>Printers' Ink</u>), <u>Publishers' Weekly</u>, and <u>Television</u>.

605. <u>The Industrial Arts Index: Subject Index to a Selected List of Engineering, Trade and Business Periodicals</u>. New York: Wilson, 1913-57.

     Indexes a number of publications pertaining directly to the media or containing frequent articles about them. Among these are <u>Advertising Agency</u>, <u>Editor & Publisher</u>, <u>Industrial Marketing</u>, <u>Printers' Ink</u>, and <u>Radio and Television News</u>. In 1957 this ceased publication and was succeeded by <u>Business Periodicals Index</u> (No. 604).

606. <u>Journalism Abstracts</u>. Chapel Hill: The Editor, University of North Carolina, School of Journalism, annual.

     Yearly summary, begun in 1962, of M.A., M.S., and Ph.D. theses in journalism and communication. Published by the Association for Education in Journalism.

607. Journalism Quarterly. Cumulative Index, Volumes
1-40, 1924-1963. Minneapolis: University of
Minnesota, School of Journalism, 1964.
Special supplement to the Summer 1964 issue,
containing an index to all articles and book
reviews. Articles are listed by subject and
by author. Book reviews are by author.

608. New York Daily Tribune Index. New York: Tribune
Association, 1875-1906.
A yearly index which, for the years it was
published, serves as a valuable source for historical information about newspaper, magazine,
and book publishing.

609. The New York Times Index: The Master Key to the
News. New York: New York Times Co., semimonthly
with annual cumulation.
Since 1913 this index has summarized and
classified the contents of the New York Times
alphabetically by subjects, persons, and organizations. Within recent years the Times has
produced the index file back to the establishment of the paper in 1851. Its comprehensive
coverage makes a valuable source for information about the mass media and advertising.
The only other contemporary American newspaper with its own index is the Wall Street
Journal (No. 616). For information about mass
media and advertising in Great Britain and the
Commonwealth, the London Times Official Index
(London: Times Publishing Co. Ltd.), which
began publication in 1906, is an excellent
source.

610. Poole's Index to Periodical Literature, 1802-1891.
2 vols. Supplements 1-5, 1892-1907. Rev. ed.
Boston: Houghton Mifflin, 1882, 1887-1908. Reproduced by photo-offset. New York: Peter Smith,
1938 (6 vols. in 7).
Pioneer index, spanning the nineteenth
century and covering a total of about 590,000
articles in over 12,000 volumes of almost 500
American and English periodicals. Entry is by
subject only, with no author-title index. Even
so, the work is monumental to anyone involved in
the history of communications.

611. Psychological Abstracts. Washington, D.C.: American Psychological Association, monthly with annual
bound volume.

An important bibliography, international in
scope, abstracting current articles and books
in psychology and closely related fields. A
number of items pertain to the mass media and
still more to the communication process. Among
journals abstracted are Journalism Quarterly
and Public Opinion Quarterly. Abstracted
articles are indexed by author and subject.

612. Readers' Guide to Periodical Literature: An
Author and Subject Index. New York: Wilson,
cumulative.
An index to articles contained in general
American consumer magazines and some scholarly
and trade ones. Here one finds the articles on
the mass media contained in magazines like the
Atlantic, Commentary, Ebony, New Republic,
Esquire, Vital Speeches, Annals of the American
Academy of Political and Social Science, Common-
weal, Saturday Review, Nation, the major news
magazines, and others of this type equally well
known.

613. Public Affairs Information Service Bulletin. New
York: Public Affairs Information Service, Inc.,
cumulative.
Lists by subject current books, pamphlets,
periodical articles, government documents, and
other materials in the fields of economics and
public affairs. Includes selected publications
of all kinds from all English-speaking countries,
as well as many printed in English in non-
English-speaking countries, and gives excellent
coverage to the media and to advertising, public
opinion, and propaganda and censorship. Particularly useful because of its wide coverage
of many kinds of materials and its wide geographic coverage. Journalism Quarterly is among
the periodicals indexed.

614. Social Sciences and Humanities Index. Formerly
International Index. New York: Wilson, cumulative.
Author and subject index similar in format
to the Readers' Guide but covering the more
scholarly journals in the two fields. Formerly
contained a number of foreign titles, but since
World War II these have been dropped, so that
coverage is American and English only.

615. Topicator: Monthly Classified Article Guide to
the Advertising-Broadcasting Press. Denver, Colo.:

Thompson Bureau, monthly with quarterly and annual
cumulations.

Excellent subject index to the leading trade
and scholarly journals in broadcasting, including broadcast advertising. Although it includes
only about 20 periodicals, they are the key
ones, and their contents are difficult to pick
up elsewhere -- e.g., Variety and TV Guide.
(Music Index carries Variety, but only those
items pertaining strictly to music.) An indispensable guide to anyone needing periodical
material concerned in any way with broadcasting.

616. The Wall Street Journal Index. New York: Dow-
Jones, monthly with annual cumulations.

Index to the contents of the New York edition of the Wall Street Journal, begun in
December 1957. Useful for its leads to information about specific businesses and for articles
about trends in the mass media. Although editions in cities other than New York differ somewhat in paging and content, the references are
easy to locate.

Scholarly and Professional Periodicals*

617. <u>Admap</u>. London: Cornmarket Press Ltd., monthly.
Carries articles concerned with advertis-
ing research, trends, and theories.

618. <u>Advertising Age: The National Newspaper of Mar-
keting</u>. Chicago: Advertising Publications, Inc.,
weekly.
The title is not comprehensive enough to
indicate properly the contents of this valuable
trade magazine. Advertising is broadly defined
to include detailed news of the magazine,
broadcasting, and newspaper industries. Although
a good deal of its material appears to be public relations handouts, it does some good
interpretive reporting on its own initiative
and, while accepting the existence of advertising, can be tartly critical.
From time to time issues as a regular feature contain certain information difficult to
find elsewhere. For example, one issue, usually
in mid-January, gives as a regular feature total
magazine revenue and pages and the revenue and
pages for individual magazines for the past
year. Another issue capsules reports on bil-
lings and accounts of most individual advertising agencies. A late spring issue lists studies
available to the public about listening and
viewing audiences of specific broadcasting
stations and readership studies of specific
magazines and newspapers.

619. <u>The Advertising Quarterly</u>. London: Advertising
Association, quarterly.

* Only extant periodicals are included.

Contains provocative articles, individually
rather than staff-written, and book reviews.

620. AdWeekly. London: Advertiser's Weekly, weekly.
Nonanalytical analysis of the latest happenings in British advertising.

621. The American Press. Wilmette, Ill.: Michael &
Ginsberg Publishing Co., monthly.
Concerned with offset newspaper publishing,
this trade journal is subtitled "The Nation's
Only Independent Journal for the Entire Newspaper Management." Contains notes on latest
methods and happenings and various departments -- Booktalk, which briefly reviews a
current book or two; a calendar; letters;
"idea swapshops"; a page of abstracts of current articles, pamphlets, and so on; a classified section; and a few other such features.

622. AV Communication Review. Washington, D.C. 20036:
Association for Educational Communications and
Technology, 1201 Sixteenth St., NW, quarterly.
Scholarly review carrying articles, mostly
experimental, about instructional audiovisual
materials. Contains book reviews.

623. Book Production Industry. Cleveland, Ohio: Penton
Publishing Co., monthly.
Although a trade journal devoted primarily
to various forms of book production, including
the newest, this also contains excellent articles on various phases of the book trade, like
mergers, employment of minorities, and so on.

624. The Bookseller: The Organ of the Book Trade.
London: J. Whitaker and Sons Ltd., weekly.
British equivalent to Publishers' Weekly.
Contains a section, "Publications of the Week."

625. Broadcasting Bibliophile's Booknotes. Ed. by
Christopher H. Sterling. Philadelphia 19122:
Temple University, Department of Radio-Film-TV,
monthly.
An informal essay-bibliography of about
eight pages lists and discusses recent books
about broadcasting. Although it is part of
the monthly kit of the APBE (Association for
Professional Broadcasting Education), it may
be obtained separately by writing to the
editor.

626. Broadcasting: The Business Weekly of Television and Radio. Washington, D.C.: Broadcasting Publications, weekly.

The best known of the trade journals for the broadcasting industry. Seldom critical, usually defensive of industry, it gives ample coverage to the week's happenings in more detail than depth. An extremely useful feature is "For the Record," which lists all new television stations and changes in status of existing ones.

627. Columbia Journalism Review. New York: Columbia University, Graduate School of Journalism, quarterly.

Provocative and often challenging articles by scholars, journalists, and free-lance writers who describe and often challenge the status quo. It is more concerned with exposing what is wrong than with applauding what is right. Contains book reviews and abstracts of research.

628. EBU Review. Geneva, Switzerland: European Broadcasting Union, bimonthly.

Part B of this journal of the European Broadcasting Union carries a section of articles on various aspects of European broadcasting, a section on legal aspects, and a section on EBU activities.

629. Editor & Publisher, the Fourth Estate. New York, weekly.

The subtitle of this trade journal describes it well: "Spot News and Features about Newspapers, Advertisers and Agencies." Although it attempts some interpretation, its strong point is in being a chronicle of events and trends. Coverage is good, enabling the reader to keep up with latest developments. Contains many small items about newspapers and their personnel.

630. Educational Broadcasting Review. Washington, D.C.: National Association of Educational Broadcasters, bimonthly.

Published by the National Association of Educational Broadcasters in cooperation with Ohio State University, this contains first of all an open forum for opinion on the current broadcasting scene, a few articles which can be experimental, interpretive, or both, book and

program reviews which concern educational broadcasting, and abstracts of recent research.

631. Film Culture. New York: Film Culture Nonprofit
Organization, quarterly.
Brief avant-garde articles on the underground
and experimental films and their makers.

632. Film Quarterly. Berkeley and Los Angeles: University of California Press, quarterly.
Film Quarterly started in 1941 as the Hollywood Quarterly, a scholarly journal of the
motion picture. In 1951 it broadened to the
Quarterly of Film, Radio and Television and in
1957 took its present name. It is a journal
of quality which carries articles on the state
of today's films, along with several interviews
with film personalities and film reviews. Also
contains an article on short films, entertainment, and book reviews.

633. The Gallagher Report. Ed. by Bernard P. Gallagher.
New York: Gallagher Report, Inc., weekly.
Subtitled "A Confidential Letter to Advertising, Marketing and Media Executives," this
breezy four-page newsletter is full of trends,
tips, predictions, facts, and figures on advertising media.

634. The Gallup Opinion Index -- Political, Social and
Economic Trends. Princeton, N.J.: Gallup Inter-
national, Inc., monthly.
Reports the results of the month's Gallup
opinion polls. Formerly called the Gallup
Political Index.

635. Gazette: International Journal for Mass Communication Studies. Deventer, the Netherlands, quarterly.
Scholarly articles on the press, broadcasting, propaganda, public opinion, advertising,
and public relations. Contains several comprehensive book reviews, a section on current
trends ("Current Activities"), and a bibliography of magazine articles from around the
world, broken down by subject.

636. The Guild Reporter. Washington, D.C.: American
Newspaper Guild, bimonthly.
Eight-page newspaper which is the official
organ of the American Newspaper Guild (AFL-CIO,
CLC). Reports labor happenings.

637. IPI Report. Zurich: International Press Institute, monthly.
     Monthly bulletin of the International Press
Institute. The content of its publication follows the purpose of the organization: to safe-
guard freedom of the press, to achieve understanding among journalists, to promote better
flow of news, and to improve journalism practices. Coverage is worldwide.

638. Journal of Advertising Research. New York:
Advertising Research Foundation, quarterly.
     Articles emphasize research methods and
techniques. Contains a brief section of one-
paragraph book reviews and a list of books
received.

639. Journal of Broadcasting. Washington, D.C.:
Association for Professional Broadcasting Education, quarterly.
     Articles, some empirical, about various
phases of broadcasting -- issues, research, law,
education, and literature, which includes "Books
in Review."

640. The Journal of Communication. Athens, Ohio:
International Communication Association, Center
for Communication Studies, Ohio University, quarterly.
     Articles, which are scholarly and often sta-
tistical, vary from mass media to interpersonal
communication, with considerable emphasis on
speech. Carries book reviews and a section,
"Books Received."

641. Journal of Marketing. Chicago: American Marketing Association, quarterly.
     Although devoted primarily to scholarly
articles on marketing, much of the material in
this journal is pertinent to advertising, and
some of the articles center upon it. Contains
a section of book reviews and another of abstracts of pertinent articles grouped by subject.

642. Journal of Popular Culture. Bowling Green, Ohio:
Modern Language Association of America, Popular
Literature Section (Comparative Literature II),
and Folklore Section of the Midwest Modern Language Association, quarterly.
     Popular culture is herein interpreted
broadly to include high, low, and middle --
present and past. Articles on the whole are

well written, interesting, and scholarly. They
range in subject matter over music, art, broadcasting, architecture, drama, and literature.
Contains a long section of book reviews.

643. Journalism Abstracts. Minneapolis 55455: University of Minnesota, Association for Education in
Journalism, Business Office, 201 Murphy Hall,
annual.
    Yearly summary, begun in 1962, of M.A.,
M.S., and Ph.D. theses in communications. Each
thesis is abstracted, with conclusions given
There is a subject index.

644. The Journalism Educator. Reno: University of
Nevada, Department of Journalism, quarterly.
    Published by the American Society of Journal-
ism School Administrators, this periodical contains news and informational articles in the
field.
    A useful feature is their annual directory
issue. The latest lists schools and departments of journalism, with addresses, associations and student organization affiliations,
sequences, news and broadcasting facilities,
and number of students; a schedule of work-
shops and short courses for the year; journalism education organizations; professional and
student honorary societies; collegiate and
scholastic services; media associations; national
funds, foundations, and scholarships in journalism; past and present presidents of the AEJ,
the ASJSA, and the AASDJ.

645. Journalism Quarterly: Devoted to Research in
Journalism and Mass Communication. Minneapolis:
University of Minnesota, School of Journalism,
quarterly.
    Articles cover, and often combine, both mass
media and theory. Special features include an
international communications section, book reviews, and sections on research in brief, journalism education, paperbacks in mass communication,
and a bibliography of articles on mass communication in U.S. and foreign journals.

646. Marketing/Communications. New York: Decker
Communications, monthly.
    For years Printers' Ink, along with Advertis-
ing Age, was a leading trade journal in advertising and allied fields. In July 1967 Printers'
Ink jazzed up its title to Marketing/Communica-

tions and played down its contents -- a process
which had been going on steadily for some years.
     In its heydey an outstanding feature was an
annual supplement, Printers' Ink Guide to Marketing, the name of which was later changed to
Advertisers' Guide to Marketing. This was
valuable for its analyses of marketing trends
and of advertising volume broken down by media.
Among markets analyzed were Negro, military,
religious, farm, youth, and international. It
also broke down national advertising volume
according to newspapers, syndicated supplements, magazines, radio, television, farm
publications, and outdoor. In 1965 the supplement ceased publication.

647. Media Industry Newsletter. New York: Business
Magazines, Inc., weekly.
     Subtitled "Weekly Report to Management,"
this newsletter not only reports events and
trends but also analyzes them and does so
with style and literacy. Each issue carries
an "Advertising Box Score," comparing for
selected magazines the current year's advertising pages with the previous year's. Also lists
financial figures for various corporations such
as paper, broadcasting, and book publishing,
which, though not directly part of the magazine
industry, are connected with it.

648. Monthly Film Bulletin. London: British Film
Institute, monthly.
     Analytical reviews and information about cast,
director, footage, length, producer, and so on
for about 25 full-length current films from
various parts of the world, as well as reviews
of two or three current nonfiction and short
films.

649. NAEB Newsletter. Washington, D.C.: National
Association of Educational Broadcasters, monthly.
     Six-page newsletter giving newest develop-
ments in educational broadcasting. Contains a
section, "Dates and Deadlines," and a page,
"Personnel Service."

650. Nieman Reports. Cambridge, Mass.: Society of
Nieman Fellows, quarterly.
     Articles on various aspects of contemporary
journalism, written perceptively and with style
(the authors are all Nieman Fellows).

651. The Public Opinion Quarterly. New York: American
Association for Public Opinion Research, quarterly.
    Scholarly articles concerned largely with
empirical research. A special section, "Current Research," gives "brief reports of research
in progress, discussions of unsolved problems,
methodological studies, and public opinion data
not extensively analyzed or interpreted." Carries book reviews.

652. Publishers' Weekly: The Book Industry Journal.
New York: Bowker, weekly.
    The trade journal for the book publishing
industry and one of the best of all trade
journals. In addition to giving news of the
book trade -- some of it in considerable depth --
each year a spring issue carries articles summarizing statistics of the previous year. Included in these statistics are a table of the
total number of titles published (not to be
confused with the total number of volumes),
broken down by subject, and a list of book
publishers with the total number of titles each
produced. There are also a résumé of the year's
trends and an analysis of best sellers.
    Some of this information appears later in
the Bowker Annual (No. 124), but the information
on output of individual publishers is available
nowhere else. Another special issue is the
International Edition, begun in 1970 to replace
Bowker's annual Publishers' World, which appeared
for five years from 1965 through 1970 (No.
164).

653. Quill: The Magazine for Journalists. Chicago:
Sigma Delta Chi, monthly.
    The organ of Sigma Delta Chi, professional
journalistic society, this magazine carries
articles, most of them reportorial, evaluating
the state of journalism today. Has a book review section and several pages of short items on
Sigma Delta Chi happenings and news of members.

654. Scholarly Publishing: A Journal for Authors &
Publishers. Toronto: University of Toronto Press,
quarterly.
    The only journal devoted exclusively to uni-
versity presses. In its first issue the editors
state their ambition to treat subjects which are
often technical with a philosophical regard for

the unique need for and responsibilities of
university presses.

655. Screen: The Journal of the Society for Education
in Film and Television. London: Society for
Education in Film and Television, bimonthly.
Each issue contains about five discerning
articles on directors, films, techniques, and
new trends, as well as sections on film reviews, book reviews, new film study materials
and documents, and a checklist of filmscripts
in print.

656. Sight and Sound: The International Film Quarterly. London: British Film Institute, quarterly.
Perceptive articles about trends in content
and techniques of today's film, both British
and foreign, along with about a dozen reviews
and several book reviews. Although sponsored
by the British Film Institute, it describes
itself as "an independent critical magazine"
which is "not an organ for the expression of
official British Film Institute policy; signed
articles represent the views of their authors,
and not necessarily those of the Editorial
Board."

657. Telecommunication Journal. Geneva, Switzerland:
International Telecommunication Union, monthly.
The organ of the International Telecommunication Union, giving news of activities,
studies, technological trends, and so on. Also
contains a list of pertinent articles in other
technical publications listed under the language of the publication. Published in separate English, French, and Spanish editions.

658. Telecommunications Reports. Washington, D.C.:
National Press Building, weekly.
Subtitled "Weekly News Service Covering the
Telephone, Telegraph and Radio Communications
Fields since 1934," this gives brief -- and
sometimes not so brief -- accounts of weekly
developments in the fields covered.

659. Television Age. New York: Television Editorial
Corp., weekly.
Trade journal concerned with television advertising and with radio advertising as it affects
television.

660. Television Digest with Consumer Electronics. Washington, D.C.: Television Digest, Inc., weekly.
Subtitled "The Authoritative Service for Executives in Broadcasting, Consumer Electronics & Allied Fields," the Digest capsules the week's news in all types of broadcasting, including broadcast advertising and CATV.

661. Television Quarterly. Boston: Boston University, School of Public Communication, quarterly.
The journal of the National Academy of Television Arts and Sciences. Articles tend toward the interpretive rather than the experimental and are generally thoughtful and provocative. Carries a few long reviews.

662. TV Communications: The Professional Journal of Cable Television. Englewood, Colo.: Communications Publishing Corp., monthly.
Trade journal concerned with developments, techniques, and people in the cable television industry.

663. TV Guide. Radnor, Pa.: Triangle Publications, weekly.
Annotated log of weekly programs. Regional issues take care of variations in programming throughout the country. One of the most valuable features is the articles preceding the log, which vary in quality. The good ones can be very good indeed.

664. U.S. Department of Commerce. Business and Defense Services Administration. Printing and Publishing Industries Division. Economic Summary: Printing and Publishing and Allied Industries. Washington, D.C.: Government Printing Office, bimonthly.
A four-page bulletin, with each issue devoted to a different phase of printing and publishing, which is broadly defined to cover periodicals, newspapers, miscellaneous publishing, books, binding, and various kinds of printing. Most of the information is statistical, but figures are preceded by a brief, interpretive survey. Examples of articles carried: "Size of Business as a Factor in Bulk Third-Class Mail Costs," "Metropolitan Centers of Printing and Publishing," "Expenditures for New Plant and Equipment," "The Market for Books in Industry."

665. Variety. New York: Variety, Inc., weekly.

<u>Variety</u>, of all trade journals, is unique
for both its picturesque language and its
remarkably comprehensive coverage of motion
pictures, the recording industry, broadcasting,
and "show biz" in general. In addition to
reporting news, it makes an attempt to interpret trends and is a particularly good source
for reports of government action on the entertainment industry. Carries reviews of films,
including foreign, underground, domestic, and
commercial.

Subject Index

All references are to entry numbers,
not to pages.

Asia: book publishing, 105, 117, 122, 155, 166, 168;
    broadcasting, 1, 18; film, 1; mass media, 1, 18,
    57; news agencies, 18; newspapers, 1, 18, 463;
    periodicals, 18, 105; radio, 18; research, 18;
    telecommunications, 18; training in journalism, 18
Associated Correspondents of Race Newspapers, 505
Associations: advertising, 458, 500, 603; book pub-
    lishing, 124, 151, 163; British, 488, 500; broad-
    casting, 63, 69, 186, 248, 274; Canadian, 60; CATV,
    190; film, 322, 343, 407; Indian press, 506; labor
    press, 424; library, 124; mass media, 66, 69; news-
    paper, 63, 69, 458; specialized periodical, 419; in
    Washington, D.C., 475
Australia: advertising, 184; authorship, 103; bookstores,
    161; broadcasting, 184, 244; film, 400; newspapers,
    473, 489; public relations, 566; television, 243
Austria: advertising, 541, 559; newspapers, 532;
    periodicals, 532
Authors, 99, 134. See also Authorship; Feature writers
Authorship: economics, 125; markets, 103, 104, 439,
    440
Awards: broadcasting, 175, 230; film, 322, 343, 369;
    library, 174; literary, 161; mass media, 46; news-
    paper, 458

BBC. See British Broadcasting Corporation
Belgium: advertising, 559, 566
Bermuda: newspaper directory, 495
Best sellers, 124, 134, 141, 154, 157
Biography: American Negro press, 472; film, 313, 314,
    326, 327, 343; reporters, 63, 475; television, 230;
    women in communication, 26
Black press, 449, 450, 455, 472, 501, 505, 535; bib-
    liography, 68; biography, 472; directories, 458,
    484, 495, 538
Book clubs, 125, 145, 151, 172
Book programs by U.S. for developing countries, 144
Book publishing, 91, 108, 112, 113, 127, 134, 138, 140,
    142, 150, 154, 156, 162, 171, 172, 173; acronyms,
    124; advertising, 138, 140; associations, 124, 151;
    awards and prizes, 151; children's books, 138, 172;
    direct-mail, 138; directories, 104, 107, 151, 159,
    163; economics, 108, 112, 113, 127, 142, 162, 173;
    encyclopedia, 136; foundations, 151, 172; government
    agencies concerned with, 144, 151, 172; history,
    140, 150, 153, 154, 158, 162, 169; imports and
    exports, 113, 151, 164; inactive firms, 107, inter-
    national, 134, 145, 163, 164; legal books, 172;
    medical books, 138, 172; mergers, 107, 124, 150,
    151, 154; quality, 134; reference books, 125, 138,

389, 403; lists, with filmographies, 299, 317, 318,
322, 333, 343, 372, 373, 375; music, 342, 368;
musicals, 402; Negroes in films, 379; newsreels,
304; periodicals, 322, 342; production (worldwide),
342; regulations, 322; review anthologies, 319,
323, 376; serials, 305, 354, 396; shorts, 342,
351, 355, 356; sociology, 347, 387; star system,
330, 371, 405; statistics, 100, 320, 322, 343; on
television, 333, 374; terminology, 324; theaters,
62, 100, 322, 401; training, 300, 342; violence,
406; youth, 380
Finland: advertising, 541, 559
Foreign-language newspapers in U.S.: directories, 458,
495
Foreign-language periodicals in U.S.: directory, 495
Foundations associated with book trade, 151, 172
Fowler Report, 188
France: advertising, 559, 566; advertising directory,
595; advertising rates, 595; broadcasting, 255;
film, 321, 347, 367, 389; mass media directory, 595
Fraternal newspapers and periodicals: directory, 495
Freedom of media, 11, 14, 24, 82, 87, 93

Gallup poll, 8, 27, 634
German-American newspapers, 126, 534; directory, 445
Germany: advertising, 541, 559, 566; advertising
directory, 595; advertising rates, 595; broadcasting, 255; film, 312, 341, 347, 389; history, 352;
mass media directory, 595; Nazi press, 470; newspapers, 470
Ghana: advertising, 541; mass media, 29
Government agencies and book publishing, 151, 172
Great Britain: advertisers' directories, 195, 540, 543;
advertising agencies, 540, 543; advertising associations, 488, 500; advertising effects, 600; advertising media directories, 540, 551; advertising rates,
551; advertising statistics, 543; best sellers,
106; book publishing, 91, 110, 162; book publishing
bibliography, 130; book publishing directories,
107, 488; book publishing economics, 162; book
publishing history, 115, 158, 162; book selling,
110, 114; broadcasting, 91, 102, 214, 253, 254;
broadcasting bibliography, 183; broadcasting directories, 195, 196; broadcasting effects, 216; broadcasting history, 178, 182, 253, 254; fiction, 94,
99, 106, 139; film, 321, 343, 349, 367, 389; film
biographies, 326; film catalog, 310; film directory,
195; film history, 326, 361; film monopoly, 328;
libraries, 110; mass media directories, 436, 488,
500, 533, 551; news agencies, 436, 533; newspaper
circulation, 500, 551; newspaper directories, 488,

500, 533, 540; newspapers, 106, 464, 466, 467, 468,
488, 519, 529; newspapers, year's trends, 458; outdoor and poster advertising, 540, 551; periodical
directories, 436, 488, 500, 533, 551; periodicals,
34; popular culture, 34, 99, 106; Publishers Association, 149; readership, 34, 91, 94, 99, 106;
rental libraries, 139. See also British Broadcasting Corporation; Independent Television Authority
Greece: advertising, 541; film, 400; newspapers, 469

High-school journalism: bibliography, 40
Holland. See Netherlands
Hong Kong: advertising, 566; broadcasting, 1; film, 1,
347; newspapers, 1, 486
House organs: directories, 420, 432

Illiteracy, 50, 100, 101
Independent Television Authority, 196, 214, 253, 254;
advertising code, 600
India: advertising, 496, 506, 566; book publishing,
163, 166; broadcasting, 1, 13, 176, 228; correspondents, 506; film, 1, 13, 307; journalism bibliography, 476; mass media, 513, news agencies,
446, 494, 506; newspapers, 1, 13, 446, 486, 494,
496, 506, 510; press associations, 506; periodicals,
494; periodicals' bibliography, 476; public opinion,
446; syndicates, 494; training, 494, 506, 510
Indonesia: broadcasting, 1; film, 1; newspapers, 1, 486
International book trade, 145
International Labor Press Association, 424
International mass communications, 25, 97; statistics,
100; training, 55
Iran: book publishing, 166
Iraq: advertising, 541
Ireland: advertising, 541, 559; book publishing, 135;
book publishing directory, 107; film, 343; news-
paper history, 493
Israel: advertising, 541
Italian anti-Fascist press, 511
Italy: advertising, 541, 559, 566; advertising direc-
tory, 595; advertising rates, 595; broadcasting,
255; film, 321, 347; mass media directory, 595

Japan: advertising, 541, 566; broadcasting, 1, 13, 227,
231, 478; film, 1, 13, 347; mass media, 478; news
agencies, 478; newspapers, 1, 13, 478, 486; television, 252
Jewish press, 457, 503

214

Journalism. See Mass media; individual media
Journalism: bibliographies, 40, 412, 508, 509, 537
Journalism education: directory, 458

Kenya: book publishing, 165; mass media, 29
Kitsch, 21, 74
Korea (South): advertising media directory, 554;
    broadcasting, 1; film, 1; newspapers, 1, 486

Labor newspapers: directories, 424, 495, 538
Labor periodicals: directories, 424, 495
Labor unions: broadcasting, 66, 186, 230, 235, 280;
    film, 322, 343; newspapers, 66, 458
Land mobile systems, 181
Laos: broadcasting, 1; film, 1; newspapers, 1
Latin America: advertising, 566; book publishing,
    146; broadcasting, 59, 443; film, 59; mass media,
    57, 59; news agencies, 59; newspapers, 59, 443,
    463; periodicals, 59; printing, 443; training for
    mass media, 22, 59
Law: and book publishing, 138; and mass media, 11,
    28, 61, 87; and public relations, 590. See also
    Mass media, regulation
Lebanon: advertising, 541
Left-wing periodicals: directory, 422
Legal book publishing, 172
Lending libraries. See Rental libraries
Libraries: associations, 144; awards, 124; book pub-
    lishing, 156, 173; film, 404; newspaper, 527;
    periodical, 430; statistics, 113, 124
Literacy, 50, 100, 101
Literary agents: directories, 104, 125, 140, 151, 343
Literary awards, 151
"Little magazine": directories, 414, 421, 423

Magazines. See Periodicals
Magazine sections of newspapers, 458, 556
Malawi: advertising, 541
Malaysia: advertising, 566; broadcasting, 1; film, 1;
    newspapers, 1, 486
Maori press, 152
Marketing research: directories, 550, 568
Markets for writing. See Authorship, markets
Mass media, 2, 3, 5, 9, 19, 23, 32, 36, 43, 48, 52,
    53, 67, 73, 74, 75, 77, 78, 85, 86, 91, 98, 530;
    audience, 3, 19, 77, 78, 80, 91, 102; bibliographies,
    12, 16, 33, 64, 65, 219; contents, 3, 5, 14, 23,
    77, 78, 80, 81, 85, 91, 93, 98, 100, 102; control,
    73, 97, 240, 264, 530, 531; criticism, 2, 14, 43,

215

73, 93, 98, 264; developing nations, 17, 18, 25, 29,
50, 57, 70, 89, 102, 116, 117, 122, 123, 129;
development, 23, 73, 77, 93, 98, 99; dictionary,
39; directory, 66; economics, 36, 64; effects, 3,
41, 42, 44, 48, 53, 77, 78, 91, 93, 102; joint
ownership, 240; monopoly, 24, 512; politics, 12;
regulation, 11, 14, 24, 28, 44, 58, 61, 77, 82,
87; responsibility, 2, 14, 43, 73, 77, 82, 86;
statistics, 92, 100; structure, 3, 73, 77, 78, 100,
102; tariffs, 72, 78; violence, 30, 44, 93, 95,
226, 406; youth, 95, 211, 215, 217, 219, 226, 265,
267, 380. See also Civil disorders; Readership
Medical book publishing, 138, 172
Mergers. See Book publishing, mergers; Newspapers,
  mergers
Mexico: advertising, 541; advertising directory, 595;
  advertising rates, 595
Middle East: mass media, 57
Monopoly in mass media, 24, 512
Motion Picture Association of America: code, 77, 85,
  86, 322, 343
Musical comedy films, 402

National Association of Broadcasters, 186, 280
National Association of Educational Broadcasters, 225
National Book Committee, 124
Nazi press, 470
Negro press. See Black press
Netherlands: advertising, 559, 566; book publishing,
  166; broadcasting, 255
News agencies, 17, 18, 67, 100, 498, 499, 531, 539
News coverage, 93, 97, 247, 271
Newspaper Advertising Executives Association, 458
Newspaper libraries, 527
Newspapers, 23, 67, 73, 77, 85, 86, 91, 454; advertis-
  ing rates, 578, 580; broadcast affiliates, 458;
  business and trade, 417; business and trade directories, 415, 495; change in name; 444; circulation,
  458, 491, 546, 547, 548, 577, 578, 580; trends for
  year, 458; directories, 444, 448, 458, 491, 495,
  504, 532, 533, 538, 548, 580; economics, 521;
  English-language papers published abroad, 528;
  expenditure by advertisers, 504, 514; foreign-
  language papers published in U.S., 458, 495, 538;
  free-distribution, 447; history, 461, 482, 485,
  492, 518, 520; Jewish, 457, 503; joint ownership,
  458; market analysis, 577; mergers, 444; personnel,
  458, 538; political leanings, 458, 495; ranked by
  quality, 490; statistics, 92, 100, 458, 517; suburban, 447, 471; training, 459; weekly, 458, 497,
  599. See also College press

216

Newsprint: statistics, 100, 458
Newsreels, 304, 436
New Zealand: advertising, 184, 541, 566; authorship,
    markets, 103; broadcasting, 184, 245; newspaper
    history, 152; printing, 152
Nigeria: book publishing, 129; broadcasting, 13, 246;
    mass media, 29; newspapers, 13
Norway: advertising, 541, 559; film, 321
Nyasaland: book publishing, 165

Oceania: mass media, 57
Outdoor advertising, 540, 583

Pakistan: advertising, 541; authorship, markets, 103;
    book publishing, 166; broadcasting, 1; film, 1;
    newspapers, 1
Panama: newspaper directory, 495
Paperbacks, 74, 125, 138, 167. See also Book publish-
    ing; Bookstores
Pay TV, 271; organizations, 280
Periodicals, 73, 74, 77, 85, 86, 91, 428, 430, 437, 438;
    advertising rates, 408, 432, 547, 552, 556, 573;
    bibliographies, 416, 429, 431; business and trade,
    417; business and trade directories, 495, 552, 586;
    ceased publication, 410; change in title, 410, 434;
    circulation, 408, 432, 434, 440, 491, 495, 573;
    content, 408, 425, 432, 440; directories, 66, 104,
    408, 432, 434, 440, 495, 504, 548, 552, 556; farm
    directory, 495, 556; history, 427, 428, 433, 437,
    438; Jewish, 457, 503; new titles, 410, 435;
    personnel, 440; readership analyses, 558, 585;
    scholarly, 408; specialized, 419; specialized direc-
    tories, 104, 414, 440, 557. See also College press;
    "Little magazines"; Pulp magazines
Peru: advertising, 541
Philippines: advertising, 541; broadcasting, 1; film,
    1; newspapers, 1, 486; newspaper directory, 495
Pilkington Report, 214
Poland: film, 347, 367
Polling, 8, 10, 27, 71, 634
Politics and mass media, 25, 32, 71, 78, 91; bibliog-
    raphy, 12; television bibliography, 224
Politics and television: bibliography, 224
Popular culture, 7, 9, 30, 34, 38, 53, 62, 74, 75, 80,
    81, 96, 99, 143, 157
Popular music, 34, 74, 75, 81, 91, 96
Portugal: advertising, 541, 559
Press codes, 507. See also Codes
Press councils, 507

Printing: chronology, 128; encyclopedia, 136; history, 153, 169
Private presses, 47, 136, 172, 488
Professional associations, 20, 66
Propaganda, 10, 25, 71, 83, 84, 85; bibliographies, 45, 83, 84
Public information, 2, 6
Public opinion, 3, 6, 8, 10, 49, 71, 78, 85, 86; bibliographies, 83, 84
Public relations, 10; bibliographies, 557, 581; dictionary, 598; international, 25, 566; law, 590; reference sources, 296, 439, 440, 538, 548
Public television, 85, 259
Pulp magazines, 62, 430

Radical publications. See Left-wing periodicals; Right-wing publications
Radio, 220, 234, 241, 258, 261, 269, 271; advertising rates, 579, 591; black, 210; content, 236, 258, 259, 262, 296; criticism, 258, 261; directories, 186, 230, 296, 297, 298; dissertations, 273; history, 177, 182, 218, 220, 250, 269, 287, 294; listenership, 258, 261, 269; as popular culture, 62, 77; private and point-to-point, 181; programming, 236, 258, 261, 262; regulation, 177, 181, 192, 207, 208, 220, 234, 263, 294; regulation bibliography, 223; serials, 71, 77, 80, 218, 236; shortwave, 295; statistics, 100, 197, 275, 278, 287; systems, 193, 208, 255, 269. See also Broadcasting
Radio-Television News Directors Association, 248
Readership, 77, 91, 99, 108, 134, 147, 168, 239; books, 77, 147; newspapers, 77; periodicals, 34, 558
Reference book publishing, 125, 138, 172
Regulation. See Law; Mass media, regulation
Religion: book publishing, 138; book publishing directory, 151; broadcasting, 179, 382; film, 382; Catholic directory, 413; Jewish directory, 457; newspapers, 426; newspaper directory, 495; periodicals, 426; Protestant directory, 409
Rental libraries, 107, 139, 156; directory, 107
Research: need for, 56; research centers, directories, 4, 20
Rhodesia: advertising, 541, 542; book publishing, 165
Right-wing publications: directory, 418
Rumania: book publishing, 119

Satellites, 2, 78, 185, 187, 201, 205, 237, 238, 247, 251, 264, 272, 290, 291, 298
Scandinavia: advertising, 566
Scientific book publishing, 138, 172

ownership of stations, 280; personnel of stations, 186, 280; as popular culture, 62; programming, 211, 281, 282; programming for children, 211; rating systems, 270; regulations, 223, 270, 271; research organizations, 280; sale of stations, 186, 280; station directories, 186, 230, 252, 280; statistics, 100, 198, 275, 280; subscription, 118; viewing, 180, 212, 276, 280; youth, 211, 215, 217, 219, 226, 265. See also Broadcasting

Author-Title Index